AN ARMY OF DAVIDS

HOW MARKETS AND TECHNOLOGY EMPOWER

ORDINARY PEOPLE TO BEAT BIG MEDIA,

BIG GOVERNMENT, AND OTHER GOLIATHS

GLENN REYNOLDS

NELSON CURRENT

A Subsidiary of Thomas Nelson, Inc.

www.nelsoncurrent.com

Published in Nashville, Tennessee, by Nelson Current, a division of a wholly-owned subsidiary (Nelson Communications, Inc.) of Thomas Nelson, Inc.

Nelson Current books may be purchased in bulk for educational, business, fundraising, or sales promotional use. For information, please e-mail SpecialMarkets@ThomasNelson.com.

Library of Congress Cataloging-in-Publication Data

Reynolds, Glenn H.
    An army of Davids : how markets and technology empower ordinary people to beat big media, big government, and other Goliaths / Glenn Reynolds.
      p. cm.
    Includes bibliographical references and index.
    ISBN 1-59555-054-2
    1. Technology—Social aspects. 2. Digital media—Social aspects. 3. Internet-Social aspects. 4. Freedom of expression. 5. Knowledge, Sociology of.
    6. Creation (Literary, artistic, etc.)—Social aspects. I. Title.
                                   HM846.R48 2006
303.48'33—dc22

To my wife and daughter

CONTENTS

CONTENTS

ACKNOWLEDGMENTS

Technology empowers ordinary people. But other people are the greatest source of empowerment in this world. In working on this project, I was reminded again that I have been very fortunate with regard to the people I have known.

My wife, Dr. Helen Smith, has been a source of encouragement, advice, and support throughout. Even her health problems have served as inspiration for some parts of this book. Likewise other members of my family—and in particular my parents, who encouraged my interest in technologies and in writing—have been great sources of help.

Many of the ideas in this book were first worked out in columns at *TCS Daily*, where Nick Schulz has been an unfailingly supportive and inspiring editor. When Nick first contacted me to solicit a weekly column, I was reluctant, wondering if I had enough ideas to produce a column a week. Now, nearly four years later, it turns out that he was right, and I did.

My dean, Tom Galligan, and the rest of the faculty and staff at the University of Tennessee College of Law have been uniformly positive and encouraging regarding my writing, even when it has veered from the legal-academic to the technological and sociological. At a time when we hear much about the narrow-mindedness and jealousy of the academy, it's worth noting that the University of Tennessee has been a consistently friendly and supportive place for me, despite the fact that my work is politically incorrect from pretty much any and all angles. I have never regretted choosing to join, and to remain on, the faculty.

Thanks too to my research assistants, Matt Lindsay, Josh Phillips, and Erika Roberts, who discovered typos I had missed, offered helpful stylistic advice, which I sometimes took, and located sources I was unable to find. Likewise to faculty secretaries Sean Gunter, Neal Fischer, Michelle Gilbert, Teresa Michael, and Tammy Neff. Other invaluable, and sometimes indispensable, help in various forms has come from (in no particular order) Ashley Pope, Jennifer Marks, Brannon Denning, Heidi Henning, Chris Peterson, Eric Drexler, Robert Pinson, Jennifer Coffin, Nick McCall, Ralph Davis, Leigh Griffith, John Ragosta, Doug Weinstein, David McCord, Rob Merges, and countless readers and emailers via the InstaPundit and TechCentralStation sites. If you want to understand how technology empowers ordinary people, try writing a popular blog for a while, with a published email address. And my agent, Kate Lee of International Creative Management, has been tireless, persistent, and a pleasure to know.

I hope that you enjoy reading this book as much as I enjoyed writing it and that the trend I outline will continue for the foreseeable future.

GLENN HARLAN REYNOLDS
Knoxville, Tennessee
19 October 2005

DO IT YOURSELF

About fifteen years ago, I started brewing my own beer. Nothing new about that: people have been brewing their own beer for millennia, and my grandfather was reputed to have been a pretty good brewer during Prohibition. But when I started brewing, it was unusual.

It was unusual because rather than brewing their own beer, most people—almost everyone, in fact—bought beer from huge brewing companies that made the stuff in giant steel vats. (When they say that it's "beechwood aged," they don't mean it's aged in casks made out of beechwood—they just throw a few wood chips into the vats for flavor). The industrial beer wasn't bad, exactly, and unlike most of the homebrewed stuff, its quality and flavor were consistent from batch to batch. The problem was that there wasn't much flavor left; in an effort to consolidate brands, to save money, and to appeal to the broadest tastes possible, brewing companies had gradually thinned out their product until a lot of people found it inoffensive, but unsatisfying.

That's why I started brewing my own beer. The beer I brewed was sometimes terrific—a couple of batches were among the best beer I've ever had—and sometimes not so great. But it had more character, and it was fun to brew it myself. I learned some things about brewing, I got to experiment with different recipes and approaches, and I got to make the kind of beer I wanted, not the kind that someone else wanted to sell me. It was a little bit cheaper, but that wasn't really the point. The point was that I was making something for myself, to suit me.

Lots of people followed suit, and homebrewing went from an unusual hobby to a fairly common pastime. Beer companies— and beer distributors—took note, and the range and quality of beer offerings on tap and in stores dramatically improved. In the end, even the non-homebrewers benefited.

A few years later, I started recording my own music. The technology for digital recording had improved enough that making your own professional quality CDs was possible. I recorded various bands in my basement studio, and, after a while, moved most of my own music production and recording onto a PC. I distributed CDs and downloadable music on the Internet (one of my albums made it to number one for several weeks on the MP3.com charts) and got written up in places like *Salon* and *Spiked*.[1] My brother and I even set up a small record company that, basically, consisted of a few PCs, some microphones, and the Internet. It didn't make us rich, but it did make us a little bit of money. And it made us happy.

Lots of other people were doing the same, and "Indie" music has become an important part of the scene—to the point that major acts sometimes design their CDs so that they look home-made, gaining them extra street cred. Ironically, the CDs that are actually homemade usually look, and sound, as professional as those put out by big labels. I've found a lot of bands that I like through the indie scene, bands that I would have never heard of in the old days. So have a lot of other people.

Then, in what may have been a fateful move, I decided to get into Internet journalism, via what's called blogging today. In the summer of 2001, the now ubiquitous "blogs" were then called "mezines." I had been posting regularly in "The Fray," the online forum of *Slate* magazine, and decided to strike out on my own using one of my Fray nicknames: InstaPundit. I set up a weblog on the free Blogger.com service and started posting my opinions, along with links to news items, several times a day. (My first post was on digital music, bringing in another of my interests.) I started blogging partly because I teach Internet Law and like to stay active in some sort of Internet activity, and partly because it looked like fun. I had consumed news and opinion journalism for most of my life, but it seemed that much of it had become a bit thin and flavorless (much like the beer). I thought I could produce something that I'd like better and that perhaps some other people would enjoy too.

I figured that if the blog did well, I'd have a few dozen, maybe even a few hundred, readers a day. By September 10, 2001, I had 1,600 and thought I'd hit the big time. The next day, on September 11, I had nearly triple that, and it just took off from there, though the events responsible for that growth took away a bit of the savor.

Lots of other people started blogging shortly thereafter, and you often hear the same reasons given—basically variations on "I got tired of watching the video of the towers collapsing," and "I got tired of yelling at the TV." Like me, people were unhappy with the mass-market journalistic product and wanted to try making something of their own.

Since then, blogging has exploded in popularity. As I write this, Technorati.com is tracking over 22 million blogs—and bloggers have accomplished a lot in independent journalism: bringing down Trent Lott and Dan Rather; reporting on events in Iraq, Afghanistan, and the Ukraine that Big Media have ignored; and even playing a major role in defeating ratification of the European Constitution in France and the Netherlands. Now bloggers are a normal part of national discourse, featured on TV and quoted in the press. Blogging has become such an important means to reach people that bloggers are courted by advertisers and PR people. Some of the bigger blogs have readerships that rival those of medium-sized newspapers (I get as many as a half-million pageviews some days, and often get more than 250,000, and I get more reader email in a day than *The Rocky Mountain News,* a top-ten daily, gets in a week).

So what does all this mean . . . besides suggesting that professional trendspotters ought to pay attention to my *next* hobby?

Well, all of these phenomena have something in common: the triumph of personal technology over mass technology. And that's a trend that is going to strengthen over the coming decades.

We're accustomed to thinking that big organizations are the important organizations because that's how it's been in recent centuries. Starting around 1700, big organizations became the most efficient way to do a lot of things. The main sources of power, steam engines and the like, had to be big to be efficient. And keeping track of information required armies of clerks, secretaries, etc., who needed a big organization to support them. These concepts—which economists call "economies of scope and scale"—

favored big organizations. Big companies, big governments, whatever. Mass production. Bigger was better. *Goliath rules.*

But that phenomenon was the result of technology, and technology keeps changing. We saw a hint of the new world in a bit of dark humor from the days of the old Soviet Union: making fun of its habit of boasting about size, people joked about a *Pravda* headline reading "The Soviet Microchip: Largest in the World!" The jab was, of course, that big microchips aren't better. Smaller ones are, and that joke presaged the failure of the Soviet approach and the Soviet Union itself.

In fact, those smaller microchips are one of the main factors responsible for the change. New technologies mean that big organizations aren't necessarily more efficient. The growth of computers, the Internet, and niche marketing means that you don't have to be a Goliath to get along. Like David's sling, these new technologies empower the little guy to compete more effectively. They have, in fact, spawned a veritable army of Davids, now busily competing with the Goliaths in all sorts of fields. And, as with the beer, even where that competition is no real threat to the big guys, it tends to push them to do a better job.

In the chapters that follow, we'll look at how technology is empowering ordinary people in all sorts of ways—from journalism and entertainment, to homeland security and counterterrorism, to manufacturing and scientific research—and at how it's likely to influence the world in the future. Because in the future, the efforts of individuals and small groups, acting sometimes on their own and sometimes in informal cooperation with others, are likely to make a bigger difference than they've made in centuries.

1

THE CHANGE

Sherman, set the Wayback Machine for 10,000 BC.
What does the world look like?

Except for the soon-to-be extinct cave bear or saber tooth tiger here and there, the scale is pretty small. The biggest human organizations are band- and tribe-level: at most a few hundred people, but usually only a few dozen. The line between work and play is pretty blurry. Some things are clearly work, and some things are clearly play, but many are in between, and people go from one to another as circumstances dictate, not according to a schedule. Agriculture hasn't been invented yet, though people brew beer from wild grains and are grasping the concept of reseeding: plants tend to multiply in the same places every year, making it easier to brew beer. (What, you think people invented agriculture for *bread?*)

The few material possessions that exist are homemade, except for a very small amount of stuff purchased from itinerant traders carrying rare luxuries like amber, obsidian, or dyestuffs. Children aren't sent off to school but hang around the adults as they go about the business of the day. The most dangerous activities, like big-game hunting, are off-limits to the kids, but they grow up quickly and are soon a part of all clan activities.

Even in these caveman days, there's plenty of technology around. Humans are tropical animals, and without technologies like fire and clothing, most of the world would be off limits. Finely wrought flint tools are capable of impressive feats (how do you think those saber tooths and cave bears became extinct?), but there aren't any machines as we'd understand them. Probably the most sophisticated device in general use is the spear thrower. The biggest organized human events are mass hunts and the occasional clan gathering. They're limited in size and duration because you can't feed that many people by hunting and gathering in one place for long, and it's hard to store much food: it goes bad, or it's eaten by vermin.

Fast-forward a few thousand years and not all that much has changed. Advances in agriculture and organization make some difference: more people can live closer together, thanks to the higher efficiency of farming over hunting and gathering (though because farming is hard work, those people are usually less well nourished and harder working than the hunters and gatherers). There's still not much in the way of sophisticated machinery. There are tools a caveman wouldn't recognize, but nothing he couldn't figure out in a few minutes.

Things stay pretty much this way, in fact, until the Industrial Revolution. Agriculture, written language, and a growing facility for procuring and using metals allow big empires to organize large numbers of people, but not very efficiently. Doing things on a large scale is usually less efficient than cottage industry, because coordinating all those people is so much trouble. You can build big things, like the Pyramids or the Great Wall of China, but at enormous cost, and only by making people choose between hauling bricks or being killed. For most of human history, this was the norm.

DIVIDE AND CONQUER

But the Industrial Revolution changed things. Improvements in organization, communications, and machinery meant that it was often much more efficient to do things on a large scale than on a small one, as Adam Smith observed in his famous description of a pin factory:

> A workman not educated to this business . . . could scarce, perhaps, with his utmost industry, make one pin in one day, and certainly could not make twenty. But in the way in which this business is now carried on not only the whole work is a peculiar trade, but it is divided into a number of branches, of which the greater part are likewise peculiar trades. One man draws out the wire, another straights it, a third cuts it, a fourth points it, a fifth grinds it at the top for receiving the head; to make the head requires two or three distinct operations; to put it on is a peculiar business, to whiten the pins is another; it is even a trade by itself to put them into the paper. . . . Those ten persons, therefore, could make among them upwards of forty-eight thousand pins in a day. . . . But if they had all wrought separately and independently, and without any of them having been educated to this peculiar business, they certainly could not each of them have made twenty, perhaps not one pin in a day; that is, certainly, not the two hundred and fortieth, perhaps not

the four thousand eight hundredth part of what they are at present capable of performing, in consequence of a proper division and combination of their different operations.[1]

Division of labor allowed large groups to be organized in ways that were actually *more* efficient than smaller groups or collections of individuals acting independently. Big machinery allowed big jobs to be done, but because the machinery itself was big it could *only* do big jobs efficiently. When the smallest efficient steam engine is big enough to power a whole factory, it doesn't make sense to use it for anything less: the cost is the same, but the return is smaller. Thus the "minimum efficient scale" turns out to be pretty big. And lots of capital and lots of time and energy are required to fuel these big operations.

The line between work and play is a lot sharper in the Industrial Age too. Industrialists like Henry Ford didn't think much of levity:

In 1940, John Gallo was sacked because he was "caught in the act of smiling," after having committed an earlier breach of "laughing with the other fellows," and "slowing down the line maybe half a minute." This tight managerial discipline reflected the overall philosophy of Henry Ford, who stated that "When we are at work we ought to be at work. When we are at play we ought to be at play. There is no use trying to mix the two."[2]

Most of the developments of the nineteenth and twentieth centuries followed this pattern. You can't run a railroad as a family business. The same is true for steel mills (the Chinese Communists tried backyard steel-making, disastrously, with their "little steel" program, but learned better) and, after the very earliest days of the automobile industry, auto factories. Other than a few shops serving NASCAR and very rich car collectors, people don't build cars one at a time any more.

Big organizations doing big things: it's the story of the nineteenth and twentieth centuries. In fact, it was so much the theme of those centuries that it's easy to forget what a departure this was from the rest of human history. But it was a huge departure, brought about by the confluence of some unusual technological and social developments.

And it was a mixed bag. On the one hand, it made people in industrialized countries a lot richer, healthier, and longer-lived. Really, a *lot.* In his book, *The Escape from Hunger and Premature Death, 1700-2100,*[3] historian Robert Fogel notes that the improvement in living conditions for the working classes in industrial countries during the Industrial Revolution is without any parallel in human history. Life expectancies got much longer (from thirty-two in 1725 to seventy-six in 1990 in the UK);[4] people got taller, were sick less often, with much better nutrition. The poor of today are much better off than the aristocrats of the pre-Industrial era.

THE DOWNSIDE

On the other hand, industrialization created a lot of social strain as traditional ways of living were disrupted by new ways of doing business. William Blake's "Dark Satanic mills" weren't as bad as they're remembered today—if they had been, people wouldn't have flocked to them. Or maybe it's fairer to say that, bad as they were, they were still better than life as a subsistence farmer. But this new industrial world was very different from life on the farm.

Parents and children were separated. Husbands and wives were separated. "Work" became something separate from the rest of life, something fast-paced and foreign. An old-style blacksmith made a plowshare or a sword from beginning to end. A worker in Adam Smith's pin factory, or Henry Ford's automobile factory, performed a single repetitive task with no real connection, emotional or intellectual, to the overall product. Nor—unlike those old-time craftsmen—did factory workers have much of a connection to the economics of the business. Although factory workers did much better economically than peasant farmers had done, their share of the proceeds was trivial compared to that of the people who financed and ran these large capital-intensive operations—people who became known as "capitalists."

This divide between workers and financiers led to talk about worker "alienation" and the perceived problematic separation of labor from ownership of the means of production. This was the foundation of Marxism and of efforts—universally disastrous—to replace capitalists with government-controlled capital in communist countries. Government replacements for free-market capitalists were, if anything, more rapacious. They were also much worse at actually producing wealth. Much of the twentieth century was spent in making this clear in various unfortunate and lethal ways.

The large-scale operations hit their zenith in the mid-twentieth century, with American business revolving around huge entities like General Motors and IBM. Economists like John Kenneth Galbraith[5] began arguing that big corporations were protected from failure by their size, and that the kind of massive organization and information-processing available to these huge enterprises meant that smaller businesses couldn't possibly compete. Bigger was better, and the power resulting from the managerial class "techno-structure" that ran these big corporations was more important than crude things like profits. Or so the theory went.

This turned out not to be the case. Even as Galbraith's book, *The New Industrial State*, was appearing in 1966, the seeds of change were taking root. The year before, in the thirty-fifth anniversary issue of *Electronics* magazine, Gordon Moore had first proposed "Moore's Law"—essentially saying that computing power was doubling every two years and would continue to do so for the foreseeable future. Giant corporations weren't nimble enough to keep up such a pace.

DESKTOP REVOLUTION

It was a while before the impact of this trend on Galbraith's formulation became obvious, but the growth of cheap computing power has already undercut the importance of big organizations in many areas. That cheap computing power is now being coupled with cheap manufacturing—including, increasingly, what Neil Gershenfeld calls "personal fabrication," in his book *Fab: The Coming Revolution on Your Desktop—From Personal Computers to Personal Fabrication.*[6] But even without the kinds of progress that Gershenfeld describes, manufacturing, including custom manufacturing, has become cheap and versatile enough to neutralize many of the advantages that large organizations once held.

For activities that, ultimately, are about processing information, the computer revolution itself has drastically reduced the minimum efficient scale. A laptop, a cheap video camera, and the free iMovie or Windows Movie Maker software (plus an Internet connection) will let one person do things that the Big Three television networks could only dream of in Galbraith's day, and at a tiny fraction of the cost.[7] The same laptop with a soundcard, a couple of microphones, and software like Acid, Cubase, or Audition can replace an expensive recording studio. Change the software to Lotus or Excel and it can replace an office full of Galbraith-era accountants with calculators, pencils, and paper, and access—filtered through a priesthood of programmers and machine operators—to big 1960s mainframe computers.

This observation is commonplace now, of course, but its implications for Galbraith-era economics have gotten somewhat less attention. It's not just that fewer people can do the same work, it's that *they don't need a big company* to provide the infrastructure to do the work, and, in fact, they may be far more efficient *without* the big company and all the inefficiencies and stumbling blocks that its bureaucracy and techno-structure tend to produce.

Those inefficiencies were present in Galbraith's day too, of course. People have been making jokes about office politics and bureaucratic idiocies long before *Dilbert.* But in the old days, you had to put up with those problems because you needed the big organization to do the job. Now, increasingly, you don't. Goliath's strength compensated for his clumsiness. But now the Davids can muscle up without all of the unnecessary bulk.

So why be a Goliath? As technology moves toward smaller,

faster, and cheaper approaches to many jobs, we're likely to see an army of Davids taking the place of those slow, shuffling Goliaths. This won't be the end of big enterprises, or big bureaucracies (especially, alas, the latter), but it will represent a dramatic reversal of recent history, toward more cottage industry, more small enterprises and ventures, and more empowerment for individuals willing to take advantage of the tools that become available. We're likely to see a movement from the impersonal, imposed means to an end to a more individualized, grassroots way of doing things. In fact, we're already starting to see that, as many people—laid off or voluntarily departed from big organizations—start small businesses. Working from home, their daily lives look more like what we saw in the pre-Industrial Revolution era than like the classic *Man in the Gray Flannel Suit* lifestyle.

YOU HAVE NOTHING TO LOSE
BUT YOUR CUBICLES

One of the most significant consequences of this shift is that the empowerment of individuals may lead to an interesting twist on Karl Marx's goal: workers control the means of production, all right, but it's a far cry from communism. Marx's view was tied to an outdated technological paradigm, but his desired outcome, a world in which "capital" is in the hands of the masses, not just the few, may ironically come about through the technological capitalism that Marx's heirs (though not Marx himself, really) despised.

Technologies that are still on the horizon, like molecular nanotechnology (whose enthusiasts predict will lead to machines that can make anything out of "sunlight and dirt") and biotechnology, may bring this trend to complete fruition, but everyday technologies are already moving us a long way in that direction.

The worker's paradise may turn out to be a capitalist creation after all.

In the coming chapters, I'll look at the way this change is playing out in the worlds of business, media, the arts, and even national security. I'll also look at the downside of empowering individuals: if amateur musicians or bloggers are empowered by technology, so in a different way are terrorists.

Overall, I consider the trend to be a positive one. Whether you agree with that assessment or not, the existence of this empowerment is undeniable and irreversible. Love it or hate it, it's worth close consideration.

As William Gibson has remarked, "The future has already arrived—it's just not evenly distributed." The pockets of the future that we'll be surveying are not only interesting in themselves, but provide a look at how a lot more of the world is likely to operate before long.

2

SMALL IS THE NEW BIG

A while back, blogger Jeff Jarvis noted a press release saying that eBay's sellers were threatening to overtake Wal-Mart's employment numbers:

> eBay is fast becoming one of the largest employers in America. Of course, it hardly employs anyone, but it enables a lot of people to employ themselves and run their own businesses: 724,000 people are using it as their full- or part-time employment, up 68 percent from a year ago; another 1.5 million use it to supplement their income. Wal-Mart is America's largest employer with 1.1 million workers. Sure, the eBay-self-employed don't have Wal-Mart's crappy benefits and uniforms (if eBay were really smart, they'd institute group health insurance!) but all those folks are their own bosses. As industry gets bigger and bigger, small becomes more and more of an economic force.[1]

Yes, this is something of an apples-and-oranges comparison, *but not entirely*. And it captures an important point: lots of people don't like their jobs, their bosses, or their offices—just read any selection of *Dilbert* comic strips.

What's more, a lot of people responded to the 2000 recession by starting their own businesses. For some it was a case of necessity—"If I can't *get* a job, I'll *make* one!" For others it was a case of being given a push toward something they wanted to do anyway. In fact, quite a few formerly unemployed people are now reporting that they're self-employed. Though an economist quoted by the *New York Times* discounts this phenomenon as "involuntary entrepreneurship,"[2] it seems likely that—voluntary or otherwise—we'll see a lot more of this sort of thing.

As *Slate*'s Mickey Kaus notes: "If we're entering a new economic era—one in which traditional cyclical employers won't start rehiring, . . . isn't it *likely*, even, that workers will adjust by pursuing entrepreneurial opportunities? And if entrepreneurship is real, what does calling it 'involuntary' mean? I might prefer to have a full-fledged 'job' at Microsoft, complete with stock options, health insurance, etc. Instead, I'm a freelance contractor. Calling my entrepreneurship 'involuntary' might be accurate, but it doesn't mean I'm not working and feeding myself. In the 'newer' economy, you'd expect such self-employment to increase, no?"[3]

Yes.

For whatever reason, many people have decided to join the ranks of the entrepreneurial classes, and technology has made it a lot easier. What's more, a lot of people really *want* to live that way. If they didn't, I wouldn't see and hear so many advertisements offering people ways to work at home. Sure, the ads are often scams—but the demand they're responding to is quite genuine.

Before the Industrial Revolution, artisans worked in or alongside their homes, often with children observing and even helping. After the Industrial Revolution, workers were segregated in factories, where specialized facilities took advantage of new technologies and of the economies of scope and scale that those technologies made available. Blacksmiths could make steel or work iron in small quantities, but foundries could do it better, and cheaper.

The results of this shift reverberated through every level of society. Of course, with the workers off at factories learning the kind of skills—like punctuality and the ability to follow orders— that factories required, something had to be done with the kids. This led to two major changes: women often specialized in child-rearing to a much greater extent than previously, when child-rearing was just part of the household work; and children were segregated into massive "educational factories" of their own: public schools organized, quite explicitly, to mimic factories and assembly lines, with students envisioned as the products. (What's more, the student-products were designed to be good factory employees themselves.)

And that was mostly a good thing. The techniques of industrialization took precedence because they worked better and faster than the methods they replaced. And that made everyone richer and, overall, freer. The social transformations—in families, in workplaces, and in neighborhoods—that came on the heels of these changes, on the other hand, were adopted not because they worked better than what they replaced but were necessary to survive in and accommodate this new work environment.

ARMCHAIR WORKERS

Now, it may be that things are starting to change. I was struck by this passage from the writer John Scalzi's blog, describing the impact of Wi-Fi on his life, and how it has freed him from depending on his home office:

> At the moment, I'm writing this in [my daughter] Athena's room, on the floor, the computer propped up on my lap; Athena is behind me on her bed making up a Powerpuff adventure. Three weeks ago I would have to be in my [home] office to type this and Athena would be coming in about every six seconds to ask me something or to ask me to do something or whatever, which means I would actually have a difficult time getting work done when she was around; now she's happy to let me work because I have proximity to her. She still asks me questions and such, but once I've answered she's off on her own thing.
>
> Interestingly, this also works with Krissy [his wife]; she's more content to let me do work if I'm in line of sight. There's a real psychological difference between being in the office all the time, away from the family while I'm doing work, and being in the room, doing work while the family is doing stuff around me. It's useful for me (especially when I'm on deadline, like I am right now), and it's better for the family.[4]

I've noticed much of the same thing in my work. I work at home more often now, thanks to the combination of a laptop computer and wireless Internet. I work all over the house, often sitting in a chair while my daughter plays with dolls or does homework. She spends a lot more time around me than I spent with my dad, and this is one reason why.

It's a mixed bag, of course. You can look at it as *getting* to spend time with your family while you take care of work, or you can look at it as *having* to work when you're with your family, and no doubt both perspectives are valid from time to time. But it's certainly better for many kids than the frequent absences required by the much less flexible office job.

I'm not alone in this. Many people are doing the same thing as technology makes it easier to do many kinds of jobs at home. How far we'll move in the direction of what Dan Pink calls a "Free Agent Nation"[5] isn't clear: obviously, some jobs are more amenable to the cottage-industry approach than others. Our neighbors tried running a coffee service from home but met with some neighborly resistance when coffee-bearing semitrailers began backing down the street at all hours. Operating a car-repair business or a blast-furnace out of your home might also pose challenges.

But many jobs will move back home, at least in part. And if you believe, as Virginia Postrel suggests,[6] that more jobs in coming years will have an aesthetic component (which is the sort of work that lends itself to a cottage-industry approach), then that trend may accelerate even more. New advances in computer-aided design and manufacturing, along with things like nanotechnology further down the line, may help the trend as well.

How will this change society at large? Schools, of course, will have to adjust to train kids for different career options. But this will just be part of it. The new freedom and flexibility will also change the mix of political issues somewhat: self-employed people tend to hate red tape and taxes (pundits have been predicting a "1099 revolt" for a while, as the percentage of self-employed people grows), but on the other hand, the difficulty of getting things like health insurance when you're not affiliated with a large company (as Jeff Jarvis noted) might make them more amenable to some proposals from the Democrats.

COMING ATTRACTIONS

We'll save that speculation for another time, though, because I want to look at some social changes that may come with increasing self-employment and home-based work. The Industrial Revolution, after all, remade our society—and the boom in white-collar jobs after World War II did it again. Now a new revolution is dawning: How will it change us for good or ill? Here are some thoughts:

Crime: Crime in the suburbs increased once the population of stay-at-home moms was diminished. Neighborhoods had fewer sets of adult eyes around, teenagers got less supervision, and two-career couples were more distracted. Will that change? Likely. "Latchkey" kids are increasingly coming home to a parent who works at home, or whose schedule is irregular enough that his/her absence can't be taken for granted. And irregular schedules mean that thieves can't assume that neighborhoods will be deserted during the day. That's certainly true in my neighborhood, where quite a few of the people are professionals who set their own calendars, and who can often be found mowing the lawn, or lounging by the pool, in the middle of a weekday because they'll be working at night or on the weekend or whenever their schedule best fits.

Family: One of the standard negative depictions from the Gray Flannel Suit era featured a disconnect between the world of work and the world of family. Fathers trudged off en masse to downtown office buildings where they performed inscrutable tasks, from which they returned exhausted and in need of martinis. Kids had little idea what their fathers did; fathers knew little about what their kids did. Husbands and wives moved in different worlds.

The entry of women into the workforce in large numbers has helped this a little, I suppose, but not a lot, especially where the kids are concerned. But kids who get to watch their parents work up close—the way that kids did in the pre-Industrial Revolution, cottage industry days—are likely to have a much greater appreciation of how the world of work operates. Perhaps, like the kids in the pre-Industrial Revolution days, they'll mature more quickly as a result, though here I may be overly optimistic. At the very least, however, they'll see work behavior modeled in their presence. Instead of "take your daughter (or son) to work" day, it'll be "take work to your kids" every day. Spouses also tend to know a lot more about the work of their self-employed beloveds, for better or worse. I'm not enough of a sociologist—or a psychic—to analyze all the changes that may result from this phenomenon, but I feel pretty confident that many of these significant changes will be for the better.

Nobody was that thrilled with the Gray Flannel Suit era.

Economy: If more people are free agents, working at home or out-and-about rather than in traditional offices, then businesses that provide them with useful services and amenities will flourish. We're already seeing some of that, with businesses featuring amenities like free wireless Internet connections in order to attract "gypsy workers" who aren't chained to offices and who like to combine work with pleasure. (I often write at one or another local establishments offering free Wi-Fi along with other lures, and I've noticed that I'm not the only one.)

Obviously, other businesses catering to the self-employed crowd—from Kinko's to Office Depot—are likely to do well too. On a macro level, self-employment will make economic statistics more difficult to decode: instead of the binary distinction between "employed" and "unemployed," we'll have the fuzzier distinction between "good year" and "not-so-good year" that small businesses tend to experience. As the reports from Jeff Jarvis and Mickey Kaus quoted above indicate, this will make it harder to figure out what's going on in terms of employment.

Traffic: Proponents of light rail and other sorts of mass transit tend to portray these systems as the wave of the future. But the "commuter-rail" model assumes the presence of, well, commuters: traditional gray-flannel-suit types who head downtown in flocks, spend a day at the office, and then return home. The driving pattern for work-at-home types is different: lots of quick, parcel-laden errands to different destinations (like Office Depot or Kinko's). It's much harder to design a commuter-rail system that works for people like that. As Ralph Kinney Bennett notes, the automobile's flexibility and independence are unmatched by other forms of transportation.[7]

Politics: This topic deserves a chapter of its own, and I'll come back to it later. But here's one note: people who are self-employed are far more aware that there's no such thing as a free lunch and far more likely to look at the bottom line. As more of the electorate becomes self-employed, this is likely to produce an overall attitudinal shift in politics, over and above any changes in specific policies. Both state and local governments—now basically organized along a Henry Ford sort of model—might want to take a lesson from eBay and Wal-Mart and look for ways in which they can help individuals do their own thing more effectively.

Likewise, political parties, and other political organizations designed around old-fashioned industrial approaches to politics, are unlikely to flourish in a new world of fluid coalitions and issue-oriented constituencies. They, too, may want to look more like eBay, and less like Ford, if they are interested in holding on to their members and influence.

DOWN WITH *DILBERT*?

Will people miss things about the old-fashioned employment market? Absolutely. Though "job security" under the old system was always a lot less than it appeared (ask any steelworker or airline pilot), the constant need to hustle up new business that successful self-employment requires is a very different way of life. And though big companies are subject to *Dilbert*-style inefficiencies and stupidities, they take advantage of division of labor in a way that the self-employed can't. On the other hand, most people who are self-employed, in my experience, tend to like it. Most people who work for big organizations don't. So perhaps, overall, job satisfaction will be higher. I hope so. Because, for good or for ill, this is the trend. And I think that it's here to stay awhile.

Jarvis's initial observation about big and small raises some interesting points of its own. It turns out that eBay *does* make health insurance available to its "Power Sellers"—basically, people who sell over $1,000 a month for three months and get good customer reviews—on terms that aren't bad.[8] (Wal-Mart's benefits also aren't as bad as Jarvis makes them sound.[9]) It's not the best deal in the world, but it's better than many full-time employers offer, and—unlike, say, auto workers—eBay Power Sellers don't have to worry about being laid off or fired because they've offended a boss.

Amazon.com has similar online programs for independent sellers via its zShops affiliates (which let individuals and small companies sell through its website) and its Amazon Associates program, which pays people referral fees for sales by customers they refer to Amazon.com's website. Their PR people were pretty unforthcoming when I asked them for information, but they did tell me that there are hundreds of thousands of people in both programs. No health insurance yet, but that could change.

This really isn't a question of big versus small; the key is to have both working together. It's easier to be small because outfits like eBay are big: eBay's buying power lets it make group insurance policies available to its sellers on terms they'd be hard-pressed to equal on their own. And by aggregating lots of minor sellers into one big marketplace, eBay makes it much easier for individuals to make a living buying and selling things via the Internet. Likewise, other big operations like Wal-Mart, Sam's, Office Depot, Staples, and Costco—which offer low prices, big selections, and support to small businesses—do the same kind of thing. By being big, they make it easier for other people to be small.

I think that there's a big future in this cooperation between the two. Many people like the idea of being self-employed, especially as technology makes it so much easier. But while you may not want to work for Dilbert's pointy-haired boss, you probably would want Dilbert's health plan. In a way, sites like eBay and Amazon are replacing or "disintermediating" the pointy-haired boss, and all other organizational layers between the people who do the work, and the actual customers. Similarly, music sites like GarageBand.com (which I'll discuss in more detail in Chapter Four) are disintermediating the record companies (and producers and A&R people) who sit between the musicians and their audiences.

But they're also *re*-intermediating by putting themselves in the role formerly occupied by the companies and management. To the extent that they're doing things that traditional companies used to do—dickering with health insurance companies and providing a trusted reputation that makes customers feel better about dealing with strangers they'll never meet—they're filling that niche. But they're doing so in a very different way, with very different implications for the economy, and for employment.

The secret to success in big business and politics in the twenty-first century, I think, will involve figuring out a way to capitalize on the phenomenon of lots of people doing what *they* want to do, rather than—as in previous centuries—figuring out ways to make lots of people do what *you* want them to. The eBay and GarageBand examples are just the beginning. I suspect that more enterprising folks will figure out ways to make money along the same lines.

ARE YOU BEING SERVED?

Another way that small is the new big, of course, doesn't have much to do with the Internet. As people have more money and more stuff, they often become more interested in buying services: purchases that buy time, like a cleaning service, or a certain kind of experience, like a spa retreat. Sometimes those services are substitutes for goods that people once bought, and sometimes—and I think this will be the wave of the future—the services are bound up with the goods themselves. And sometimes when we buy the goods, it's really the service we're after.

I'm a big fan of Virginia Postrel's work, not least because it seems to resonate with things that happen in my everyday life. Not long ago, her *New York Times* column eerily predicted a weekend shopping expedition of mine with my daughter.

I've bought my ten-year-old daughter countless shoes at big discount places: Target, Kohl's, Shoe Warehouse. When she was little, that was fine. Now that she's older, she's become a bit harder to please. Finding shoes that she likes, shoes that fit well (it's harder to keep her size straight now), is not so easy. So one Saturday we went to Coffin's Shoes, a venerable Knoxville outfit that's been selling shoes the old-fashioned way since the 1920s. A friendly salesman, who had obviously been doing his job for quite a while, measured her feet, listened to her talk about what she liked, had her try on a couple of shoes made on different-shaped "lasts" to get an idea of what she found comfortable, and then disappeared into the back, reemerging with a tower of shoes for her scrutiny.

After about half an hour of individual attention, we departed with two new pairs of shoes that she pronounced "the best shoes ever." And, she reported, they were comfortable. Of course, they cost more than it would have cost to buy shoes—even the same shoes, if that had been possible—at Target. But we wouldn't have gotten the service.

Now comes Postrel's column in the *New York Times,* where she notes that Americans are consuming more services and relatively fewer goods. "Listen to the economic debate carefully, and you might get the idea that the problem with the economy is that Americans just are not materialistic enough," she writes. It's a counterintuitive notion. So how does that square with reality? Pretty simple, really. "We spend too much of our income on restaurant meals, entertainment, travel and health care and not enough on refrigerators, ball bearings, blue jeans and cars. . . . As incomes go up, Americans spend a greater proportion on intangibles and relatively less on goods. One result is more new jobs in hotels, health clubs and hospitals, and fewer in factories." According to Postrel, between 1959 and 2000 the percentage of income that Americans spent on services jumped from about 40 percent to 58 percent. And, she says, "That figure understates the trend, because in many cases goods and services come bundled together."[10]

In fact, that's what I was really buying at the shoe store: goods and services bundled together. At places like Target, they're unbundled—you get goods, but not much in the way of service. (You get even less service at Wal-Mart or Costco). I bought the shoes at an old-fashioned shoe store. In the process I paid extra for the service, and I got my money's worth.

But that's only part of the story. There's more to this than simply choosing to spend money for a massage instead of a TV. As consumers become more interested in the total buying experience, the appeal of Big Box stores—whose approach consists of giving you *much* less service in exchange for *somewhat* lower prices—may decline; in turn, the appeal of old-fashioned specialty stores, where the salespeople know their products and their customers, may come back.

If people want a "dining experience" more than they want a cheap meal—and, as Postrel notes, nowadays they often do—then they're likely to want a shopping experience, not just cheap shoes. And they'll be willing to pay to get it. This won't mean the end of Big Box discounters any more than the desire for dining experiences has meant the end of fast food. (Some Big Boxes, as I've mentioned above, actually facilitate small businesses). But it may mean the reappearance of a certain kind of shopping—and certain kinds of jobs—that some people thought the Big Boxes would wipe out forever. And because people can get the basics of life cheaply at places like Wal-Mart, they'll actually have more money available to spend on that sort of shopping where non-basics are concerned.

Services can also replace goods. We tend to treat manufacturing as authentic and services as, somehow, bogus—not *real* economic activity. That's a traditional view of service industries harking back to Adam Smith. Manufacturing produces something tangible. The results of services are much less obvious.

Postrel, in fact, almost seems to accept this critique in

another column: "By missing so many new sources of productivity, the undercounts distort our already distorted view of economic value—the view that treats traditional manufacturing and management jobs as more legitimate, even more real, than craft professions or personal-service businesses. Still, more and more people are recognizing that true value can come as much from intangible pleasures as it can from tangible goods."[11]

But services can produce more than just "intangible pleasures." They can displace tangible goods. In fact, even "personal services" like massage therapy can displace goods, as I can attest from personal experience.

When practicing law in Washington back in the 1980s, I was one of the early laptop computer users, and I paid the price. I developed all the usual computer problems: numbness and shooting pains in my wrists and hands, backaches, neckaches, and headaches. My health plan then was the George Washington University HMO. So I got great care at a fancy teaching hospital that, since it could use me as a guinea pig to train medical residents, had no interest in cutting corners on treatments that did me no good at all. I was examined by neurologists, immunologists, occupational medicine specialists, and orthopedists. I had nerve conduction studies and electromyelograms. I was given powerful NSAIDs that upset my stomach but provided little relief. I was tested for lupus, myasthenia gravis, and Lou Gehrig's disease.

Then I went to a massage therapist, who dug her thumb into my back just inside a shoulder blade and asked, "Does this trigger your symptoms?" It did. She prescribed some stretches and exercises, and I got much better.

A pill that gave me an equivalent amount of relief would be considered a "product," and the worker who made it would occupy a "manufacturing job." But the pill would have side effects, and it would come out of a factory that consumed resources and energy, and produced pollution and waste, in a way that a massage therapist doesn't.

So the massage therapist is, in a sense, a replacement for that manufacturing job. What's more, the reason there are more massage therapists now, in part, is that more people can afford them. And more people can afford them because increasing productivity makes manufactured stuff—computers, clothing, food—cheaper. So when companies shift to automation or outsourcing to lower their costs, it in fact does help to produce new jobs at home.

To pick another example, consider the manufacture of cheap plastic dolls—whether Barbies, Bratz, or, God forbid, Liam Flavas (a manpurse-carrying metrosexual consort to the Flava line of urban dolls). My daughter used to spend most of her allowance money on that sort of thing. But more recently she's been spending her money at places like Club Libby Lu, a Sak's franchise where she gets "starlet makeovers" and the like. These cost about as much as a doll but, to my delight, they don't add to the mountain of trash at my house that has grown big enough to worry my garbagemen. Isn't the American economy actually better off when cheap plastic dolls made in China are replaced by services performed at home? Heck, I think it's better even than my daughter's money going toward cheap plastic dolls made in America: there's no environmental damage (except for the tenacious glitter-powder) and no addition to my trash pile. And makeovers are harder to move offshore.

And where, to belabor a point, do we get the money to pay for these services? In part, money is available because technology makes manufactured goods and food cheaper. And as society becomes richer, time and energy are spent doing things rather than in production. It's probably not a coincidence that many services (massage therapy, for example) actually work better on a smaller scale. Somehow I don't think a McMassage or a Wal-Mart Massage Center would do as well. Still, your masseuse may hold prices down by buying equipment at Wal-Mart, and you may be able to afford a massage because you were able to buy a six-pound bag of pasta for $2.29 at Sam's Club. As the big guys get better at being big, it's actually easier for the little guys to stay small. That's a kind of synergy we're likely to see more of.

3

THE COMFY
CHAIR REVOLUTION

I've noticed a gradual change in public surroundings over the
past few years. Unlike the hard, unappealing settings of traditional retail space (ground rule: "*get 'em in, get their money, get 'em
out*"), more and more stores are being designed to encourage customers to linger.

Some of these transformations are obvious—the cozy coffee
bars and cafés featured by many bookstores, for instance. But
the phenomenon has spread to less obvious locales. In the mall
near my house, for example, an Abercrombie spin-off called
Hollister & Co. features comfortable leather chairs complete
with end tables and stacks of magazines. The first time I was
there I joked to a salesgirl that I might come back with my laptop and camp out. "People do," she responded. And when I
went back a couple of weeks later, the circle of armchairs near-
est the cash registers was completely occupied by teenagers with
cell phones and PDAs. A conversation with a couple of staffers
confirmed that the store was intentionally designed to serve as a
"hangout."

And I think this shift in design may be the key to understanding how personal technology has changed us. In the old days, retailers knew that most people squeezed shopping in between the office and home. The goal was to sell as much as possible to people during the small amount of time available. Hence the keep 'em moving philosophy. But people live differently now. Lots of people work independently, or part-time, or as telecommuters. The lifestyle is more fluid, in part because technologies like cell phones, laptops, and PDAs allow people to work no matter where they are while also staying connected to family, friends, and colleagues. I see a lot of folks with that kind of personal tech hanging out wherever there's a pleasant setting, checking email, returning calls, or writing. It's work that doesn't quite feel like work.

THE APPEAL OF THE "THIRD PLACE"

This fluidity gives retailers and other businesses a different kind of opportunity. Retailers have always tried to sell the idea of a certain lifestyle along with their product: a sweater can become a symbol of social status. But if you become somebody's hangout, you don't just sell the suggestion of a kind of lifestyle, you're selling a particular way of life. If price and selection are the main basis for competition, people can always buy on the Internet; but everyone—especially teenagers—will still want a place to go. By becoming a place to hang out, a store can sell both the experience and the goods.

Does it work? Well, I'm writing this on a laptop in a Borders right now, comfortably ensconced upon a leather couch and waiting for the line to thin so I can order a latte. I do a lot of writing here, especially during the summers or on breaks when the university is closed. (And they sell me more books and CDs as a result.) A few years ago, in the pre-laptop, pre-Wi-Fi era, it would have been much more cumbersome and inconvenient to work and hang out simultaneously.

Examples of this trend are ubiquitous. A new public library in my area is breaking the old library taboo against food and installing a luxurious coffee bar of the sort normally found only in chain book superstores. Some malls provide a place for tired moms to chat on their cell phones while their kids romp in elaborate play areas. Health food stores provide welcoming spaces complete with live music and kitchen access. Even many churches in my area feature coffee bars with Wi-Fi.

As the trend has continued, we've started to see all sorts of amenities added: not just comfy chairs and beverage service, but wireless broadband Internet access, fireplaces, books and magazines (already begun at Hollister & Co.), and other furnishings and services designed to keep customers around, comfy, and receptive. Businesses reap rewards in the form of impulse buys and customer loyalty. But everyone enjoys the benefits of an abundance of safe, comfortable places to hang out, something that advocates of "community" were calling for just a few years ago.

People like to go out, and providing inexpensive hangouts may draw more business in a recession than when people are feeling flush. And it may be cheaper too, even when times are good. After all, you can buy a lot of comfy chairs for the price of a single Super Bowl ad slot.

Certainly the prevalence of comfy chairs and hangout-marketing bespeaks an attempt to meet an unfulfilled need for safe and comfortable public spaces. My Borders hangout is a good example—and it also illustrates how capitalism, combined with personal technology, can promote community.

I have an office with a nice computer, and I have a study at home with a nicer computer. But I often pack up my laptop, or a book that I'm reading, or student papers to grade, and relocate to this third place: somewhere more congenial than the office, less isolated than home.

Others must feel the same way because when I'm tapping away at my laptop, I find myself surrounded by people of all sorts. On a typical day, the place is hopping: tables are filled by students, alternately studying and flirting; a parent drilling a homeschooled child on Babylonian history; one or two road-warrior salespeople catching up on scheduling and messages; a gaggle of Bible-studiers arguing about Job; and a leather-clad cyberpunk youth sitting with his more conventional mother. By now, I know all the regulars by sight, and many by name. We keep up on each others' lives in a casual sort of way.

This third place, of course, is the "Third Place" that sociologist Ray Oldenburg called essential to civilization in his 1989 book *The Great Good Place.*[1] The third place, Oldenburg observes, must possess the following characteristics: it has to be free or inexpensive, offer food and drink, be accessible, draw enough people to feel social, and foster easy conversation. Oldenburg lamented that such places were disappearing.

Back in 1989, they were. Today, they're not—and you can thank the much-maligned chain book superstores for this. Certainly when I moved to my upscale Knoxville suburb some years ago there weren't many such places. Nor had there been many in Washington D.C.: the Afterwords Café at Kramerbooks was the closest thing, but it didn't really fit the bill. When I lived in New Haven, Connecticut, the famous Atticus Books was like a poor man's Borders: cozy, but no public restrooms. (They've since added them, in the face of competition from the palatial Barnes & Noble–operated Yale co-op down the street.)

Now, within about a mile of each other in my Knoxville suburb, stand three big bookstore/café complexes: Borders, Barnes & Noble, and Books-A-Million. All seem to be thriving.

They're doing well because they've identified a need and they're meeting it. You'd think that this would make a lot of people happy—and, of course, it does, as I can tell just by looking around. But you'd think it would make more than just the customers happy; you'd think that it would please the people who are always worrying about America's need for "community."

In that, however, you would mostly be mistaken. While hostility toward book superstores has receded from its late-1990s peak, it is still very real. Independent bookstores, we are told, are genuine; chain bookstores are all about marketing. Chain bookstores are bad for small presses, bad for communities, and—as Carol Anne Douglas writes in *Off Our Backs*—bad for feminists, whose books apparently can only be bought at "feminist bookstores."[2]

I don't know about the feminists, but small-press sales appear to be up thanks to chain bookstores' larger selection of titles. Communities are surely benefiting from the introduction of pleasant third places where they didn't exist before. And what's more, with the exception of a handful of independents, chain bookstores are better at being third places.

Perhaps this is because independent bookstores traditionally have been run by people who like books. These people generally aren't interested in offering the other amenities that Oldenburg names as important and that superstores provide: coffee shops, big chairs, and live music performances. At many independent bookstores, employees like books better than people and want you to know it—the bookish version of the music geeks in the book (and movie) *High Fidelity*.[3] (Small bookstores may not have the money for these amenities, either, though they're not terribly expensive).

The chains, however, aren't in business for personal gratification. They just want to keep customers coming back.

Want coffee? *Got it!*

Want a triple mocha latte and handmade fresh sandwiches and salads? *Got it!*

And, interestingly, the extra traffic that these amenities produce means that chain stores typically can afford a better selection of books than the independents, which is why small presses are benefiting right along with latte-lovers.

Well, no surprise there. That's what capitalism is all about. Funny that it's a dirty word to some people. But put technology and capitalism together, and what we often get is an updated version of the good old days; the changes we associated with technology and capitalism—fast-food-style uniformity, alienation, and lowest-common-denominator treatment—were actually products of a particular, and transitional, stage in technology. Now that the technology has changed, so have the economics, and so has the response from business. And it goes way beyond Borders.

As a believer in markets, I think that this trend will eventually find an equilibrium point. As an observer of the current direction of technological change, I think that equilibrium point will be a lot closer to where things were in the eighteenth century than to where they were just a few years ago. And this will be on account of many forces both pushing and pulling the change along. Let's look at these "pushes" and "pulls."

FORWARD MY MAIL TO STARBUCKS, PLEASE

The "push" comes from the office environment. You have almost certainly read *Dilbert*, and I'm tempted to simply cite the comic strip and say, "Case closed." But there's more to it than that.

Yes, the office environment can be unpleasant, and the commute can be nasty and time-consuming and expensive— just a few reasons people like to work at home. But working at home has its own problems. It can be hard to maintain the work/non-work boundaries. And who wants to meet with clients in your den?

On the other hand, offices are expensive. I've noticed a lot of small business people in my area giving up their offices and having meetings in public places—Starbucks, Borders, the public library, and so on. In fact, a real estate agent recently told me that the small-office commercial real estate market is actually suffering as a result of so many people making this kind of move.

The "push" comes from people wanting to get out of offices. But the "pull" comes from the technology that makes it possible, and from businesses' desire to cash in. The existence of personal tech like laptops, PDAs, and cell phones, coupled with Wi-Fi and other technologies that allow Internet access from all over means that you don't need to be at the office nearly as much anymore.

If a home is, in Le Corbusier's words, a "machine for living," then an office is a "machine for working." But nowadays, the machinery is looking a bit obsolescent. The traditional office took shape in the nineteenth century, largely due to new technology. People needed to be close to each other to communicate and make use of services like telegraphs, telephones, and messengers (and later copy and fax machines and elaborate computer equipment). You can pretty much carry all that stuff with you now. And people are doing just that.

Consequently, a market has arisen for places that cater to this more fluid workstyle. Right now we're seeing the early phase of that, with amenities that focus on Wi-Fi and lattes. In time, we're likely to see much more than that. A recent article in *Salon* by Linda Baker finds that many urban-design types are looking beyond connectivity to interconnectivity. For example, she points to pervasive urban networks that let people access the Web, determine whether their friends are in the area via a tool called FriendFinder, and arrange meetings:

> "I can come into downtown Athens [Georgia] with a PDA, send a text message that I'm going to be in Blue Sky Coffee for two hours, then turn it off and put it in my pocket," explains Shamp. "Then when one of my buddies comes into downtown, he can use the WAG zone to find out where his friends are."[4]

Various target groups will get different amenities; business users might like readily available Internet printing, for example, more than friend-finding—or maybe not. But my guess is that the end result will look more like the eighteenth-century coffee-houses, in which so many of that day conducted their business (Lloyd's of London started in Lloyd's coffee-house), than like the office towers where the twentieth century's men in the gray flannel suits encamped.

In the eighteenth century, the coffee-house was a hotbed of activity: "There," according to British newsweekly *The Economist*, "for the price of a cup of coffee, you could read the latest pamphlets, catch up on news and gossip, attend scientific lectures, strike business deals, or chat with like-minded people about literature or politics." These coffee-houses even served as offices—Richard Steele, editor of London's popular periodical, the *Tatler*, requested that his mail be delivered to his favorite coffee haunt. Londoners would drop in at several coffee-houses to participate in all kinds of conversation. "Regulars could pop in once or twice a day, hear the latest news, and check to see if any post awaited them. . . . [M]ost people frequented several coffee-houses, the choice of which reflected their range of interests."[5]

THE GENIUS OF BUILD-A-BEAR

I believe this is part of a larger phenomenon. Nineteenth- and twentieth-century technology seemed to favor aggregation, uniformity, and large size. Twenty-first-century technology seems to favor diversity, variety, and small size—along with a much higher degree of interconnection. From politics to work, from factories to malls, I think there are quite a few revolutions along these lines yet to come, and I think they'll go well beyond comfy chairs.

In fact, they're moving the factories into the malls. Build-A-Bear, a place where I've spent a lot of time, is a good example. My daughter had her birthday recently, and during her party I experienced what I'll call a Virginia Postrel moment. The party was at Build-A-Bear, a place that I thought was sure to go out of business when it first opened. *Why put a factory in a mall?* Who, I asked, would pay top dollar to assemble their own teddy bear or other stuffed animal when you could buy perfectly good ones off the shelf? Well, that was before I had a daughter, and now I know the answer: lots of little girls!

During the party it was interesting to watch the girls picking out animals with the help of the friendly salespeople. (Note: The phrase "Would you like me to stuff your monkey?" sounds, somehow, *er*, inappropriate.) As my wife pointed out, the animal-and-clothing combinations that the girls put together reflected their own personalities and styles.

The girls were very happy, but I couldn't help thinking that quite a few bluenoses would have disapproved. Customized bears (or monkeys!) that you put together yourself? An endless array of bear-pants, bear-glasses, bear-hats, bear-dresses, bear-briefcases, and even bear-roller skates to go with them? Who needs it? Rotten kids, spoiled rotten!

Except that actually they're rather nice girls, who with no prompting spent considerably less than the party budget allowed for, and who cooperated sweetly in picking things out and complimenting each others' choices. So as I was paying the bill (the cashier was an Albanian Kosovar refugee, who seems to have settled in rather well in that most inclusive and most American of institutions: the shopping mall), I had a Postrel moment: I realized why I was so thoroughly wrong about the prospects for Build-A-Bear.

Virginia Postrel has argued in her book, *The Substance of Style*,[6] that aesthetic values are becoming a major driver—perhaps the major new driver—of economic activity. It's easy to scoff at this because aesthetics seem divorced from function: an ugly car gets you where you're going just as quickly and reliably as a pretty one, an ugly coat keeps you just as warm as a handsome one, and an ugly house keeps the rain off just as well as a showplace.

Nonetheless, attractiveness matters. We all know that an ugly spouse can be just as faithful and loving as a gorgeous one—even, if popular legend is to be believed, more so—but we nonetheless tend to choose mates whose looks we like. To my daughter and her friends, it's natural to spend a lot of time thinking about what looks good. And, judging by the attention that my nephews pay to the subjects of their interests (automobiles, airplanes, and other vehicles, mostly), looks matter there too.

So does customization. What the folks at Build-A-Bear figured out, and what I missed entirely when I scoffed at their business plan, is that people don't just want things to look good. They want them to look good *their way*. That's what makes Build-A-Bear work.

Other stores have stuffed animals that are just as attractive, but the buyers don't feel that they are *unique*. So where will this lead? People talk about "customizing" outfits with accessories, but how long before on-the-spot manufacturing of clothing lets people design clothing themselves, or download designs from the Internet and produce truly one-of-a-kind outfits? People are already experimenting, and I suspect that a "Build-An-Outfit" will be coming soon to a mall near you.

I also suspect that it's just the beginning. (Design your own car? Why not?) But I also have another suspicion that verges on certainty: when it happens, people will complain. Just as people complained about the enforced conformity of old-style mass-production, people (often the same people) will complain about the multiplicity of choices offered by new technologies.

But then, complaining is an aesthetic style too, of a sort—though it's one that, for better and worse, may not fit in as well at malls as it does elsewhere. And as malls develop (beyond comfy chairs and Build-A-Bear) that may become much more significant.

Reportedly, the new trend is toward a different kind of mall, the "lifestyle center," which fits the beyond-comfy-chairs description pretty well. Changes in shopping habits and an increased competitiveness due to the Internet and other local specialized boutiques have motivated retailers in shopping centers to be more imaginative in order to keep bringing in customers.[7] And people are specifically invoking the "third place" point in pitching these facilities, as this account of one such venture makes clear:

> His idea for Camano Commons, a 3.3-acre gathering place, is to try to capture that European spirit of places where private commerce and public leisure mix readily, said the project's marketing director, Theresa Metzger.
>
> "In Paris, you have the sidewalk cafe. In England, you have the neighborhood pub," Metzger said. . . .
>
> "Americans are so unfamiliar with third places, so I always like to describe it this way: Remember the TV show,

'Cheers'? They didn't always get along, but when somebody was missing, they got concerned," Ericson said.[8]

I think we'll see more of that. In my local mall, blue-haired Goths with multiple piercings cluster in one area, while Dungeons & Dragons-playing teens stake out their territory in another spot. All the while, senior citizens and families stroll around them. It seems to me that the traditional downtown is being replaced by commercial spaces. And that has its ups, its downs, and its lessons.

The "up" is that Americans are getting the kind of safe, diverse, and communal public space that critics of suburbanization have long called for. Rather than being locked in their tract homes, watching television and not knowing their neighbors, Americans are increasingly spending their time in public spaces surrounded by all sorts of other people.

Another upside is that—unlike the cumbersome white-elephant "downtown revitalization" projects envisioned by urban planners and funded by massive quantities of taxpayers' money—these public spaces are market-driven and actually generate tax dollars rather than consume them. And, because it's market driven, the comfy-chair revolution can turn on a dime to meet consumer needs and interests.

FREEDOM OF . . . SHOPPING?

The downside is that the traditional downtown has been replaced by corporate-controlled space. What's wrong with that? Well, in the traditional downtown, things like the First Amendment's guarantee of free speech apply. In malls, they generally don't. (One of my former students has written an interesting law review article on this subject.[9]) But that's where the people are, meaning that First Amendment guarantees of the right to protest downtown are increasingly meaningless when nobody goes downtown. Indeed, here in Knoxville the antiwar protests, such as they were, were held on the sidewalk in front of West Town Mall when the protest organizers realized that a weekend protest downtown would be the proverbial tree falling unheard in the forest. Malls often have such offensive characteristics as omnipresent security cameras coupled with draconian bans on picture taking. It's not like Singapore, exactly, but it's not your old-fashioned downtown square either.

But there's a lesson too. One reason why people go to malls instead of downtown is that they feel safe. Part of this is physical safety. Though that's partly an illusion. Mall crime doesn't get reported much—all those advertisers make it easy to persuade local media to keep it quiet—but there's lots more of it than you'd think. Makes sense: criminals go where the money is, and a mugger would starve to death in most downtowns.

But more important than the desire for physical safety, I think, is the desire to go un-hassled by unpleasant people. Vagrants (relatively safe from prosecution in light of Supreme Court decisions), panhandlers, and accosters of pedestrians ranging from Bible-thumping street preachers to various political activists are free to express themselves in downtowns, thanks to the expansive First Amendment jurisprudence of the past half-century. But, except in a few states where the state constitution has been interpreted to treat malls as public space, they're barred from these spaces. And, in a curious coincidence, that's where people tend to go. (How do people really feel about this? I've observed that in the movie

Airplane, the audience always cheers when the airport solicitors get beaten up.)

So what's the lesson? Free speech absolutists (and I'm pretty much one myself) may tell people that being hassled by loud-mouths is part of democracy. And people may even agree—but they'll still choose the mall over downtown if the hassle-factor gets very high. What that means, among other things, is that public-sector rules are always subject to private-sector competition. It also suggests that you can enact rules that promote free speech at the cost of people being hassled—but if you go too far, people will vote with their feet by choosing a controlled environment with fewer hassles.

This sort of market-constrained approach to rights may trouble some people, though it's really just a public-private version of the sort of competition among states that federalists have always supported. Either way, it's a reality worth keeping in mind when planning rules and regulations for public and quasi-public spaces—especially since we are likely to see the latter increase as a result of the comfy-chair revolution.

The upside, though, is that the traditional lonely orator, try-ing to get his (it was almost always "his") message across in the public square, isn't so important as a symbol of free speech any-more. The Supreme Court once wrote, "The liberty of the press is the right of the lonely pamphleteer who uses carbon paper or a mimeograph just as much as of the large metropolitan publisher who uses the latest photocomposition methods."[10] But more recently, the Court noted, "Through the use of Web pages, mail exploders, and newsgroups, the same individual can become a pamphleteer."[11]

But, actually, technology has made it possible for individuals to become not merely pamphleteers, but vital sources of news and opinion that rival large metropolitan publishers in audience and influence. Since these independent sources are both *less* expensive and usually less annoying, perhaps First Amendment doctrine will take the difference into account.

Charles Black once wrote of "the plight of the captive auditor," who is subjected to messages that "he cannot choose but hear."[12] Limits to technology may have required us to overlook the captive auditor's plight in the past in the name of free speech—causing many people to vote with their feet in favor of controlled private space. But newer technologies may justify a different approach today: the First Amendment often requires the government to pursue the least restrictive means in regulating speech. Perhaps there should be at least an implicit requirement that speakers use the least *annoying* means of speaking too, or at least abide by limits when choosing the most annoying. This doesn't strike me as a bad thing. While the Internet makes publishing—and hence a free press—easier and cheaper, technologies like The Cloud and FriendFinder should make free speech, and public orations, easier and cheaper too, without the need to annoy. They'd better, anyway, because people's willingness to put up with annoyance is limited, while people's choices are, thanks to technology and the market, growing all the time.

What makes this issue difficult is that the tidy division between public and private spaces that we've taken for granted in recent years is breaking down. Traditional public spaces, like town squares, usually lack amenities. Even public restrooms are often hard to find. Private-public spaces like bookstores and coffee-houses have amenities and are open to everyone; but people tend to develop a proprietary interest in the places they frequent most. (No surprise to anyone who has ever heard a Londoner refer to "my pub.") Likewise, as people develop more control over their environments, they tend to have less tolerance for things that threaten that control. Americans tolerate TV commercials but hate popup ads, accept junk mail but despise spam, and, I suspect, will respond even less favorably to interruptions by strangers in public places once they become accustomed to meeting mostly with people they know or have something in common with. The "third place" may be a partial remedy to that, but as with the pub, we're likely to see people who don't fit in get a somewhat chillier reception. Determining the boundaries for acceptable public conduct, especially in private-public places, may prove a challenge in the future.

Working it out won't be easy, but then all revolutions have their difficulties.

4

MAKING BEAUTIFUL
MUSIC, TOGETHER

The popular media are obsessed with news about how technologies like Napster, Grokster, and BitTorrent are making life hard for musicians. But what they rarely report is how technology affecting everything from the latest equipment to file swapping and podcasting is also empowering ordinary people to create, not simply to copy.

That's certainly been my experience. Back in college I had a band. It wasn't a great band, but it was good enough to get gigs in all the local clubs. We recorded a couple of demo tapes, but to do that we had to rent time in a studio, pay an engineer, and then produce copies on cassettes. If I remember correctly, a demo cost about five hundred bucks, which was real money back in the Reagan years.

The studio had a big Tascam mixing board, which cost thousands of dollars, and a big Tascam reel-to-reel deck that tracks were recorded on. It cost thousands of dollars too. The recording heads had to be cleaned, demagnetized, and aligned regularly. The tapes were very expensive—a hundred bucks apiece for the good ones.

MUSIC BOXES

Things are different today. You can buy a "studio-on-a-shelf" (Tascam's trademark for its compact all-in-one recording devices) with infinitely more capability, and it costs you about a thousand bucks. And where Terry Hill's Camel Studios, the studio that we used, had eight tracks, the do-it-yourself model will have sixteen or twenty-four. I had to look hard to find a do-it-yourself-recording device limited only to what Camel Studios offered. The Musician's Friend website does list a Fostex 8-track all-in-one studio for $399, but it still does things that Camel Studios couldn't, like emulate different expensive microphones and guitar amplifiers using built-in computer models. Unlike Camel Studios, you can't get Terry Hill to sit in on guitars or offer unsolicited (and usually good) production advice, but on the other hand, the Fostex doesn't produce endless clouds of cigarette smoke either.

And the Fostex lets you burn CDs and transfer .wav files to a computer so that you can convert them to MP3s and upload them to the Internet. Despite his technical sophistication (Terry Hill was buddies with guitar gadget geniuses like Brian Eno, Robert Fripp, and Alvin Lee), mentioning any of those capabilities would probably have elicited a "Huh?" from Terry.

I've taken advantage of all of these kinds of capabilities myself. With some friends, I have a genuine studio with an eight-track digital tape deck, an impressive mixing console, and racks of effects boxes. I use the studio sometimes, but most of my recording is done at my house, on a computer, using an interface box by Echo audio; software like Cubase, Acid, and Audition; and various pieces of software that emulate actual instruments—programs that take the place of the old effect boxes with wires and glowing lights. My ReBirth RB-338, for example, emulates the old Roland TB-303 synthesizer that produces the sounds associated with classic techno—and it sounds cleaner than the real thing, which was originally designed as a cheesy accompaniment to lounge bands, not a studio instrument. My Native Instruments Pro-52 emulates a Prophet 5, a classic '70s-'80s synthesizer. And Cubase comes with all sorts of virtual instruments, including a surprisingly good electric guitar. Propellerhead's Reason is an entire studio and collection of virtual instruments aimed at producing trance and hip-hop; it costs about $400. Many of these software emulations do a surprisingly good job of capturing the sound and feel of the original instruments, often even offering graphic recreations of bakelite control knobs and analog meters on the computer screen.

These things let you make music easily and cheaply—although you still have to be able to make it sound good. When my wife made a documentary recently, I did the soundtrack entirely on the computer. I licensed a handful of loops (about ten seconds each) from Brian Transeau, a musician and sound designer I like a lot (he did the soundtrack to *Monster*), assembled them with some stuff I recorded myself, and created a soundtrack in a couple of weeks. Doing it the old-fashioned way would have cost thousands of dollars.

What's more, the new music often sounds better, if it's done right. I've always been a big fan of vintage equipment—my favorite keyboard is a Roland Juno—but the fact is that music recorded on computers often sounds cleaner and richer than music recorded on tape in studios. And software comes to the rescue there too—in my case, in a way that offers some broader lessons.

Polish software engineers are making me very happy. I know, I know: this sounds like some sort of punch line. But it's not, and here's why.

My brother and I have a small record label. It's not a non-profit, though it might as well be, but we have fun, and we're able to release things that a bigger record company—one whose share-holders actually cared about making money—might not touch, from Nebraska tractor-punk to native Ugandan music.

I'm the main sound engineer, and one of my tasks is to "master" everything. That means performing a variety of transformations to the finished mixes before they're turned into CDs: adding compression, adjusting the stereo image, normalizing levels, applying frequency equalization, etc. Mastering is more of an art than a science. When it's done right, everything on the song sounds just like it did before, only more so: "As if somebody cleaned the wax out of your ears" is a standard definition.

Nowadays there's even more to mastering. People object to what they judge to be the cold and harsh sound of digital recording. But the coldness isn't really caused by unpleasant digital distortion; rather, it's just the opposite: analog tape recording actually distorts the sound in ways that people *like*. Recording to tape adds even-numbered harmonics, smoothly rolls off the extreme highs, and because it doesn't respond linearly to increased volume it produces what's called "tape compression." All these distortions result in a feeling of warmth, fullness, and general ear-pleasing goodness. The harshness that people blame on digital technology actually comes from the absence of pleasant artifacts, not from any new quality that the digital recording process injects.

When mastering was done with rooms of equipment driven

by racks of glowing vacuum tubes, printing to half-inch-wide magnetic tape, this wasn't an issue. But now that we master on computers it is, and all sorts of software has appeared to generate the kind of warmth previously supplied by huge racks of vintage gear.

My favorite software—one of the many good programs of this kind—is produced by a Polish company called PSP Audioware. The sound is great, the software is very intuitive to use, and it's dirt cheap.

The cheapness comes from the way PSP does business: it's two guys, in Poland, who write the software themselves and distribute it via downloads from their website. They also provide tech support themselves (at least they've answered the few questions I've had), and since they're also the guys who wrote the software, they do a better job providing support than most computer users get from behemoth companies.

TRADING IN ELECTRONS

This is a mode of doing business that was impossible until recently, and it's one that's wonderfully suited to countries like Poland (and India) that have lots of smart people but suffer from mediocre infrastructure and a shortage of investment capital. I'm sure that shipping the software, on disks, from Poland to the rest of the world could be a much bigger headache, and produce far fewer sales, but Internet downloads solve these problems.

What's news about this is that it isn't news. Ten years ago, the notion of quality software from Poland would have been a joke to most people, and the idea of selling it to consumers over the

Internet would have seemed equally far-fetched. Yet now such ventures are commonplace. In the audio software field alone, there are literally dozens of companies like this—small shops, selling excellent software via download at very attractive prices, often from places not generally associated with computer leadership.

Twenty years ago, the guys at PSP would have been miserable drones in some horribly run state software enterprise, if they were able to work in software at all. Ten years ago, they would have been wondering how to sell their skills to the West without emigrating. Now they're earning hard currency from buyers around the world without having to manufacture or ship any tangible goods at all.

Remember this when people tell you that the whole Internet thing was just a bubble. But the impact doesn't stop there. With that software, I mastered some recordings by a Ugandan band called Afrigo. My brother is an African historian and travels to Africa regularly. He found out about Afrigo, the most popular band in Uganda, and offered to help them get some broader exposure.

Internet access was lousy in Kampala then, so they mailed us some CDs (they record their music on one of those studio-on-the-shelf setups). I mastered it using the PSP software and uploaded their songs to the MP3.com website. Back then, before it was destroyed by music-industry lawsuits, MP3.com was the place to go for interesting independent music. (There's still an MP3.com site, but it's nothing like what used to exist.) What's more, bands got paid based on how much their songs were downloaded. Afrigo's music turned out to be pretty popular, and it earned a few hundred dollars a month. That's not a lot of money to an American band, but it's a pretty good chunk of change in Uganda.

What's more, their exposure on the site got their music noticed elsewhere. If MP3.com had lasted longer, I think it would have helped more African bands, but the Internet will do the job anyway, given time. Perhaps the world's greatest reservoir of wasted human talent—that is, ability that was never developed and recognized to the degree it deserves—is Africa. And, because of that, Africa may have the most to gain from the communications revolution.

Africa has been exporting music to the world for centuries, of course. Almost every musical form of the past century—from gospel, to ragtime, to blues, to jazz, to rock and roll, to reggae, to techno—has its roots in African musical styles. And African art has influenced Western artists from Picasso to Modigliani to Renee Stout.

The world has gotten a lot from Africa. Africa, however, has gotten much less from the world. But that may change now that Africans are working in media that can make money with the Internet and other communications technologies, making it easier to get work out and other people's money in. It's not just Afrigo. Other bands like Ilay Izy from Madagascar (playing a mixture of tribal vocals and hip hop), Ras Shaheema from Namibia (reggae), or Co. Operative from Zimbabwe are taking advantage of new technologies. We get the benefit of the diversity of African music today while their chance of financial viability greatly increases.

It's not just music. Awhile back I watched a Nigerian movie called *To Rise Again*: an enterprising mixture of *Scarface*, *Sliding Doors*, and *It's a Wonderful Life*. Nigeria's film industry is booming and is now a regional threat to India's third-world film capital of Bollywood.

To Rise Again is a well-done and interesting picture, with a budget probably in the neighborhood of $20,000. Africans, Nigerian expatriates around the world, and American film buffs in the States have all been able to participate in its success. Thanks to DVD and Video CD technology, distributing a movie is nothing like the challenge it was a couple of decades ago. And film-making—thanks to digital video cameras and PC-based editing—is not nearly as expensive as it was even a few years ago.

Given that Africans have as much talent and ambition as you'll find anywhere else, these lowered barriers are likely to mean that African musicians, actors, producers, and directors will enter the global market at a growing rate. And given that, historically, African culture has been very intriguing, even appealing, to the world at large, the growth of inexpensive communications technologies is likely to mean a greater Africanization of world culture in general.

African culture has taken the world by storm even in the face of drastic economic and transportation barriers. Imagine what it may accomplish now that those barriers are falling. While it may be a long time, if ever, before Africa becomes an entertainment center to rival, say, California, its share of the world market seems likely to grow dramatically, while California's influence shrinks.

The consequences are likely to be interesting. Antiglobalization types accuse American culture of spreading Western ideas that corrupt "traditional" cultures. Yet, if you listen to African songs, you find more religious influence than you find on the American charts, including many Christian-influenced songs.

Likewise, the Nigerian film industry, based in Christian southern Nigeria, is heavily Christian-influenced, producing works that make the "Left Behind" films look downright secular by comparison. Its continental rival, the Ghanaian film industry, has a similar orientation, with a heavy inclination toward Pentecostalism.

If these industries grow, the result could well be a far more Christianized Third World. What will the antiglobalization folks say if the growth of Third World entertainment industries leads to a far more conservative media climate around the world?

Regardless, new technologies have created jobs and prospects in Africa that were almost unimaginable back in 1985. Which raises a question: While the rock stars who gave of their time to perform at Live Aid and Live 8 received much public praise for their selflessness, what of the engineers and scientists whose work made these new technologies possible? Will they get similar praise? Probably not, though reportedly Bill Gates was cheered like a rock star at the Live 8 concerts.[1]

APPLE STARTED IN A GARAGE, TOO

MP3.com is gone, but its successor, in many ways, is a company called GarageBand.com. GarageBand, like MP3.com, provides a website that hosts music for bands and allows bands and their fans to connect in various ways. GarageBand draws about 150,000 bands—a pretty large fraction of the million or so bands in the United States—especially when you allow for the fact that GarageBand's artists are all writing and recording original music. These aren't the bands that play "Proud Mary" at weddings.

I spoke with GarageBand's CEO, Ali Partovi, about where all this is going.[2] Partovi is an open-faced entrepreneur whose previous venture, LinkExchange Inc., wound up being bought by Microsoft for $265 million. (It's still around as bCentral.) Partovi spoke so rapidly that I had to ask him to slow down, but it seemed like the excitement of an enthusiast, not the fast talk of a salesman. And there's a lot to be excited about.

The key to GarageBand's approach is filtering, but with a human touch. Lots of people listen to the music and review it. Every band gets a chance: musicians upload music, then review each other's work. You don't know much about the artist until after you've done your review; and unlike certain MTV stars, you can't make it on looks alone. A song can rise on the charts very rapidly if people like it; or it can languish for a long time, with no help from big-label payola, if they don't.

Partovi says that this appeals to two things that motivate musicians. "It's both money and a desire to be heard. An increasing number just want to be recognized. There's a mixture of both on our site." The most serious people, he says, usually want to make money: "Music production is time consuming, even with the best technology, so if you're serious you want a payoff. On the other hand, there are lots of people just below the top level who just want to have fans."

GarageBand has already had some success in moving its stars off the Internet and into the wider world. Geoff Byrd's pop-rock songs, which topped the GarageBand charts, were getting enough radio airplay to drive them, at the time of my Partovi interview, to the top 40 on Billboard's radio charts. Another artist, Jenna Drey, was number 23 on the Billboard dance chart. Both made it without the big promotional investments that record companies usually make to get artists on the charts.

What's the secret? Partovi says that it's simple: people tend to like what other people like. The GarageBand songs are pretested on a lot more people than the songs of unknown artists who are signed by record labels. "The role that GarageBand is increasingly playing is as a filter that can predict radio success. That's a very important role. Instead of 'invest first,' the Internet allows us to 'test first' before a big investment. That changes things for both artists and labels."

This probably doesn't mean doomsday for record labels, but it certainly does change things. Partovi thinks that record companies will have less to offer musicians, and consumers, in the future. "Twenty years ago there was no alternative [to the record-label route], because production and distribution were so capital-intensive. Those aren't anymore, but promotion has become much *more* capital-intensive because there's so much more music out there. Major labels have been reduced to providing the capital for promotion, and the Internet will cut into that too." Record labels' days of holding the whip hand are over. Contrary to what the record industry people thought, Napster wasn't the threat; it's out-fits like GarageBand.com that provide rival services to musicians and listeners alike that pose a real problem for their industry.

The same may be true for radio. Partovi is very enthusiastic about podcasting, which lets pretty much anyone get into the Internet "radio" business by recording broadcasts that are auto-matically downloaded and copied onto people's iPods and other portable music players. Podcasters, he says, are becoming a new route for people to discover music they like. "It's the cultural trend of amateur DJs discovering new music—performing the role that radio DJs should have performed for the last twenty years but haven't. A regular FM DJ could get fired for playing a song by a new artist. Podcasting unlocks that."

Interestingly, he thinks that DJs may thrive in this new atmosphere: "DJs play an important role. Consumers want new music, but most don't want to take the trouble to find it on their own. They want someone else to do the filtering, and the human touch is key."

What's more, podcasting is a better promotional tool than radio in some ways. If you hear a song you like on the radio, you have to figure out what it is, then go find out about the artist. With podcasting it's different: "Once you discover an artist you like via a podcast, the technology makes it easy to find out more about the artist. You can find a band via a DJ's podcast, follow a link to subscribe to the band's podcast, and then the band doesn't need a middleman to get in touch with you. You'll know when they have something new."

That's not only important for the little guy, but for established artists like Paul McCartney who are no longer darlings of the radio. All musicians benefit from a way to reach their fans that doesn't depend on the radio business; the Internet provides one. And it's not just GarageBand or podcasting getting in on the act—another site, CDBaby.com, has sold 1.7 million CDs and made over $16 million for its artists.

GarageBand offers a lot of podcasting tools on its website, allowing bands to communicate with their fans—and allowing anyone else who wants to set up a podcast, musical or otherwise, to do so. The *Wall Street Journal*'s technology columnist, Walt Mossberg, tried it and found it easier than most other systems for creating podcasts; there's even a feature that lets you create a podcast by telephone. Still, he concluded (and I agree) that creating podcasts remains a lot harder than creating text-based blog entries.[3] That's likely to change soon, though.

On the receiving side, podcasts have gotten a lot more user-friendly. Apple has upgraded its iTunes to let users subscribe to podcasts via a point-and-click interface, so that anyone who owns an iPod will find it easy to subscribe. Once that's done, iTunes will check for new podcasts from that source and then download them every time a user plugs in the iPod. And GarageBand is thinking of creating a podcasting site that specializes in nonmusical subjects, like interviews and news reporting.

THE FCC WON'T LET ME BE

One of the biggest things holding podcasting back—and protecting commercial radio—is the copyright barrier. Radio stations operate under so-called "blanket licenses." By paying an annual fee to clearinghouse organizations like ASCAP or BMI, they can play songs without having to get permission for each one. The clearinghouses then divide the money according to a formula and forward payments to artists. (Nothing wrong with that; I'm an ASCAP member myself and occasionally get a check when somebody uses one of my songs.)

On the Internet, however, things are much harder. In a recent column in *Wired* magazine, Larry Lessig reports on how copyright concerns made it effectively impossible for a nonprofit he works with to put a recording of "Happy Birthday" (yes, it's still under copyright and will be until 2030) on the Web. At first, they thought they could purchase a "mechanical license" (which operates under a similar sort of clearinghouse arrangement). But then the lawyers decided that they needed a separate permission from Warner/Chappell Music, which manages the rights to "Happy Birthday." Warner first agreed to grant them a license for $800, but then changed its mind. By that time, the lawyers were worried that people would take Lessig's performance and remix it, making him an accessory to copyright infringement. Lessig concludes: "The existing system is just workfare for lawyers."[4]

Yes, it is. And it's likely that commercial broadcasters—who are seeing their audiences shrink because, not to put too fine a point on it, their programming stinks—will oppose any legal changes that might eliminate this sort of barrier. Anything that makes life easier for podcasters, and Web music in general, is likely to make things worse for them. At this point, their comparative advantage isn't technological or creative: it's the advantage conferred by a friendlier legal environment.

Of course, radio stations are relying on such legal protection, even from their old-media competitors, in the form of low-power radio. Because as things stand now, the Federal Communications Commission is a major barrier to free speech, and the only justification for its position has been exploded.

How big a barrier? This big, where radio is concerned:

Freedom to create means more than that: not just the right to choose among 500 TV stations instead of three, but fewer barriers to setting up a station of your own; not just greater ease in joining the officially licensed elite, but the right to operate outside it. Like the freedom to choose, the freedom to create is being withheld by an alliance of policymakers and professionals. The technical cost of starting a station has been within most Americans' reach for years. The legal cost, however, is much higher: thousands of dollars to purchase an existing license, thousands more to cross various regulatory hurdles. With very few exceptions, the FCC won't even issue licenses to noncommercial stations of less than 100 watts. Class A commercial stations require at least 6,000 watts of power.[5]

Some years ago, the FCC decided to license low-power radio as a separate category. Powerful broadcasting interests—including, ironically, National *Public* Radio—responded to the threat of competition by lobbying successfully for legislation that made the licensing of low-power stations far more difficult. In particular, the spacing between stations that the bill required made the creation of low-power stations in urban areas very difficult. One of the requirements of the bill, however, was a technical study on interference, with a provision for removing the spacing requirement if the study showed that interference wouldn't be a problem.

Now the study, done by the MITRE Corporation, has been released with little fanfare and only after the threat of a Freedom of Information Act demand. Such reluctance suggests that the FCC didn't much want to hear the study's results. And that may be because the study finds that low-power FM radio doesn't pose a significant interference problem. Here's an excerpt from the study:

Based on the measurements and analysis reported herein, existing third-adjacent channel distance restrictions should

be waived to allow LPFM operation at locations that meet
all other FCC requirements [after four small revisions]. . . .
Perceptible interference caused during the tests by temporary LPFM stations operating on third-adjacent channels
occurred too seldom . . . to warrant the additional expense
that those follow-on activities would entail.[6]

Here's the question a lot of people have been raising lately: Is the
FCC really devoted to efficient and diverse communications, or is
it just a bureaucratic flunky for the big broadcasting companies?
The FCC's response to the MITRE report—which was buried in
the comment section of the FCC's website and not publicly
announced—suggests that the cynics may be right. But it's not too
late for the FCC to prove them wrong.

Former FCC Chair Michael Powell's justification for relaxing
the rules on broadcast media concentration was that new media—
the Internet, satellite broadcasting, etc.—would ensure that concentration in commercial broadcasting would be offset by new
sources of information. As James Plummer wrote awhile back,
ending the suppression of microradio is a better way of promoting diversity than more regulation.[7] If the FCC really believes in
broadcast diversity, then now that the bogus interference concerns
raised by NPR and the National Association of Broadcasters have
turned out to be, well, bogus, it should endorse the growth of low-
power FM stations. Sure, Clear Channel and NPR don't want to
face the competition. But protecting fat cats from competition
isn't what the FCC is all about, is it?

Or maybe it is. But as more and more people get access to the
tools of creation and distribution, it's more likely that politicians

will recognize that there are more voters who want to create than voters who want to stand in their way. The FCC has made some moves of late to make low-power FM stations easier to establish, but it is still treating them as second- or third-class citizens: unprotected from interference and often overridden by "translators" used to extend the range of big commercial and public stations. Legislation before Congress might change that, but it's strongly resisted by broadcasters, as you might expect.

Anxious to hold on to its piece of the pie, Big Media encourages restrictions that make the field—movies, music, broadcasting, whatever—less attractive to consumers.[8] So customers leave the field entirely or substitute goods that are less regulated. Unable to get permission to use commercial music on the Internet, people often turn to independent bands that license their music freely. Radio gets duller and more boring, so people turn to podcasts. Movies are more restricted so people turn to videogames or independent films. As Princess Leia said to Grand Moff Tarkin: "The more you tighten your grip, the more star systems will trickle through your fingers." That's a lesson—taken from one of its own products, no less—that the entertainment industry would do well to learn.

5

A PACK, NOT A HERD

Unfortunately, technology empowers the bad people as well as the good. Take terrorists, for example. Modern explosives, computers, and communications magnify the damage that an individual or a small group can do. On the other hand, technology also makes the rest of us better equipped to face such threats. Dealing with both sides of that equation will be one of the big challenges of the twenty-first century.

Right now, we're not dealing with it especially well. Governments want to keep this sort of power to themselves, and they're not very good at taking small-scale approaches to, well, anything. For governments, bigger is almost always better.

But, in fact, responding to attacks and disasters is something that individuals and small groups may be better situated to deal with than governments. Certainly the amateurs on the scene have one big advantage that the government usually lacks: they're on the scene. In all sorts of circumstances and capacities.

PRIVATIZING THE CYBER WAR

It is no secret that Al Qaeda and other Islamic terror groups make extensive use of the Web. Some websites provide coded messages, in the same way radio stations used to broadcast coded messages for spies in enemy territory. Others play a role in recruiting, disseminating propaganda, and soliciting donations. Some may serve all of these functions.

No doubt various official U.S. government agencies are looking at these sites in order to gather intelligence and identify enemies. But they're not alone. In fact, a surprising number of ordinary citizens have gotten involved as well.

Sometimes, the stings are quite elaborate. For example, the pseudonymous hacker "Johnathan Galt" appears to have set up a phony pro-terrorism site that solicited support and donations from those sympathetic to Islamic terror. After operating for several months (with, apparently, the assistance of Islamist bin-Laden sympathizers who thought it was genuine), the site became a new and improved anti-Islamic terror site sporting the legend, "We've changed our mind: Jihad is crap!" No doubt Mr. Galt also harvested a great deal of information useful to the authorities, including IP addresses, cookie-tracking information, and, of course, identity information via the PayPal donations he accepted.[1]

Similarly, Internet entrepreneur "Jon David," who runs a number of Internet porn sites as his day job, has made a hobby out of hijacking pro-terror websites. Most recently he scored a coup by successfully taking over the Al Qaeda website.[2] Visitors were redirected to a mirror page operated by David, from which he harvested 27,000 IP addresses per day, along with other information he has shared with the FBI. (No big surprise in one discovery: 90 percent of his visitors came from Saudi Arabia.)

Not as James-Bondian but still pretty important, webloggers like Charles Johnson ask their readers to look for pages containing support for terrorism, publicize the results, and attempt to bring pressure on the ISPs to shut the sites down. And other folks have jumped in with ideas for disinformation and pranks that will spread confusion among jihadists at very low cost.

At the very least, website monitoring helps keep people informed of what's going on, and website hacking means that terrorists and terrorist wannabes have to constantly worry about whether their Web operations have been compromised. Both kinds of actions serve to make life much tougher for terrorists and their supporters.

It's hard to know how these actions compare to whatever is being done by government agencies. Possibly, far more sophisticated operations are underway by skilled and well-equipped government hackers. On the other hand, Jon David's experience suggests otherwise. When David approached the FBI to tell them that he had captured Al Qaeda's website and that he was eager to cooperate, the FBI's response was glacial:

> It literally took me five days to reach anyone in the FBI that had an even elementary grasp of the Internet. By that time, the hostiles realized the site I had up was a decoy and then advised everyone away from it. I still gave the FBI all the log information and link information to the hostile boards and whatnot, but it's far from what could have potentially been done if they would have acted more quickly.[3]

The good news is that the Bush administration seems to be figuring out that creative individuals may be able to complement law enforcement's more traditional approach. Richard Clarke, when he was White House computer security adviser, publicly encouraged white-hat hacking and offered to put the administration's weight behind any legislative changes needed to protect good-guy hackers from prosecution or litigation. That's a good start, especially in light of the software industry's tendency to punish those who point out flaws in fear of bad publicity. But Clarke was mostly concerned with probing friendly systems for weaknesses. Clarke's long gone now, and I'm not sure that his successor is as supportive. What we really need is a counterterrorist program that harnesses the energy and innovation of good-guy hackers. Terrorism is a decentralized, fast-moving threat, which means that a decentralized, fast-moving response makes sense. Bureaucracies aren't good at that, but ordinary Americans are.

Electronic privateering, anyone? It's an idea whose time may have come.

LEARNING CURVES

But, of course, the role of involved citizens, empowered by technology, goes well beyond that. In fact, we saw it on 9/11.

Albert Einstein once said that the most powerful force in the universe is compound interest. Arguably so. But I think that the most powerful force in the human universe is the learning curve.

The war on terrorism provides good examples of this phenomenon on both sides. Before September 11, the terrorists were the ones with a learning curve. Although there is plenty of evidence that the Al Qaeda crowd isn't especially bright, over the years they demonstrated the salutary (for them) qualities of persistence and willingness to learn from mistakes. When truck bombing the World Trade Center failed, they started looking at airplanes. When initial efforts to hijack airplanes failed, they changed their approach.

The aviation-security establishment, meanwhile, was much less adaptable. It concentrated on stopping 1970s style skyjackings, where the chief goal was publicity (and perhaps money) rather than murder. Later, efforts began to turn toward blocking Lockerbie-style bomb smuggling. And because the security system was blocking such efforts with a fair degree of efficiency, it didn't change its approach even when confronted with indications that the terrorists were changing theirs. Bureaucracies are supposed to be about sharing information, but information is power in bureaucracies, and people are not all that keen about sharing power.

The result was that, on September 11, the terrorists held all the cards. They carried only items that did not violate carry-on rules. They avoided scrutiny designed to thwart bomb-smugglers—scrutiny based on the assumption that terrorists wouldn't want to die with their victims. They took advantage of a stay-passive philosophy that urged (indeed, required as a matter of policy) cooperation rather than confrontation with hijackers.

But no sooner did the first plane strike the World Trade Center than the hijackers had to confront someone with a swifter learning curve. As Brad Todd noted in a terrific column written just a few days later, American civilians, using items of civilian technology like cell phones and twenty-four-hour news channels, changed tactics and defeated the hijackers aboard United Airlines' Flight 93. These civilians overcame years of patient planning in less than two hours.

Just 109 minutes after a new form of terrorism—the most deadly yet invented—came into use, it was rendered, if not obsolete, at least decidedly less effective.

Deconstructed, unengineered, thwarted, and put into the dust bin of history. By Americans. In 109 minutes.

And in retrospect, they did it in the most American of ways. They used a credit card to rent a fancy cell phone to get information just minutes old, courtesy of the ubiquitous twenty-four-hour news phenomenon. Then they took a vote. When the vote called for sacrifice to protect country and others, there apparently wasn't a shortage of volunteers. Their action was swift. It was decisive. And it was effective.[4]

No one has successfully hijacked a Western civilian airliner since—and, as "shoe bomber" Richard Reid learned, those terrorists who threaten civilian airliners now tend to emerge rather the worse for wear. Against bureaucracies, terrorists had the learning-curve advantage. Against civilians, they did not.

No surprise there. American civilians, perhaps even moreso than counterparts in Europe, Japan, and the rest of the industrialized world, are used to making rapid changes based on new information. Accustomed to a steep learning curve in business and in life, we should be able to out-adapt those who, after all, are ultimately committed to returning the world to a simulacrum of the twelfth century.

There's a lesson here. Societies that encourage open communication, quick thinking, decentralization, and broad dispersal of skills—along with a sense of individual responsibility—have an enormous structural advantage as opposed to societies that don't, an advantage that increases in a world of high technology and unconventional war. But tyrants and fanatics of whatever stripe cannot afford to encourage those traits in their citizens if they want to remain in power. The message that this should send to our adversaries is one they should find disheartening: The only way you're likely to beat us is by becoming like us—at which point, more than likely, you won't want to beat us anyway.

The Americans acting aboard Flight 93 were not an aberration. In fact, Americans responded to the 9/11 attacks in similar fashion elsewhere.

One barely reported story from September 11 illustrates this better than any other. The improvised navy evacuated roughly a million people by boat from Lower Manhattan, in an operation that some have called an American Dunkirk. Ferries, commercial boats, and pleasure craft spontaneously assembled to carry people away from the scene of the attack and to return with needed supplies:

People at Ground Zero, the Manhattan Waterfront, nearby New Jersey, Staten Island and Brooklyn waterfronts, and crews on the numerous vessels repeatedly used the phrases "just amazing," "everyone cooperated," and "just doing what it took" to describe maritime community responses. Individuals stepped up and took charge of specific functions, and captains and crews from other companies took their direction. . . . Private maritime operators kept their vessels onsite and available until Friday, Day Four, when federal authorities took over.[5]

"Day Four, when federal authorities took over." There's a lesson in that phrase, isn't there? This wasn't just an evacuation: it was a whole alternative logistic system, improvised on the fly by people who didn't work for the government. Fuel, water, and food were brought in; when there were problems moving big pieces of steel at the site, the boats brought structural ironworkers from New Jersey along with boots, oxygen, and acetylene cylinders, and whatever else was needed. This effort got some coverage at the time but has largely been forgotten in the aftermath since ad hoc groups don't have PR agents to keep their deeds in the public eye. Still, it was one of the most amazing feats of human self-organization ever, and it deserves more attention than it got.

Of course, many of the players in the New York evacuation and supply effort already possessed the technical skills that they needed—it was just a question of applying them to the job at hand. Such might not be the case among a group of ordinary citizens at the scene of another disaster.

GETTING READY

But things don't have to be that way. With a modicum of effort, it might well be possible to ensure that people at the scenes of disasters are prepared and possess the necessary skills for quick action on their own. How? By training them now.

Both the prevention of and the response to terrorism might be handled, at least in part, on a dispersed-among-the-citizenry basis. Prevention could be done by training volunteers to watch for suspicious indications that might warn of terrorism, and perhaps even inform certain select (but large) groups of intelligence data.

The September 11 hijackers and D.C. shooter John Muhammad displayed lots of warning signs. The problem is that we were not ready to read those signs.[6]

Citizens could do much more in response to terrorism. Many have suggested encouraging people who are licensed to carry guns (an early technology for empowering individuals) to do so. After all, it was armed individuals working for El Al, rather than a law enforcement agency, who stopped Mohammed Hadayet's Los Angeles International Airport shooting spree almost as soon as it started. Armed citizens, especially if trained in what to look for, could be a very valuable line of defense against terrorism. In almost every instance of terrorism, the true first responders will be the people already on the scene. And, as Flight 93's passengers reminded us, that response can be decisive.

In addition, people trained in first aid (especially the specific skills likely to be useful in the aftermath of a terrorist attack), in recognizing the signs of chemical or biological attack, and in various other disaster-recovery skills could contribute a lot. Even in the case of such relatively "mundane" events as truck bombings and shooting sprees, individuals on the scene will have to wait crucial minutes before aid even begins to arrive.

People should also be encouraged to carry cameras, or video cameras, and use them in the immediate moments after an attack to gather potentially valuable data. Would people remember to use them? Probably. They often take video of disasters anyway (there's something about a viewfinder that tends to steady the nerves); it wouldn't take much to get people to do that.

In the case of the D.C. sniper attacks, even a massive law

enforcement presence couldn't prevent terror attacks it knew were about to happen. But an informed and prepared citizenry—the likes of which stopped "shoe bomber" Richard Reid, helped stop Mohammad Hadayet, kept Flight 93 from smashing into the Capitol, and finally caught D.C. snipers Muhammad and Malvo—can be everywhere. It already is.

After repeatedly slipping through the fingers of law enforcement, John Muhammad and Lee Malvo were caught because leaked information about the suspects' automobile and license number was picked up by members of the public, one of whom spotted the car within hours and alerted the authorities. He even went so far as to block the exit from the rest area with his own vehicle to make sure they didn't escape. "You can deputize a nation," said one news official after the fact.

With proper information, the public can act against terrorists—often, as we found on September 11, faster and more effectively than the authorities. The key, as blogger Jim Henley noted, is to "make us a pack, not a herd."[7]

The problem is that this goes against the very grain of intelligence agencies, law enforcement agencies, and the rest of the bureaucratic infrastructure. Within bureaucracies in general—and doubly within intelligence and law enforcement bureaucracies—information is power, and power isn't something you want to share. If you deputize a nation, doesn't that make the *official* deputies feel just a little bit less special?

The problem with this mindset is that it's all about bureaucratic turf, and not about getting the job done. Otherwise we'd have learned the lesson long ago. As Canadian journalist Colby Cosh remarked:

I'd have thought the Unabomber case would have taught
police, I don't know, *everywhere* that it is better to be liberal
than stingy in releasing information to the public. Remember the Unabomber—the serial killer who was caught
because his *prose style* was recognized? Yeah, that guy. If
Charles Moose and his merry men had actually succeeded in
sitting on the information they wanted sat upon,
Muhammad and Malvo might have been popping another
D.C.-area shopper's head like a grape while you read this.
Keep this in mind as you hear their police work praised in
the days to follow.[8]

That's a bit harsh, but the point is clear. There are good reasons
police might want to keep some kinds of information confiden-
tial—they need details that will let them screen out calls from nut-
balls other than the real killer (though that didn't work very well
in the D.C. sniper case), and they don't want to create an unnecessary panic or provoke an orgy of finger-pointing and suspicion.
These are actions based on legitimate concerns, but they can actually facilitate crime if overdone. And police are overdoing them.

It seems pretty clear that the authorities, overall, view the citizenry as a herd, not as a pack. They see ordinary people as sheep,
with themselves in the role of shepherd. Without close supervision, they assume, people will erupt into mob violence, or scatter
in fear.

The evidence, however, doesn't support this assessment. As
sociologist Kathleen Tierney writes, contrary to what pop portray-
als of disaster might have predicted, the response of ordinary New
Yorkers to the 9/11 attacks was "adaptive and effective":

Beginning when the first plane struck, as the disaster literature would predict, the initial response was dominated by
prosocial and adaptive behavior. The rapid, orderly, and
effective evacuation of the immediate impact area—a
response that was initiated and managed largely by evacuees
themselves, with a virtual absence of panic—saved numerous lives. Assisted by emergency workers, occupants of the
World Trade Center and people in the surrounding area
helped one another to safety, even at great risk to themselves. In contrast with popular culture and media images
that depict evacuations as involving highly competitive
behavior, the evacuation process had much in common
with those that occur in most major emergencies. Social
bonds remained intact, and evacuees were supportive of one
another even under extremely high-threat conditions.[9]

What's more, such responses are typical, even though they often
infuriate outsiders. For the government it's upsetting, because
people aren't asking it what to do. For the media it's frustrating,
because there's no one in charge to interview. But we shouldn't
assume that these frustrations have anything to do with effectiveness. As Tierney notes, people improvising on the scene often *look*
disorganized because there's nobody in a uniform running things.
But their on-the-spot improvisations and local knowledge often
make them more effective than a more impressive-looking operation made up of people in uniforms.[10]

So while Chief Moose and the other talking heads were holding press conferences in which they castigated the press for
reporting information, they should have been figuring out how

to take advantage of the vast resources that a mobilized public can command. But the officials didn't want to, for fear of "vigilantes." Luckily for them, a leak saved the day.

Regardless of whether or not the D.C. snipers count as "terrorists" under your particular definition (they do under mine, but the authorities seem to have been shooting for a much narrower standard), there seems little question that in coming years we're going to be dealing with a lot of fast-moving, dispersed threats of the sort that bureaucracies don't handle very well. (Every dramatic domestic-terrorism victory so far, from Flight 93 to bringing down the LAX shooter to spotting the D.C. killers was accomplished by non-law-enforcement individuals). Rather than creating new bureaucracies, we need to be looking at ways of promoting fast-moving, dispersed responses, responses that will involve members of the public as a pack, not a herd. Even if doing so reduces the career satisfaction of the shepherds.

As David Brin points out, the trend over the past century was to put this sort of thing into the hands of "official" organizations. But with technology empowering people in new ways, that's changing, and it's time we changed our approaches to take account of this difference.[11] I hope that people in Washington are paying attention to this. But the evidence so far isn't too encouraging. On the other hand, some people are catching on.

Responding to the 9/11 Commission's report released in 2004, J. B. Schramm wrote in the *Washington Post*: "A first review of the Sept. 11 commission's report indicates that the system failed, but that is wrong. While the U.S. air defense system did fail to halt the attacks, our improvised, high-tech citizen defense 'system' was extraordinarily successful. . . ." The important question, according to Schramm, is not "How did the government/CIA/ FAA fail us?" But rather, "How did the networked citizens on the ground and in the sky save us?"[12]

We shouldn't let this fact make us overconfident, of course. Structural advantages are a wonderful thing, but no one is invincible. However, as we look at how to order our society in the wake of September 11, and with the prospect of other disasters as unanticipated now as the September 11 attacks were on September 10, we should not lose sight of what it is that makes us strong—the flexibility and decentralization that make American society great, and that drive bureaucrats nuts. Bureaucrats like centralization and control. But even fundamentalist terrorists can outthink bureaucrats. It's up to the rest of us to make sure that neither the terrorists nor the bureaucrats get their way.

MAKING READY

When I've written on this subject in the past, readers request that I write on what, specifically, individual citizens can do to prepare for a role in responding to, and preventing, terrorism. Okay.

I will say up front, though, that although I'm totally in favor of individual citizens taking the initiative to prepare themselves, such self-help measures would do more good if the federal and state governments actually took a role in encouraging and facilitating them. But if you want to get a leg up on the process before the much slower bureaucracy gets the ball rolling—if it ever does—here are a few things you can do to help. Odds are that you'll never use them or even come close to needing them. Terrorist attacks are pretty rare. But you'll probably never need your smoke detector either. And, anyway, many of these skills and behaviors may turn out to be useful otherwise.

Prevention: Where terrorism is concerned, an ounce of prevention is worth a metric ton of cure. But what can you do to prevent terrorism?

Well, you can't intercept Al Qaeda communications unless you're an unusually skilled cyberwarrior of the sort discussed above. But terrorists tend to give off warning signals before they strike: they profess sympathy to Al Qaeda (a pretty good giveaway), they make threats, they brag to strippers, and they engage in other behaviors that don't add up. In the past, people have failed to report these warning signs for fear of seeming prejudiced. Those days are over, I think, and you should certainly be prepared to report to authorities things that seem odd—especially as you, unlike the authorities, needn't worry too much about being charged with ethnic profiling. (Whether the authorities will listen or not is another question—they didn't where John Muhammad was concerned—but there's only so much you can do about that.)

Aside from reporting any potential terrorists you might run across at strip clubs ("Honey, I was just *protecting 'homeland security!'*" probably won't work as an excuse), you can maintain situational awareness, especially in public places like airports, shopping malls, and so on. Jeff Cooper's book *Principles of Personal Defense*[13] contains a number of games and mental exercises designed to promote that sort of awareness. Short of that, just get into the habit of noticing what's going on around you. Scan for people who look suspicious or are acting oddly, unattended bags or packages, and so on. (For practice, try to notice something distinctive about each person you see—a tattoo, a crooked nose, whatever. Really look at people instead of just skimming the crowd.)

Also, consider what you'd do if you saw something unusual. Obviously that depends on what you see—if you see a guy pulling out a gun, you're not going to have time to call security—but if you see an unattended package you probably will. But you should know whom to call, and what to say, or what to do if there's not time to call anyone. No need to get obsessive, but do play a few of these scenarios out in your mind and you'll be prepared if the situation actually comes up.

Response: How do you prepare to respond once it's too late to prevent something? Carrying a cell phone is something anyone can do, and experiences ranging from Flight 93 to the more recent Moscow theater incident and the London bombings demonstrate that having people on the scene with cell phones is enormously valuable. Be prepared to report what's going on clearly and concisely. Think about what information is valuable to authorities trying to respond—exactly what you're seeing, how many people are in the area, how many terrorists (if any) are present, how they're armed, and so on. (Example: "There are four guys wearing black, they've shot several people, and they're carrying AK-47s and pistols" is a lot more useful than "There are some guys shooting!" or "Help! It's terrorists!")

If you can legally carry a gun, you may want to consider doing so on a regular basis. But remember that there's nothing magical about a gun. If you're going to carry it, you need to be good at hitting what you shoot at, and—just as important—you need to practice in situations that will help you formulate judgment about when and how to shoot. Training courses along these lines are available most places, and if you're planning to carry a gun regularly they're a good idea. (In fact, given the woeful nature of most law enforcement officers' training and practice, if you take one of these courses and practice regularly, you may actually be better prepared than many of the professionals.) Of course, many places forbid guns—and, not surprisingly, they're often prime terrorist targets. So you may want to brush up on your unarmed-combat skills too. Courses in those are even more common and provide good healthy exercise anyway.

Preparation: Sadly, many terrorist events will involve things that no degree of prior awareness or self-defense skill will do much to prevent. Terrorists, not exactly paragons of bravery or fair play, tend to choose methods that are hard to stop by such means: bombs, for example. Unless you spot the bomb or bomber in time for people to be evacuated, you probably won't be able to do much in response until after it goes off.

So brush up on your first aid skills too. If there's a mass shooting, or if a bomb goes off, help will be on the way within minutes. But "minutes" can be a very long time in the aftermath of a bomb or a shooting. The Red Cross and other organizations offer first aid courses, though most of them focus more on responding to isolated individual accidents than in dealing with the massive trauma that often occurs after a terrorist attack. (Maybe these courses should be updated.) I once took an advanced course that did cover this sort of thing (along with a lot of other stuff I hope I'll never use, like improvised traction and bone setting), however such training is a bit harder to find. But simply applying direct pressure to wounds and keeping airways clear can go a long way toward keeping someone alive until more advanced help comes.

Getting in the habit of having a video camera or small still camera around can be helpful too, as I suggested earlier. If it's a cell-phone camera, you may even be able to send pictures to the authorities right away. Photos during, or in the immediate aftermath of, a terrorist attack may well reveal useful information, as well as making you a temporary celebrity—and perhaps a few bucks. Just be sure your batteries are charged! (And don't get so interested in taking pictures that you forget to duck.)

And what about your home? The disruptions caused by terrorist attacks tend to be short-lived, but anyone should be ready to live without power, food, or water for at least a few days. The Red Cross website has a list of recommendations for disaster preparedness that is a good starting point. Gas masks and Geiger counters are, it seems to me, overkill unless you live next to a hazardous waste facility or somesuch. If you disagree, lots of places on the Web offer to sell and advise on this kind of merchandise. But being able to take care of yourself, your family, and perhaps a few others for a week or more is a good idea and will do much to ease the burden on disaster services.

These recommendations just scratch the surface, of course, but they should at least point you in the right direction. Many of them will also prove useful even if you never encounter a terrorist: being aware of your surroundings may prevent a rape or mugging (both more likely, statistically, than terrorism anyway); having emergency supplies at home will pay off in the event of a blizzard, hurricane, earthquake, or other natural disaster. Perhaps most importantly, if you formulate the habits of mind that will keep you alert and focused in an emergency (instead of paralyzed or panicky), you improve your odds in all sorts of unfortunate situations, regardless of whether terrorism is involved. Even before 9/11, the "leave it to the professionals" approach to safety and security was obviously a bad idea. And that will remain true even after the last Al Qaeda sympathizer is pushing up daisies. Let's just hope that the government catches on to this, sooner or later, and offers the kind of support that will move these suggestions from the category of "self-help" to the category of "national defense."

INSTITUTIONAL LEARNING

There are some promising signs in that direction at the moment. A recent article from the *Christian Science Monitor* describes a trend toward terrorism vigilance—mostly by volunteer groups—in the years since September 11. Pennsylvania has been training citizens, ranging from business owners to members of the Rotary Club, in antiterrorism preparedness and response since 2002. Over sixty thousand have received courses in how to recognize terrorism and how to respond.[14]

At the federal level, the Coast Guard has set up "America's Waterway Watch,"[15] encouraging recreational boaters and maritime workers to be alert to any suspicious behavior that might indicate possible terrorism. Volunteers are trained to be wary when people pay cash to rent boats, don't take bait when "fishing," and show inordinate interest in things like naval bases or chemical plants. Sounds suspicious to me, all right. Similarly, the Air Force's "Eagle Eyes Program" trains people who live and work on and around air bases to be aware of suspicious conduct.[16] And Highway Watch is a program organized by the Department of Homeland Security and the American Trucking Association to get truckers to recognize and report suspicious activity—especially important given that a truck, particularly one loaded with gasoline or other dangerous cargo, can be a dangerous terrorist weapon all by itself.[17] Sometimes this kind of thing helps. A few years ago, a truck driver noted that twenty-five boxes set to be shipped to Saudi Arabia contained suspicious information; he tipped off authorities, and it turned out that the shipment did have terrorist connections.[18]

Meanwhile, guarding against another sort of threat entirely, NASA is enlisting amateur astronomers to help search the skies for killer asteroids so that we'll know they're coming in time to prepare. This recruitment of amateur astronomers is relatively new, though these "non-experts" have been researching asteroids for a while. Much of the collaboration, as one reporter notes, occurs on an Internet message group called the Minor Planet Mailing List. The group boasts over eight hundred members and is run by Richard Kowalski, "a forty-year-old baggage handler at US Airways in Florida by day and an astronomer by night."[19]

Harnessing the passion and persistence of such amateurs seems a smart way to deal with a diffuse but real threat like killer asteroids. And it's made possible by a world in which technology and economic growth allow a forty-year-old baggage handler to own a telescope setup better than many universities would have possessed a few decades ago. ("Kowalski observes the skies through an eleven-inch, computer-driven telescope. He houses it in a backyard garden shed with a retractable roof. Amateur setups like his can cost as much as $25,000; but, like most amateurs, Kowalski put it together himself, without the benefit of NASA endowments."[20])

We're still a long way from the sort of broad-based disaster preparedness I propose above, but this is a start. And, in some ways, we may be closer—even without government programs—than we realize.

KEEPING THE FIRE ALIVE

I've just been reading Steve Stirling's recent novel, *Dies the Fire*,[21] in which every piece of technology more sophisticated than a waterwheel or a crossbow quits working. In Stirling's story, lots of people die, of course, but civilization doesn't, quite. And though some might find the extent to which his leading characters are able to draw on expertise gathered via the Society for Creative Anachronism and various back-to-the-land hippie movements a bit convenient, I actually know many people with those sorts of skills. And there seem to be a lot more floating around out there. (Just look at the website for the Roman reenactment group, the XXIVth Legion[22]—and be sure to check out the ballista page.) It's almost as if, as we move up the technological curve, interest in old innovations is growing.

Why is that? Cultural explanations no doubt exist for why geeks in particular are fascinated with obsolete technologies, but it's certainly the case that any gathering of geeks or science fiction fans will find a lot of people interested in old technologies: from arms and armor, to brewing and viticulture, to seafaring and agriculture.

It's not just geeks, by any means, who make a hobby of such undertakings. All kinds of people find such archaic arts interesting and apply their surplus time and money to them. As a side effect, though, we have a large bank of people possessing all sorts of skills (and not just the out-of-date kind, but modern skills like astronomy or obscure languages) that aren't especially useful now. But they might be someday.

This is the real lesson. We have such a diversified collection of skills because our society is rich enough and free enough that people have leisure time for such pursuits. No plausible government program could prepare us adequately for the kind of unlikely cataclysm Stirling envisions—but, in fact, if we should ever find ourselves needing people who can construct a *lorica segmentata,* we've got them. In fact, thanks to the wonders of the free market, such folks are already supporting themselves, without government money. (See, for example, the website of Albion Arms, which will happily sell you a *lorica segmentata* or a broadsword, for a substantial sum.[23])

A society that's rich and free will have citizens who—entirely on their own—develop a wide range of skills. Most of these skills will never provide more than hobby-level amusement for their owners, but in the aggregate they provide a resource that could not easily be developed through any sort of government program. And that's a kind of disaster preparedness too. The kind that's not available to a herd.

Of course, sometimes we get a herd, not a pack, and the disgraceful behavior of the looters (and the not-very-admirable behavior of the people who refused *either* to prepare themselves *or* to evacuate the city) produced nasty results in New Orleans after Hurricane Katrina. Part of this is, of course, that the citizens with skills, resources, and public spirit did mostly evacuate, leaving the city occupied by those with none of these. Such a situation also underscores the point that some sort of infrastructure—whether created by the government or someone else—helps a lot. People often self-organize, but it's easier to do under some circumstances than others.

Such self-organization did happen in New Orleans, in neighborhoods where community ties were stronger. In the French Quarter, for instance, people formed "tribes" and divided up the various chores required to survive the recent hardships. An excerpt from an Associated Press account shows how effective these informal groups were:

> As some went down to the river to do the wash, others remained behind to protect property. In a bar, a bartender put near-perfect stitches into the torn ear of a robbery victim.
>
> While mold and contagion grew in the muck that engulfed most of the city, something else sprouted in this most decadent of American neighborhoods—humanity.
>
> "Some people became animals," Vasilioas Tryphonas said Sunday morning as he sipped a hot beer in Johnny White's Sports Bar on Bourbon Street. "We became more civilized."[24]

For residents of the French Quarter, loyalty to an established neighborhood—and familiarity with each other—made this sort of thing easier. (Likewise, in Houston, armed citizens banded together to prevent looting after Hurricane Rita.[25]) Rich societies, like richer neighborhoods, will generally have more of this sort of mutual trust and cooperation than poor ones. But it's something we should foster everywhere, not only as a good in itself but because it helps to protect society from all sorts of problems—including, and perhaps especially, the kinds of problems that nobody even foresees today.

6

FROM MEDIA TO WE-DIA

Nothing is so unsettling to a social order as the presence of a mass of scribes without suitable employment and an acknowledged status.

—Eric Hoffer[1]

Zeyad was a twenty-eight-year-old dental student in Baghdad. He had never worked as a journalist, but American journalist-blogger Jeff Jarvis found his weblog, Healing Iraq, and liked it. Jarvis, the president of Conde Nast's Internet division and a huge fan of Iraqi and Iranian bloggers, had Federal Expressed him a digital camera the week before, paying more in shipping than the camera cost. Zeyad was still learning to use it when he covered a mammoth antiterrorist/anti-Baath demonstration in Baghdad, posting pictures to his blog.[2]

Over twenty thousand people marched. Western media ignored the story, but in spite of this neglect, Zeyad's pictures and reporting attracted the notice of Americans. Hundreds of thousands saw his reports on the Internet, and the next week the *Weekly Standard* reprinted them, photos and all.[3] It was a swift move: from an obscure website to coveted print real estate in less than a week. Even more striking, the left-leaning webzine *Salon* was inspired to run a story on how Zeyad had "scooped" the *New York Times,* which had published a context-less photo from the march but otherwise ignored it.[4] Before the Internet, and blogs, the *Times'* omission would have kept us ignorant, but this time it left the *Times* embarrassed and readers aware that stories were going unreported.

DAVID'S SLINGS AND ARROWS

The Zeyad story points up a typical pattern in the relationship between Big Media and blogs. Before Zeyad embarrassed the *Times,* bloggers had noticed remarks made by then Senate Majority Leader Trent Lott at Strom Thurmond's 100th birthday party, remarks suggesting that Lott would have preferred to see the segregationist Dixiecrat Party (on whose ticket Thurmond had run) win the presidency in 1948. Although these comments were made at a gala event with numerous reporters in attendance, they weren't reported in the news until several days later, after bloggers on both the left and right had made a stink. By the time it was over, Lott was an ex-majority leader.[5]

During the 2004 election, blogs and online media played a major role both in spotting stories that the Big Media had missed and in correcting stories that the Big Media got wrong. The most famous example involved the so-called "RatherGate" scandal, in which CBS relied on documents that turned out to have been rather clumsily forged, in a story alleging that President Bush had been given special treatment while serving in the Texas Air

National Guard. Another example involved Democratic candidate John Kerry's claim to have been in Cambodia on Christmas Day 1968, which turned out not to be the case either. Yet another involved a false Associated Press report that a pro-Bush crowd had booed former President Bill Clinton when Bush reported that Clinton was having heart surgery. Bloggers who had attended the rally responded with firsthand reports that included audio and video, making it clear that the AP story was false.

These examples are some of the most famous, but focusing on them misses the point, which goes well beyond the occasional scoop. The trouble is encapsulated in Ken Layne's now famous statement that this is the Internet, "and we can fact-check your ass."[6] Where before journalists and pundits could bloviate at leisure, offering illogical analysis or citing "facts" that were in fact false, now the Sunday morning op-eds have already been dissected on Saturday night, within hours of their appearing on newspapers' websites.

Annoyance to journalists is the least of this; what is really going on is something much more profound: the end of the power of Big Media.

For almost a hundred years—from the time William Randolph Hearst pushed the Spanish-American War, to the ascendancy of talk radio in the 1990s—big newspapers and, later, television networks have set the agenda for public discussion and tilted the playing field in ways that suited their institutional and political interests.

Not anymore. As UPI columnist Jim Bennett notes, what is going on with journalism today is akin to what happened to the Church during the Reformation.[7] Thanks to a technological revolution (movable type then, the Internet and talk radio now), power once concentrated in the hands of a professional few has been redistributed into the hands of the amateur many. Those who do it for money are losing out to those who (mostly) do it for fun.

Beware the people who are having fun competing with you!

Nonetheless, weblogs are not likely to mark the end of traditional media, any more than Martin Luther marked the end of the popes. Yet the Protestant Reformation did mark an end to the notion of unchallenged papal authority, and it seems likely that the blog phenomenon marks the beginning of the end to the tremendous power wielded by Big Media in recent years. Millions of Americans who were once in awe of the punditocracy now realize that anyone can do this stuff—and that many unknowns can do it better than the lords of the profession.

In this we are perhaps going full circle. Prior to the Hearst era—and even, to a degree, prior to World War II—Big Media power was countervailed by other institutions: political parties, churches, labor unions, even widespread political discussion groups. The blog phenomenon may be viewed as the return of such influences—a broadening of the community of discourse to include, well, the community.

And it's possible that blogs will have a greater influence than these earlier institutions for a simple reason: they're addictive, and many of the addicts are mainstream journalists, who tend to spend a lot of time surfing the Web and who like to read about themselves and their colleagues. This means that blog criticism may have a more immediate impact than might otherwise be the case.

If so, it will be a good thing. Americans' trust in traditional

Big Media has been declining for years, as people came to feel that the news they were getting was distorted or unreliable. Such distrust, while a natural phenomenon, can't be a good thing over the long term. In this, as in other areas, competition is the engine that will make things better.

THE COSTS OF CORNER CUTTING

And it had better. For the sad truth is that although bloggers are often criticized for producing more opinion than original reporting (some critics call them "parasites" on Big Media's hard-news reporting), even top-of-the-line mainstream news institutions like the *New York Times* are becoming more like the bloggers all the time, reducing staffs, cutting the size and number of foreign bureaus, and relying more and more on wire services for original reporting to which they add commentary and "news analysis" (it's "value added" rather than parasitism when Big Media does it). But the real appeal of this reduction to management is that it's cheap, while reporting is expensive. Decades of cost cutting and corporate consolidation at newspapers, magazines, and television networks have caused them to sharply reduce their core competency of news gathering and reporting.[8] Where they used to have bureaus in all sorts of places, now they don't. Like the industrial beer makers, they've watered down their product over a series of individually imperceptible cost-cutting stages, until suddenly it's reached a point where a lot of people have noticed that it lacks substance and flavor. That opens an opportunity for a widely dispersed network of individuals to make a contribution.

Traditionally, the big things that mainstream journalism offers are reach and trustworthiness. Critics of media bias may joke about the latter, but though reporters for outlets like Reuters or the *New York Times* may—and do—slant their reporting from time to time, their affiliation with institutions that have a long-term interest in reputation limits how far they can go. When you rely on a report from one of those journalistic organs, you're relying, for better or worse, on their reputation. And when they ask you to believe their reports, they're relying on their reputations too.

But big institutions aren't the only way to have a reputation anymore. As Web-based outfits like Amazon.com and Slashdot are demonstrating, it's possible to have reputation without bureaucracy. Want to know whether you can rely on what someone says? Click on his profile and you can see what other people have said about him, and what he's said before, giving you a pretty good idea of his reliability and his biases. That's more than you can do for the person whose name sits atop a story in the *New York Times* (where, as with many Big Media outfits, archives are pay-only and feedback is limited).

An organization that put together a network of freelance journalists under a framework that allowed for that sort of reputation rating, and that paid based on the number of pageviews and the ratings that each story received, would be more like a traditional newspaper than a blog, but it would still be a major change from the newspapers of today. Interestingly, it might well be possible to knit together a network of bloggers into the beginnings of such an organization. With greater reach and lower costs than a traditional newspaper, it might bring something new and competitive to the news business.

AD HOC JOURNALISM

In the meantime, we tend to see this dynamic mostly when bloggers self-organize around a particular big event: the Indian Ocean tsunami, hurricanes or terror attacks in the United States, and so on. Like the "flash crowds" that gather by text-message and email, the bloggers swarm around a topic and then disperse.

This "flash media" coverage does a lot of good. Sometimes— as in the Trent Lott case, documented in a lengthy case study by Harvard's Kennedy School of Government, or in Iraqi blogger Zeyad's coverage of pro-democracy rallies in Baghdad,[9] scooping the *New York Times*—this sort of coverage gets Big Media entities interested. But even when Big Media snubs such coverage, bloggers let hundreds of thousands of people read about, see, and sometimes even experience via video a story that they would otherwise miss.

I don't think that weblogs and flash media will replace Big Media any time soon. But I keep seeing evidence that they're doing a better and better job of supplementing, and challenging, Big Media coverage. I think that's a wonderful thing, and it's one reason why I'm such an evangelist for the spread of enabling technologies like Web video and cheap digital cameras. The more people there are with these sorts of things, the more of a role there will be for flash media in covering news, and for more sophisticated ways of drawing this sort of coverage together on a more routine basis. Just another thing for the Old Media guys to worry about.

The end result of the blog revolution is to create what blogger Jim Treacher calls "we-dia."[10] News and reporting used to be something that "they" did. Now it's something that we all do. This is sure to irritate the traditional press, which has always seemed to favor exclusivity—just read any of the journalism trade papers for an example of the guild mentality that seems to pervade the field—but it may also save press freedom from the problems created by the press.

I worry that freedom of the press—which in its modern extent is basically a creature of the post–World War II Supreme Court—is likely to be at risk if people see it as merely a special-interest protection for a news-media industry that is producing defective products that do harm.

But, as Alex Beam notes in the *Boston Globe,* media folks often encourage such a view, by failing to stand up for the free-speech rights of non-Big-Media folks:

> Apple Computer sued 19-year-old journalist Nicholas Ciarelli in January for disclosing trade secrets on his Apple news website Think Secret. A typical Think Secret annoyance: The site correctly predicted the appearance of the Mac Mini, a small, low-cost Macintosh computer, two weeks before the product was officially announced.
>
> Ciarelli is accused of doing exactly what reporters all over America are supposed to be doing: finding and publishing information that institutions don't want to reveal. . . .
>
> Where are the always-vocal guardians of the First Amendment? Where is the American Civil Liberties Union? Where is the American Society of Newspaper Editors? Where, for that matter, is Harvard's Nieman Foundation.[11]

Apparently, Ciarelli's status as "non-traditional media" has cost him support. But that's a mistake. Big Media outfits have been squandering their credibility and public regard for decades (see, for example, Dan Rather and Jayson Blair, or the exaggerated stories of death and lawlessness after Hurricane Katrina[12]), and I suspect that this is likely to put free-press protections at risk. It's easier to support freedom of the press when you think the press is responsible. Ironically, their greatest hope for salvation is for lots of nontraditional media to get involved in publishing too, giving the public at large a greater stake in freedom of the press.

SAVING THE FIRST AMENDMENT—FROM US?

If Americans regard press freedom as someone else's protection, they're likely to be much cooler toward the First Amendment than if they regard press freedom as their own. And that sense of ownership is more likely to develop if the explosion of self-published Internet media, often sniffed at by traditional media folks, continues. If Big Media is to be saved, it may be Little Media that is responsible.

Another question is whether Little Media can be saved from itself. Some people, invoking the usually sad fate of email lists and online bulletin boards, wonder if Web journalism is doomed to be overrun by trolls and flamers who ruin things for everyone else. I think the answer is no. In legal and economic analysis, a "commons" is a resource that anyone can use. The classic example is the common grazing field shared by everyone in a village. As long as there's enough to go around, its common character is a benefit: there's no need to waste time dividing it up and assigning rights when there's enough for everyone.

The problem is when there are more people wanting to use

the resource than it can support. Everyone could just cut back—
but since there's no guarantee that other users will cut back, a
rational user won't cut back but will try to grab as much as possible before someone else gets it. Grazing becomes overgrazing in
a hurry under these circumstances, and everyone is worse off.
Soon, there's nothing to do but to move elsewhere, as the previously settled area becomes a desert. The classic term for this problem is "the tragedy of the commons," after a famous article by that
name.[13]

This model wouldn't seem to fit the Web very well, though.
There aren't many commonly held resources, and most of them
aren't really limited. Bandwidth, maybe, in shared networks, but
that's pretty easy to address. (Actually, the use of overall Net bandwidth for spam may fall into the "overgrazing" category, but that's
a topic for another day.)

But if there's one scarcity that everyone will agree on, it's time.
Napoleon told his generals, "Ask me for anything but time," but
he didn't know the half of it. For my own blog, I try to get around
to as many sites as possible, but it's a hopeless effort: the number
of new sites is expanding far faster than I can follow. And email is
worse. I get hundreds of emails.

But that difference—between visiting sites and receiving
email—is one reason why I think that the blog world, and the new
journalism that resembles it, won't succumb to the tragedy of the
commons the way that email has. Think about an email list: everyone can post freely to the list, but by doing so they consume readers' time. In a sense, there's a common pool of reading hours
available, determined by the number of hours the average reader
is willing to devote to mail from the list, multiplied by the num-

ber of readers. Each post to the list consumes some of that time, but at minimal cost to the poster in relation to the amount of time consumed. And the bigger the list, the greater the payoff (other people's time consumed) versus the cost (the poster's time).

Left to themselves, then, you'd expect that email lists and similarly structured systems would succumb to a tragedy of the commons: excessive posting that consumes so much time that people abandon them and they die. (As a corollary, it would seem likely that the people whose time is the least valuable will post the most—since they incur the lowest cost in doing so—and if you assume that their time is less valuable because they're, well, dumb or crazy, then the more posts you see, the lower their likely value.) This does seem to describe the fate of many email listservs, which start out well, with a few members, flourish and grow for a time, but then degenerate into flamefests and collapse. A similar phenomenon seems to affect chat rooms, message boards, and the like. Some people are suggesting that even well-established sites like Slashdot may suffer from this kind of thing, though I think the jury is still out on that one.

So, despite all the blogosphere hype, is the world of blogs headed the same way? It could be, but I'm going to predict that it isn't. The reason is that people who post on blogs can't commandeer the time of others: nobody will read their stuff except voluntarily since—unlike email on a listserv—reading a weblog requires a deliberate act. As a blog reader, you control your time; as the member of an email list, you don't. So although individual blogs may collapse into Usenet-style flaming, they'll either lose their audiences or accumulate a reader base that wants to read flaming, in which case it's not really flaming—for our purposes—at all.

As Nick Denton says: "[T]his is the way to deal with flamers: let them post on their own damn sites. And then let everyone else ignore them. Weblogs are a gigantic interlinked discussion forum, in which it's trivially easy to route around idiots."[14]

It's another example of what some people (well, Jeff Jarvis, and now me) are calling Jarvis's Laws of Media:

> Jarvis's First Law: Give the people control of media, they will use it. The corollary: Don't give the people control of media, and you will lose. Jarvis's Second Law: Lower cost of production and distribution in media inevitably leads to nichefication. The corollary: Lower the cost of media enough, and there will be an unlimited supply of people making it.[15]

I think that he's right, and that the implications go beyond routing around idiots. And so, I suspect, does Jonathan Peterson, who wrote:

> At a very fundamental level, the Big Content companies don't understand the revolution that is happening in the digital media realm. They still see us as consumers only capable of digesting their offerings and handing over money. They really don't seem to understand that the reason we are buying PCs, video cameras, digital cameras, broadband connections and the like is that we want to create and share our creations. The quality of "amateur" content is exploding at the same time that Big Media companies are going through one of their all-time lows in music and television creativity.

No wonder we're spending more time with our PCs than we are with our TVs.[16]

And when "making" media is cheap, and an unlimited supply of people are "making it," what happens to journalism? Something that journalists may not like: Journalism, right now, is in the process of reverting to its earlier status as an activity, rather than a profession.

Which brings me to my last prediction. Actually, it's one I've made before: "[I]f Big Media let their position go without a fight to keep it by fair means or foul, they'll be the first example of a privileged group that did so. So beware." In the wake of the humiliation visited on Big Media by such debacles as RatherGate, I think we're already beginning to see signs of that backlash, complete with the growth of alarmist articles (like a recent cover story in *Forbes*) on the dangers posed by bloggers.[17] And the press establishment's general lack of enthusiasm for free speech for others (as evidenced by its support for campaign finance "reform,") suggests that it'll be happy to see alternative media muzzled. Big Media outfits haven't been very enthusiastic about extending the "media exemption" of the McCain-Feingold campaign finance "reform" act to bloggers, for example. You want to keep this media revolution going? Be ready to fight for it. I think people will be. Am I too optimistic? We'll see.

I could write more about the role of blogs in changing politics and media, but that task has been admirably performed by Dan Gillmor in *We the Media*,[18] Joe Trippi in *The Revolution Will Not Be Televised*,[19] and especially by Hugh Hewitt in his book *Blog: Understanding the Information Reformation That's Changing Your*

World.[20] But what I can do is give you an insight into some of the people who are going beyond blogging and into independent journalism—doing the kind of thing, thanks to technology, that only Big Media employees used to be able to do.

One of them is J. D. Johannes, whose blog, Faces from the Front (FacesFromTheFront.com), and documentary has attracted a lot of attention. There's been lots of unhappiness with media reporting from Iraq. But where people used to just complain about that, now people are doing something about it. Johannes is one of them. I interviewed him recently.

> *Reynolds:* What's your project all about? How did you come up with the idea?
>
> *Johannes:* The project is about telling a story that otherwise would have gone untold. The story of one platoon of Marines, all of which are volunteers, as they root out insurgents in Iraq's Al Anbar province. The story is told through three mediums: Web, at www.facesfromthefront.com, local TV news stations in Kansas and Missouri, and a long form documentary for local PBS tentatively titled "Outside The Wire." Washburn University has partnered with me for the documentary, making me an adjunct professor in the Military and Strategic Studies Department. The PBS station, though licensed to the university, has been a challenge.
>
> Local TV affiliates were not going to Fallujah to follow a group of Reserve Marines from their area. Local PBS stations were not going to Fallujah

to produce a long form documentary about Reserve Marines from their area. The big networks were never going to cover a group of Reserve Marines from Kansas City. The daily newspapers were not going to cover them. The story of the courage, dignity, and compassion of this group of Marines would never be told, unless I went.

The only time local stations or newspapers cover a local Marine or soldier is if they die in combat. That is an outrage.

The idea sprang to me in late December 2004. I was dissatisfied with the coverage of the war. I had an idea turning in my head about how coverage could be improved through syndication targeted for local TV markets. My college roommate and occasional business crony, David Socrates, thought the idea was a bit crazy, but jumped on board. When I learned that an infantry platoon from my former Marine Reserve unit was being deployed to Iraq, everything became clear. I knew what I had to do. I did it because I knew no one else would. A lot of others could, but no one else would.

Reynolds: How has technology played a role in letting you do this sort of thing? Would it have been possible twenty years ago? If possible, feasible?

Johannes: This project, the way it was thrown together, would not have been possible ten years ago. The major technological leap forward is in the low cost availability of 3CCD cameras that shoot broadcast-quality video and off-the-shelf video editing software that rivals television production equipment. Ten years ago, a production quality camera would cost $25,000–$40,000. The editing equipment would have been a Video Toaster or two bulky decks and two bulky monitors. The total cost being around $100,000. But now, it's $4,000 for a 3CCD camera, $1,000 for Adobe Premiere software plus features, and $2,000 for a laptop computer. We ship video from Iraq using a combination of FedEx and NorSat KU band satellite transmissions. Neither of which would have been feasible twenty years ago.

The Web end of things obviously wouldn't have worked twenty years ago. Ten years ago, the Web part of the project would have been slower, with fewer and shorter video clips. The facesfromthefront.com website would not be nearly as rich in content ten years ago; server space would have been too expensive.

Ten or fifteen or twenty years ago, a person with a large, well-established video production company could be doing what we are doing. But a small company or a start-up company? Not a chance. The initial capital investment would have been too great.

Reynolds: Do you see a trend toward independent news gathering and filmmaking of this sort? Should the Big

Media folks be worried, or should they see it as an opportunity?

Johannes: The technological trend should result in more independent news gathering and filmmaking. I once had a conversation with Hernando De Soto about how technology made the U.S. look so different from parts of Europe, especially in the red states. In Kansas, where I live, everything is spread out. The roads are wide, suburbs and cities distant, and the farms massive. The railroads were the first bit of technology that allowed this, as cities were built around rail terminals. Then came cars. The cities of the American Midwest were built for cars. Farms expanded as the tools of production (tractors, combines, etc.) became larger allowing one person to do more work.

The availability of the cameras, recorders, affordable server space, and affordable software will open up the news game to more people.

Over time, news gathering will reflect the technology that makes it available, but the Big Media will resist it. Not the business end of Big Media, they will adopt it, but the reporters, producers, and editors will resist it.

The second phase, and this will be the angle TV is likely to take, is in specialized syndication.

Every local TV station has a "Statehouse" reporter. What makes these reporters so special that their coverage should be respected? Nothing, other than they work for an identifiable and reliable media outlet.

Do they have any special knowledge of law, politics, government, economics, policy, etc.? No. They have a bachelor's degree in mass media or journalism, possibly the worst education possible outside of a teaching degree.

I worked in television for four years producing newscasts every day. These reporters are some of the least equipped individuals to be covering important topics that affect people's lives. And in TV news, performance abilities are rewarded more often than analytical ones.

And there is a "paying your dues" aspect to TV news. Everyone must start at the bottom and work their way up, unless they have a patron or a well-placed uncle.

The concept of some guy with a camera being able to produce stories and analysis superior to that of the Big Media is a threat to the status quo, and humans hate threats to the status quo, especially if it affects their livelihood.

The news directors and producers would be incredulous at the idea of some lawyer covering the statehouse. That would be an infringement on their turf.

But upper management could see the economy of scale. If one man and a camera could cover the statehouse under a syndicated contract for

$6,000 and get one station in four markets to buy in, he could make $24,000 a year for working just six months. If he had something else on the side, he could make a respectable living.

The resistance would not come from upper management, but from the news director, who would see this freelance interloper as an invader. In a newspaper, the same resistance would come from the lesser editors.

Indeed, I experienced this firsthand a few times with the Iraq project. But most original news coverage by bloggers resembles first person rambles, not news. A mere change in style would go a long way.

Because most bloggers are hobbyists, serious citizen journalist hobbyists, they are not able to devote the resources necessary to original reporting. The bloggers provide the best background information and in-depth analysis, but they rarely produce fresh news.

When enough bloggers take the leap, and start reporting on the statehouse, city council, courts, etc., firsthand, full-time, then the Big Media will take notice and the avalanche will begin. . . . If it can be done in Iraq, it can be done in statehouses and city hall.

Johannes is right. Technology has made all sorts of things possible. Twenty years ago, or even ten, it took a huge infrastructure to allow one guy in a safari jacket to report from places like Baghdad and pretend he knew what was going on there. Now it can be a do-it-yourself project, and unlike the "bigfoot" reporters of major media, who tend to drop in for a few days and then move on, the do-it-yourselfer is more likely to stay on the ground long enough to actually learn what's going on firsthand. This is probably bad news for terrorism, which is an information warfare operation disguised as a military one, and one that is based on taking advantage of the kind of reporting (hysterical and shallow, for the most part) that traditional mass media tend to do.

I suspect that the growth of guerrilla media—ranging from operations like Faces from the Front, to reporting by freelancers like Michael Yon (interviewed below), to reports from Iraqi bloggers and even emails from soldiers—has made the terrorists' task tougher, as the reporting is by people who are much closer to what's really going on and are much more closely connected to their audiences.

I also agree that the local-reporting angle is likely to be big. Most media coverage is wide but shallow. Individuals can actually outperform big news organizations when it comes to reporting on a single topic, and as it becomes easier for individuals to develop and market niche expertise, we'll see more of that. How will Big Media respond? It will be interesting to find out.

Meanwhile, another journalist, Michael Yon, is covering Iraq in a different way at his blog (www.michaelyon.blogspot.com). His first person reporting reads like Ernie Pyle's, and he often takes photos in the midst of combat. I interviewed him, too, to see what he thinks about the new approach to news gathering.

Reynolds: Please tell me a bit about your background, and how you decided to embark on this project.

Yon: I was born and raised in Florida, where I learned at a young age how to successfully hunt, kill, and eat alligators much larger than I am. I was different than the other boys in that my favorite three subjects were physics, physics, and physics. I also was very serious about sports, mainly because I was small and got beat up by my big brother a lot, and wanted to put an end to that, which I eventually did. I joined the Army for university tuition. I volunteered and was selected for Special Forces, which I enjoyed immensely, except that I hated wearing uniforms. After running several businesses, I started to write, more as a way to get perspective than as the first step toward finding out that what I most enjoy is traveling the world, exploring fascinating places, and writing about them. As for Iraq, I maintain friendships with former Special Forces teammates and other service members, most of whom are still active duty. The war is a major event for this and future generations. I had, and continue to have, complex and sometimes contradictory opinions about this war. What made me embark on this project was the need to see things firsthand, to find out for myself what is going on, what it means, and how it is going to affect all of us for a very long time.

Reynolds: What are you trying to accomplish with your reporting? What will the final result be? A book?

Yon: I am chronicling my observations of this war over an extended period. My independence is important on many levels. I am beholden to no agency and I don't need to produce copy on a deadline. So I can write about what I am seeing and take time to do so properly. Journalists of many sorts fly through here for short times, and there are a handful of semi-permanent reporters from a few majors such as CNN and *Time.* Some of these are good and serious folks, but I think they are hobbled by working for agencies and are not free to roam and follow their instincts. Being completely independent allows freedom to roam the battlefield from north to south, from Iran to Syria, and to describe without filters what I see. The events in Iraq are singularly critical to the futures of billions of people. Given that such incredible events are taking place, and that I am committed to being here as long as I still have unanswered questions . . . definitely, I will write a book.

Reynolds: What kind of a role does technology play in making your reporting possible? Could you have done this sort of thing twenty years ago?

Yon: The Internet makes wide and near-instantaneous reporting simple. Also, satellite and cell phones in Iraq allow for real-time reporting by nearly anyone. I do not "report" in real time—I am not actually a reporter—but am able to post dispatches that are being read all around the world. I think a generation earlier my background might have afforded access that the embedded reporter system now grants just about any reporter, journalist, or filmmaker. But the military's attitude toward the media has changed almost as dramatically as the technology around communications has developed. So I might have been able to tag along and observe and later write a book about my experiences, but I definitely couldn't have blogged it.

Reynolds: Do you see independent reporting as the future of news? What role do you think it will play? Should Big Media folks be worried, or should they see it as an opportunity?

Yon: I don't think anyone can predict the future of news. Some question whether it's even really still news in the classic Edward R. Murrow sense. Clearly we are shaking the tree where the Big Media has been perched. The "little guys" are increasingly not so little, they have grasped the power of the Web, and they have increasing credibility and exposure.

It's still a little wild in the streets in terms of what passes for credible information. Sometimes blogs seem like the transcripts for radio talk shows. But lately mainstream media is getting the story leads for Iraq from independents and bloggers. I get contacted frequently by an assortment of big players such as the *New York Times, Washington*

Post, LA Times, FOX, and just a couple weeks ago I "scooped" a major story from the grips of CNN (quite by accident).

When I want firsthand and nitty-gritty information about an area in Iraq, I search for bloggers in that area and then decide for myself if they sound credible. For firsthand information in Iraq, the best sources definitely are not mainstream media, all of which have become fixated with counts: numbers of car bombings, numbers of dead, numbers of insurgents captured, etc. But for real stories, the majors have lost the battle in Iraq. There is no question that the best sources for detailed information in Iraq tend to be bloggers. Mainstream media straggles further behind every day.

Should they be worried? If they really care about the legacy of solid journalism, probably yes. But if they only care about the bottom line, they are probably already thinking up some "reality TV" version of the news, maybe some program where they gather bloggers from around the world, put them in a wired house, and film them finding and reporting news. . . .

Reynolds: You write in a personal voice, more like the old-time reporting of Ernie Pyle than like most modern war correspondents. Why did you decide to take that approach? Is it part of reporting in your own name?

Yon: This is the easiest question to answer. Firstly, I never studied journalism, so I have little frame of reference past or present. I write in first person because I am actually there at the events I write about. When I write about the bombs exploding, or the smell of blood, or the bullets snapping by, and I say "I," it's because I was there. Yesterday a sniper shot at us, and seven of my neighbors were injured by a large bomb. These are my neighbors. These are soldiers I have borrowed camera gear from (soldiers who have better photo gear than I have). These are the people who risk their lives for me. I see them bleed, I see them die, I see them cry for their friends, and then I see them go right back out there on missions, and I see them caring for Iraqi people and killing the enemy. I feel the fire from the explosions, and am lucky, very lucky, still to be alive. Everything here is first person.

Yes, it is. And that first-person character is one of the strengths of the independent journalism that the Internet and other technologies make possible. Over the coming decade, we'll see the growth of alternatives to traditional Big Media, and—if we and Big Media are lucky—we'll see Big Media moving to ally itself with the Davids, rather than positioning itself against them.

We've seen a few signs of that. After the Indian Ocean tsunami, and again after hurricanes like Katrina and Rita, we've seen newspapers and television stations incorporate citizen journalism into their coverage via blogs, chat boards, and other mechanisms. In a crisis, the value of having thousands of potential correspondents out there with computers, digital cameras, and other technology is obvious. But in fact, the value is there all the time. Noticing *that* may take them a bit longer, but I suspect that they will notice it in the end. Those who don't may wind up being replaced by those who do.

Interlude

GOOD BLOGGING

So what makes a blog good? First the inevitable, though sincere, dodge: it depends. Blogs come in many different flavors and styles—though political and tech blogs get the most attention, there are many other varieties (including the huge but largely ignored mass of gay blogs), and what makes one good or bad naturally varies accordingly. What's more, there's a way in which blogging, like jazz, always succeeds: if it's reflecting the feelings of the blogger, it's a success on some level, regardless of whether anyone else likes it. (There's only one hard-and-fast rule: Get rid of the typos. No blog that's full of typos looks good.)

But that said, there are some things that, in my opinion, make good blogs good. And the most important of those things are (1) a personal voice and (2) rapid response times. By this token, some blogs aren't really full-fledged blogs: my MSNBC weblog, GlennReynolds.com, has a personal voice, but since MSNBC's antiquated publishing platform means that I have to email my entries in and then wait hours until they appear on the site, it doesn't offer the kind of rapid response—and on-the-fly editing and revision—that more typical blogs, powered by things like Movable Type, Blogger, or WordPress, offer. On my InstaPundit blog, which is powered by Movable Type, I can post something, think better of it moments later, and change it, or add an update in response to a reader email that comes in sixty seconds after it's posted. I can't do that at GlennReynolds.com—a significant lack in a medium that thrives on lively forums of cumulative dialogue and witty repartee.

On the other hand, a number of house blogs have rapid response, but no personal voice. TomPaine.com's blog, for example, used to be timely and interesting, but anonymously institutional—so they added names. The same is true for the *American Prospect*'s blog, Tapped, and the *New Republic*'s blog, &c. And the 2004 presidential campaign blogs were tedious—basically just a series of press releases.

By contrast, the *National Review Online* house blog, The Corner, features signed entries by many different NRO writers and rather a lot of back-and-forth disagreement and personal reflection, which makes it far livelier and far "bloggier" than its more staid competitors. The *Huffington Post* is an online blog-collective that's all about having named contributors. The same is true for *Reason*'s house blog, Hit&Run, which also has signed entries and considerably more life to it than the anonymous house blogs. It's no wonder that the latter have become less common.

So while you can have an anonymous "institutional" blog with rapid response, it's bound to have an institutional voice, which isn't as interesting or, I suspect, as much fun for the writers. The Corner, and to a lesser degree Hit&Run, seem to attract posts at all hours too, while the anonymous institutional blogs seem to operate on a more 9-5 or, really, 10-2 basis, with postings not only less personalized, but less frequent. I suspect that means that the anonymous house blogs feel like work to their writers, rather than like self-expression. So the personal voice seems to be awfully important to good blogging, and to frequent blogging. (Note that you can have a personal voice in an anonymous blog, but not in an anonymous institutional one—there are plenty of anonymous non-institutional blogs with strong personal voices.)

Then, most importantly, there is the link. And here, I'll quote James Lileks:

A wire story consists of one voice pitched low and calm and full of institutional gravitas, blissfully unaware of its own biases or the gaping lacunae in its knowledge. Whereas blogs have a different format: Clever teaser headline that has little to do with the actual story, but sets the tone for this blog post. Breezy ad hominem slur containing the link to the entire story. Excerpt of said story, demonstrating its idiocy (or brilliance). Blogauthor's remarks, varying from dismissive sniffs to a Tolstoi-length rebuttal. Seven comments from people piling on, disagreeing, adding a link, acting stupid, preaching to the choir, accusing choir of being Nazis, etc.

I'd say it's a throwback to the old newspapers, the days when partisan slants covered everything from the play story to the radio listings, but this is different. The link changes everything. When someone derides or exalts a piece, the link lets you examine the thing itself without interference. TV can't do that. Radio can't do that. Newspapers and magazines don't have the space. My time on the Internet resembles eight hours at a coffeeshop stocked with every periodical in the world—if someone says "I read something stupid" or "there was this wonderful piece in the *Atlantic*" then conversation stops while you read the piece and make up your own mind.[1]

When hypertext for computers was first invented (lawyers invented hypertext for paper back in the Middle Ages, but that's another topic) the inventors thought it would revolutionize discourse, and it has. People who write on dead trees can still (sort of) get away with mangling quotes to produce a desired meaning—though bloggers will quickly call them on it—but bloggers tend to link to original sources wherever possible. The result, as Lileks says, is that you can follow the link and make up your mind for yourself. A blog that doesn't have links is less interesting. The link isn't a guarantee of accuracy, of course—the source you're linking to can always be wrong—but it does let the readers evaluate the source themselves.

The best links, usually, are to things the reader would never have found otherwise. Fred Pruitt's Rantburg blog specializes in interesting information from obscure military and regional sources. Meanwhile Caterina Fake's blog—probably my favorite of the largely non-political, day-in-the-life blogs—has posts on things like what to do in Finland and is full of links and reader comments. In both cases, the selection of links has to do with the "personal voice" thing: Fred and Caterina are (very) different people. Both have built blogs around their own knowledge and interests, instead of trying to imitate someone else, and the result, in both cases, has been something very interesting and useful indeed.

Bloggers who don't unearth unusual news, on the other hand,

can still stand out and contribute by having—as James Lileks does—a unique perspective on the stories people have already read. In this light it's no surprise that bloggers who are successful generally bring something special to the table. For famous journalist-bloggers, it's their journalistic smarts and connections, as evidenced in the work of Mickey Kaus, Virginia Postrel, and Josh Marshall.

For some, like Lileks, it's that they just flat-out write better than anyone else. Still others, like the various bloggers at The Volokh Conspiracy, or Howard Bashman at How Appealing, or Jeralyn Merritt at TalkLeft, offer academic or legal expertise. For others, like famed Baghdad blogger Salam Pax, or Zeyad, or the various bloggers who chronicled the "Orange Revolution" in Ukraine, it's their proximity to events. (And local blogging, I think, is something that's likely to take off, since it provides something—knowledge of one's hometown—that's comparatively scarce and hard for others to match.)

In every case, though, what brings success is knowing something other people don't know and expressing it well.

All of this means, of course, that if you came to this chapter looking for blogging secrets, well, there aren't any. The key to good blogging is simple: have something interesting to say, and say it well. Kind of like every other sort of writing—just faster, and with links. There's nothing new about that, but it's still a kind of magic, as good writing always is.

7

HORIZONTAL KNOWLEDGE

The Internet is a powerful tool. But most attention seems to focus on its use as a means of vertical communications: from one to many. Even when we talk about how it allows individuals to compete on an even basis with Big Media organizations, we're usually talking about its ability to facilitate a kind of communication that's akin to what Big Media has always done.

But as important as this is—and it's very important indeed—it's probably dwarfed by the much more numerous horizontal communications that the Internet, and related technologies like cell phones, text messaging, and the like permit. They allow a kind of horizontal knowledge that is often less obvious, but in many ways at least as powerful, as the vertical kind.

Horizontal knowledge is communication among individuals, who may or may not know each other, but who are loosely coordinated by their involvement with something, or someone, of mutual interest. And it's extremely powerful, because it makes people much smarter.

People used to be ignorant. It was hard to learn things. You had to go to libraries, look things up, perhaps sit and wait while a book was fetched from storage, or recalled from another user, or borrowed from a different library. What knowledge there was spent most of its time on a shelf. And if knowledge was going to be organized and dispersed, it took a big organization to do it.

TINY BUBBLES

Guinness became a publishing sensation by cashing in on that ignorance. Bar patrons got into so many hard-to-settle arguments about what was biggest, or fastest, or oldest that Guinness responded with *The Guinness Book of World Records*, bringing a small quantity of authoritative knowledge to bear in a handy form.

Things are different today. I'm writing this in a bar right now, and I have most of human knowledge at my fingertips. Okay, it's not really a bar. It's a campus pizza place, albeit one with twenty-seven kinds of beer on tap, a nice patio, and, most importantly, a free wireless Internet hookup. With that, and Google, there's not much that I can't find out.

If I'm curious about the Hephthalite Huns[1] or the rocket equation[2] or how much money Joe Biden[3] has gotten from the entertainment industry, I can have it in less time than it takes the barmaid to draw me a beer.[4]

What's more, I can coordinate that sort of information (well, it might be kind of hard to tie those particular three facts together, but you take my meaning) with other people with enormous speed. With email, blogs, and bulletin boards, I could, if the topic interested enough people, put together an overnight coalition—a flash constituency—without leaving the restaurant. (And in fact, some folks did pretty much just that recently, and succeeded in killing the "super-DMCA" bill before the Tennessee legislature. Alarmed at a proposed law that would have made it a felony to connect a Tivo without permission from a cable company, they organized, set up a website, and shot down a bill that the cable companies had put a lot of time and money into.)

So what? Everybody knows this stuff, right? It has been the subject of countless hand-waving speeches about the revolutionary potential of the Internet, blah, blah, blah, yada, yada, yada. Well, sort of. Everybody knows it. But they don't *know* it, yet, down deep where it counts. And even those who kind of get it at that level tend to forget—as even I sometimes do—just how revolutionary it is. And yes, it really is revolutionary, in ways that would have defied prediction not long ago.

Just try this thought experiment: Imagine that it's 1993. The Web is just appearing. And imagine that you—an unusually prescient type—were to explain to people what they could expect by, say, the summer of 2003. Universal access to practically all information. From all over the place—even in bars. And all for free!

I can imagine the questions the skeptics would have asked: How will this be implemented? How will all of this information be digitized and made available? (Lots of examples along the line of "a thousand librarians with scanners would take fifty years to put even a part of the Library of Congress online, and who would pay for that?") Lots of questions about how people would agree on standards for wireless data transmission—"It usually takes ten years just to develop a standard, much less put it into the marketplace!"—and so on, and so on. "Who will make this stuff available for free? People want to be paid to do things!" "Why, even if we start planning now, there's no way we'll have this in ten years!"

Actually, that final statement is true. If we had started planning in 1993, we probably wouldn't have gotten there by 2033, much less before 2003. The Web, Wi-Fi, and Google didn't develop and spread because somebody at the Bureau of Central Knowledge Planning planned them. They developed, in large part, from the uncoordinated activities of individuals.

Why can you find all sorts of stuff, from information about the Hephthalite Huns to instructions for brewing beer (yes, it always comes back to beer), and even recipes for cooking squirrel, on the Web? Because people thought it was cool enough (to them) to be worth the effort (on their part) of putting it online. We didn't need a thousand librarians with scanners because we had a billion non-librarians with computers and divergent interests. Wi-Fi sprang up the same way: not as part of a national plan by the Responsible Authorities, but as part of a ground-up movement composed of millions of people who just wanted it and companies happy to sell them the gear they needed to pull it off.

There are two lessons here. One is that the skeptics, despite all their reasonable-sounding objections, would have been utterly wrong about the future of the Web, a mere ten years after it first appeared. And the second is *why* they would have been wrong: because they didn't appreciate what lots of smart people, loosely coordinating their actions with each other, are capable of accomplishing. It's the power of horizontal, as opposed to vertical, knowledge.

As the world grows more interconnected, more and more people have access to knowledge and coordination. Yet we continue to underestimate the revolutionary potential of this simple fact. Heck, forget *potential*—we regularly underestimate the revolutionary *reality* of it, in the form of things we already take for granted, like Wi-Fi and Google.

But I'm not a wild-eyed visionary. As a result, I'm going to make a very conservative prediction: that the next ten years will see revolutions that make Wi-Fi and Google look tame, and that in short order we'll take those for granted too. It's a safe bet.

Of course, not everyone is happy. The spread of horizontal knowledge is discomfiting big organizations that have depended on vertical organization. Not surprisingly, some of the first to be affected are those in the media.

In the old days, if you didn't like what you read in the newspaper, you could either complain to your neighbors, or send a letter to the editor that—maybe—would be published days or weeks later, when everyone had forgotten the story you were complaining about. And if you worked at a newspaper, you couldn't even do that. Newspapers aren't very enthusiastic about publishing letters from unhappy employees.

INSIDE, OUTSIDE, UPSIDE DOWN

For the *New York Times,* though, it became painfully obvious how that old system has broken down as the career of editor-in-chief Howell Raines came to an end. From the outside, bloggers like Andrew Sullivan and Mickey Kaus, along with specialty sites like TimesWatch, kept up constant pressure. Every distortion and misrepresentation (and there were plenty, of course) was picked up and noted. The result was a steady diminution of the *Times's* prestige among the opinion-making classes, something that opened it up for criticism in a way that it once didn't have to face because of the quasi-mystical awe in which many journalists have traditionally held it.

Meanwhile, the Internet also opened things up from the inside. Unhappy *Times* staffers in previous years could have grumbled to their colleagues at other papers, but such grumbling would have been largely futile. Now, on the other hand, thanks to email and websites such as Jim Romenesko's (and quite a few blogs that got leaked information), they could grumble to a major audience. They could also engage in that most devastating of insider activities, the leaking of sanctimonious and dumb internal memos from the bosses. (Note to bosses: If you distribute your dumb and sanctimonious memos on paper instead of via email, you'll face less of that because people can't just hit "forward" and send them on. Of course, another approach might be to write memos that aren't dumb and sanctimonious.)

Nick Denton, however, warned shortly after Raines's departure that there's a downside to this, what he calls "organizational terrorism" via Internet, a sort of asymmetrical warfare that's not necessarily a good thing.

> Raines, sometimes crassly, was trying to institute change; the organizational reactionaries didn't like it. In a previous era, a manager would have been able to execute the ringleaders, and ride out the discontent. But Raines was up against a powerful combination of old labor unionism, and the new industrial action: a leak to a weblog, tittle-tattle over the IM, whispered conversations to Howard Kurtz. . . . [M]anagers

may sometimes have the power to hire and fire, but the peasants have the Internet now.

Is that a good thing? I'm not sure. I can imagine large organizations—all large organizations—becoming more conservative, so concerned to maintain a happy workplace that they avoid change. For smaller organizations, in the media and other sectors, this may be an opportunity.[5]

Nick was right to warn about this possibility. Things will be different, and already are. Even in the military, email and chat rooms are flattening hierarchies and changing power dynamics. On the other hand, what the Internet peasantry hates most is not just power, but bogosity. Raines was disliked as much because he played favorites (and it was seen as a favoritism not based on performance) as because he was dictatorial: tough, but unfair. And—just as students resent a professor who won't shut up their over-talkative peers more than they resent one who will—employees don't necessarily resent managers who run a taut ship, so long as they feel that merit is being rewarded over sucking up.

So it may be that managers who do a good job have less to fear, and that it will be in the interest of the people who ultimately run many large organizations, like boards of directors, to pay closer attention to the performance of managers, and to what the employee samizdat is saying about them. That's one way in which horizontal knowledge could work to improve organizations, not sabotage them as Nick suggests, so long as the board members apply some good sense.

On a smaller scale, the new *Times* editors may want to look at putting horizontal knowledge to work for them in another way. It would be child's play to take RSS feeds from a number of blogs (say, via Technorati), filter them to extract the references to stories in the *Times*, and then have an ombudsman look at those references to see if correction, amplification, or investigation is called for. A newspaper that did that (and it could just as easily be done by any major paper, not just the *Times*) would be enlisting a huge (and unpaid!) army of fact-checkers, and could fix mistakes within hours of their appearing, thus turning inside its competition and enhancing its reputation, all at very low cost. I first suggested this three or four years ago, but it hasn't happened yet (though *Times* rival the *Washington Post* is making links to blogs mentioning its stories available to readers, which is a first step).

Will it happen? That depends on whether Big Media folks want to ride the wave of horizontal knowledge, or just try to keep their heads above water.

So far the signs aren't entirely promising. A lot of folks around the blogosphere got angry at the *New York Times's* John Markoff for comments he made to the *Online Journalism Review*, in which he likened blogs to CB Radio in the 1970s. But although Markoff meant to be dismissive, he was actually onto something, because CB radio was an early enabler of horizontal knowledge, with some pretty significant social and political consequences.

BIG BROTHER VS. THE CONVOY

Citizens' Band radio gets a bum rap nowadays—in most people's minds, it's associated with images of Homer Simpson (in the flashback scenes where he had hair) shouting, "Breaker 1–9" and singing C. W. McCall's "Convoy!" loudly and off-key. In other words, something out of date and vaguely risible, like leisure suits or Tony Orlando.

But, in fact, CB was a revolution in its time, whose effects are still felt today. Before Citizens' Band was created, you needed a license to be on the air, with almost no exceptions. Radio was seen as Serious Technology for Serious People, nothing for normal folks to fool around with, at least not without government approval. Citizens' Band put an end to that, not by regulatory design but by popular fiat. Originally, a license was required for Citizens' Band too, but masses of people simply broke the law and operated without a license until the FCC was forced to bow to reality. It was a form of mass civil disobedience that accomplished in its sphere what drug-legalization activists have never been able to accomplish in theirs. No small thing.

And it didn't stop there. Citizens' Band radio became popular because of widespread resistance to another example of regulatory overreach: the unpopular fifty-five-mile-per-hour speed limit. Actually passed in 1974, but reenacted on Jimmy Carter's watch and popularly identified with Carter's "moral equivalent of war," speed limits were for the first time set not for reasons of highway safety, but for reasons of politics and social engineering. Americans rejected that approach in massive numbers and entered into a state of more-or-less open rebellion. CB was valuable—as songs like "Convoy!" and movies like *Smokey and the Bandit* illustrated—because it allowed citizens to spontaneously organize against what they saw as illegitimate authority. Before CB, the police—with all their expensive infrastructure of radio networks, dispatchers, and patrol cars—had the communications and observational advantage, but with CB each user had the benefit of hundreds or thousands of eyeballs warning about speed traps in advance. This made breaking the speed laws much easier and enforcing them much harder.

And it worked: the fifty-five-mile-per-hour speed limit was repealed. That (plus the gradual introduction of cheap and effective radar detectors, which allowed citizens to watch for speed traps while still listening to their car stereos) gradually ended the Citizens' Band revolution. *Sort of,* because like many fads, Citizens' Band didn't really go away. It just faded from view and turned into something else.

CB radio primed a generation that was used to top-down communication on the network-news model for peer-to-peer communication, getting people in the right frame of mind for the Internet, cell phones, and text messaging. It also served as a vehicle for spreading countercultural resistance to authority beyond the confines of hippiedom, taking it deep into the heart of middle America.

In fact, it's probably not too much of a stretch to say that this combination of resentment over Big Brother intrusiveness, coupled with the means of resisting those intrusions, laid the groundwork for the antigovernment explosions of the 1980s. A lot of people used CB radio to evade the unpopular speed limit, and Carter wound up losing to Ronald Reagan, who preached individual freedom and deregulation. It's hard to know which way the causality runs here—did CB make Reagan's election more likely, by fanning the flames of antibureaucratic sentiment? Or was it just an early indicator of that sentiment? Who knows?

But either way, it was something important. And so it is with more modern technologies, like blogs and text messaging and

Internet video. Like CB, they may well vanish from public attention, if not from the actual world (plenty of CB radios still get
sold, after all—in fact, after being stuck in an endless traffic jam
on I-40 a couple of weeks back, I just ordered one myself). And
they'll probably be replaced, or absorbed, by new technology
within a few years. But they're popular right now because people
want to get around Big Media's stranglehold on news and information, just as CBs were popular with people who wanted to get
around speed limits. And, like Jimmy Carter, Big Media folks
seem largely clueless about what's going on.

Of course, it's not just the media who face threats from insid-
ers. Governments, too, face new kinds of pressure from horizontal knowledge in a way that the CB revolution didn't foreshadow.

That seems to be the case for the United States government,
the ultimate large organization. According to a report by Bill
Broad in the *New York Times,* employee-bloggers have been giving the Los Alamos National Lab and the Department of Energy
fits:

> A blog rebellion among scientists and engineers at Los
> Alamos, the federal government's premier nuclear weapons
> laboratory, is threatening to end the tenure of its director,
> G. Peter Nanos.
>
> Four months of jeers, denunciations and defenses of
> Dr. Nanos's management recently culminated in dozens of
> signed and anonymous messages concluding that his days
> were numbered. The postings to a public weblog conveyed
> a mood of self-congratulation tempered with sober discus-
> sion of what comes next.[6]

And that's perhaps an appropriate mood for the blogosphere as a whole. On the one hand, we've started to see a switch: where an earlier generation of articles on employee blogging warned employees about the danger of retribution from employers, a newer version of the story warns employers about the power of bloggers in their midst.

On the other hand, it's hard for organizations to operate when dissent becomes easier, and more popular, than actually running things or doing work. Whistle-blowing is all very nice, but no organization made up largely of whistle-blowers is likely to thrive. While "organizational terrorism" may be a bit strong, Nick was certainly right to note that one of management's major advantages was informational—it could know more, and communicate more to more people, than dissident employees hanging around the water cooler could.

That's changed now, and there's no doubt that it makes managers nervous. Still, I think the Los Alamos case also underscores what I wrote above in response to Nick Denton: The flattening of hierarchies that easier communication produces is a bigger threat to bad managers than to good ones, and in fact it's a useful tool for managers who want to know what's really going on.

Say what you will about the Los Alamos scandals, but no one has accused the lab of being a taut ship, or of rewarding merit above all else. While Internet samizdat may pose a threat to managers, it still seems to me that the threat is biggest where the management is the worst, and that exposing bad management and unhappy employees isn't necessarily such a bad thing.

The biggest danger, at any rate, won't come from the internal blogging. It will come from management's overreaction to internal blogging. If managers are afraid of internal bloggers and respond either with witch hunts and efforts to shut them down, or—perhaps worse, from a standpoint of organizational health— try too hard to appease dissidents by trying to run their companies or organizations in ways that won't offend anyone, the damage will be far greater than the damage done by bloggers.

With or without bloggers in the mix, management requires a backbone. The smarter managers will read blogs, looking for real problems that need to be fixed, and they'll respond (perhaps on their own blogs?) to the critics. The smartest ones will even realize that employees know the difference between the chronic belly-achers and the people who have serious complaints and will respond accordingly. Easier communication is actually a useful asset to managers who wonder whether the folks below them are reporting the truth or presenting a rosy scenario designed to cover their asses. Some have figured this out already, and a *Wall Street Journal* study in October of 2005 found that many CEOs encourage open email communication with staff precisely for these reasons.[7] Extending that to reading blogs is a logical next step for the smart managers.

How many managers are this smart? I guess, thanks to the Internet, we'll find out.

THE INSIDE-OUT PANOPTICON

But of course—as the CB era demonstrated—there's more to horizontal knowledge than workplace carping. Dictators, and even democratic governments not terribly enthused about opposition, have traditionally discouraged communication among the citizenry. Vertical communication is just, well, safer for those in power.

That's certainly what happened when Philippine President Joseph Estrada was ousted in a "people power" revolution organized by cell phones and text messages: Over 150,000 protesters appeared on short notice, thanks to technologies that allowed a flash mob to appear without the kind of big, central organization it would have taken in the past. Other technologies are doing the same kind of thing. Musician Peter Gabriel founded a human rights group called Witness that distributes video cameras to human rights groups. Activists say that government and private thugs who might have taken violent action against them have often been deterred by the fear that video of their actions might become public.[8]

Combining video cameras and cell phones, as technology is in the process of doing, only intensifies the effect. An ordinary video camera can be confiscated and its tape destroyed, but a video camera that can transmit video wirelessly can be relaying the information to hundreds, thousands, or millions of people—who may react angrily and spontaneously if anything happens to the person doing the shooting.

This represents the political future, for good and ill. I'm inclined to think that it's mostly good, but there are two sides to what Howard Rheingold calls "smart mobs." If the toppling of dictators via people power is one side, then riots by mobs of the ignorant are the other. As Rheingold observes:

On the political level, you're seeing peaceful democratic demonstrations like the ones [that brought down President

Joseph Estrada] in the Philippines. You're also seeing riots, like the Miss World riots in Nigeria. Not all forms of human cooperation are pro-social. Some of them are antisocial.[9]

Absolutely. As Clive Thompson noted, the Miss World riots in Nigeria were organized by Muslim fundamentalists who took umbrage at a newspaper story they regarded as insufficiently respectful of Islam (it said that one of the contestants was pretty enough to have been chosen by Mohammed). Word spread by cell phone and text message, and the result was a mob attack on the newspaper offices. Mobs can take down dictatorial governments, Thompson pointed out, but they can also engage in lynchings.[10]

Well, yes. Communications can make it easy for democrats and human-rights activists to coordinate via cell phone and the Internet—as they did in the Philippines, in the Ukraine, and in Lebanon—but it can also make it easy for mobs of the ignorant or vicious to coalesce in response to bogus rumors. (These might be called "dumb mobs," I suppose.) The tools empower the individuals and make them "smarter" in terms of coordination and access to information. But they're smart mobs, not wise mobs. Wisdom comes from other sources, when it comes at all.

Still, we've certainly managed to hold riots and organize dumb mobs in the absence of technology since, well, the beginning of human history. What is new isn't the potential for mob action (Hitler used a mass medium, radio, to put together the ultimate dumb mob), but the potential for constructive and spontaneous group action. Nonetheless, like most technological changes that promise good, it won't happen all on its own. We need to be looking for ways to maximize the upside, and minimize the downside, as these things spread.

That may not be as hard as it sounds. Riots are sometimes spontaneous, but they're usually more organized than they look. Somebody—gangs hoping for loot, religious zealots trying to raise a mob to smite unbelievers, government officials wanting to crush dissent—gives things a push, usually figuring that their responsibility for doing so will be lost in the fog created by the riot and its aftermath. Then the mob forms, and the individuals who make it up do things, secure in the anonymity of the mob, that they would never do on their own.

Pervasive cameras and reporting make both aspects harder, and riskier. (And readily available information means that potential victims can avoid riots, and law enforcement authorities will have a better idea of what's going on, if they make proper use of what is available.) Like everything, it's a mixed bag, but I think it's unlikely that technology will do as much to empower dumb mobs as it does to promote smart ones.

And, as it happens, I have a few thoughts on how to help maintain that imbalance. Wherever possible, we should look for opportunities to inject truth and moderation into the web of horizontal communications. Rumor-debunking sites like Snopes.com are a good example—in a Web-based world, Snopes serves as a sort of anti-*Guinness Book*, helping to neutralize false claims of the outrageous or upsetting.

It's also the case that, as with management in companies, government and antihate organizations can take advantage of what mass horizontal communications have to offer in the way of transparency. What bubbles up through blogs, chat boards, and email lists may be wrong, but it's a useful guide to what people are thinking, offering opportunities to counter rumors, incitements, and falsehoods before they reach critical mass. (I also suspect that emergency authorities could get a lot of useful information—and not only in terms of pending riots—just by watching for a sudden spike in text-messaging.)

What's more, to the extent that people can organize for constructive things as they've done with matters ranging from tsunami relief, to hurricane relief, to such collaborative research projects as SETI@home (where number-crunching is parceled out to members' computers, creating a massively parallel computing project on the cheap), to political efforts like FreeRepublic or DailyKos, the result is to discourage destructive efforts in favor of constructive ones. Not perfectly, of course, but more often than not.

At any rate, we'd best be thinking of ways to capitalize on horizontal knowledge, because it's likely here to stay. Turning back the clock on the communications revolution would probably be impossible and would certainly be vastly expensive. I don't expect that it will happen, which means we'd better figure out how to live with the change.

8

HOW THE GAME
IS PLAYED

Once upon a time, breadth of experience—both firsthand and through books, anecdotes, and institutional wisdom—was one of the things that separated the aristocracy from the peasantry. Peasants knew their daily lives and surroundings, but not much else. Only the nobility—and its hanger-on cultures of soldiers, scribes, clerics, and scholars—had experience in the broader world.

That's not so true anymore. Mostly, of course, that's because ordinary people travel more, meet more people, and accomplish more than any peasant (or king) could have imagined a few centuries ago.

But the virtual world promises to do even more to expand the range of human experience. Not everyone is happy about that, but it's a trend that, in my opinion at least, can't be stopped, and shouldn't be stopped. Shaping it, on the other hand, may be worth some thought.

XBOX WARRIORS

Legislators around the country are trying to ban violent video games as immoral and dangerous in their effect on children. According to *Wired News*: "Lawmakers in at least seven states proposed bills during the most recent legislative session that would restrict the sale of games, part of a wave that began when the 1999 Columbine High School shootings sparked an outcry over games and violence."[1] The article notes that the bills are supported by "pediatricians and psychologists."

Actually, other psychologists (including my wife, a specialist in violent kids[2]) disagree with this assessment regarding video games and violence. And why we should care what *pediatricians* think about video games is beyond me—what do they know about this stuff? (Most of the time they can't diagnose my daughter's strep throat correctly, which makes me doubt that their professional wisdom extends to complex social-psychological matters.)

But the move against violent video games strikes me as a bad idea for other reasons. Not only does it represent an unconstitutional infringement on free speech—as the *Wired News* story notes, "None of the measures that passed have survived legal challenge,"—but it may actually make America weaker.

American troops are already using video games in training. Some are fancy custom jobs, like the combat simulators described in this article by Jim Dunnigan at StrategyPage:

> [The simulators] surround the trainees and replicate the sights and sounds of an attack. Weapons equipped with special sensors allow the troops to shoot back from mockups of

vehicles, and they also receive feedback if they are hit. . . . One problem with the ambushes and roadside bombs is that not every soldier driving around Iraq will encounter one, but if you do, your chances of survival go up enormously if you quickly make the right moves. The troops know this, and realistic training via the simulators is expected to be popular.[3]

The Army has also developed a game called "America's Army," originally intended as a recruiting tool, that has turned out to be realistic enough that it's used by the military for training purposes.[4] These training games draw heavily on existing technology, most of it developed for consumer-market video games. (And, in fact, the military uses some consumer games in training too.) They also draw on troops' skills at rapidly mastering such simulators, skills likely honed on consumer video games.

What's more, civilians who play military video games may acquire useful knowledge. This knowledge may even have political ramifications. When television commentators second-guess things that happen in combat—often showing an astounding degree of military ignorance in the process—people who have played military video games are more likely to see through it. At the very least, they have some sense of how fast things can happen, and how confusing they can be.

(SIMULATED) WAR: WHAT IS IT GOOD FOR?

In fact, shortly after 9/11 Dave Kopel and I wondered if the spread of military knowledge via war-gaming might lead to changes in the way war is perceived by Americans. We also noted that war games have played an important educational role at all sorts of levels.[5]

As a population, the American public probably has greater expertise concerning serious military history than any previous society. This expertise has been acquired steadily over the past four decades, and it has happened largely without notice from the media, academics, or the punditocracy. What's more, people have become more knowledgeable in spite of the removal of most military subjects from the mainstream educational curriculum, and despite the PC movement's success in driving military history out of history departments.

One reason that this underground military education has gone unnoticed is that the people acquiring the expertise are mostly techno-geeks, the very people that some commentators point to as evidence of our unmartial character. Yet to anyone who knows it, geek culture is full of military aspects.

Military history is a popular interest among geeks. So is skill with firearms. As an article in *Salon* noted awhile back, geeks tend to be strong gun-rights enthusiasts, regarding both computers and firearms as technologies that empower the individual.[6] Geeks, knowing that they can program their VCR, also believe themselves capable of cleaning a gun safely.

Some geeks take their enthusiasm further, engaging in massed battles with broadswords and maces as part of the Society for Creative Anachronism's popular rounds of medieval combat. Though the weapons are usually blunt or padded, injuries are about as common as in rugby and football, and the rules are far less refined. Geeks also read military science fiction by authors like

David Drake, Jerry Pournelle, S. M. Stirling, Eric Flint, and Harry Turtledove, in which war is not glorified or simplified, but presented in surprisingly realistic fashion.

But the biggest source of geek military knowledge comes from that staple of geek culture, war-gaming. Ever since the introduction of war games in the early 1960s by companies like Avalon Hill and Simulations Publications Inc. (SPI), geeks have made war-gaming a major pastime. The games, once played on boards with cardboard counters, now often run on PCs and realistically reflect all sorts of concerns, from logistics, to morale, to the importance of troop training.

War-gaming, like chess, has always been an activity mainly for intelligent males. At the peak of board-based war-gaming, in the late 1970s and early 1980s, most good high schools had a war-game club. And you can be sure that the average member of the war-game club ended up with a job and an income far ahead of the average student at the school.

Board-based military games attracted a smaller set of the geek population in subsequent decades, as computers became a new way for geeks to have fun, and as Dungeons & Dragons (originally just a small part of the war-gaming world) became enormously popular, spawning scores of imitators.

Avalon Hill, the founding father of the industry, has been taken over by Hasbro, which has junked most of AH's once-formidable catalogue. Today, Decision Games is probably the leading war-game publisher, with the flagship magazine *Strategy & Tactics* (a military-history magazine with a game in every issue), and with a catalogue of board and computer games ranging from Megiddo (1479 BC, the epic chariot clash between Egypt's

Tuthmosis III and the King of Kadesh) all the way to the 1973 Arab-Israeli war.

Today's computer format for games works better at creating "the fog of war," since the computer can hide pieces. The computer also makes it easier to play Solitaire—and solitaire was always a major form of war-game play; the players were attracted by the ideas, not by the chance to chat while playing Bridge.

How well have war games taught war? Well enough that several war games have been used as instructional or analytical tools by the United States military.

Over the years, game designers learned how to playtest games before publication, so that players would be forced to address real strategy and tactics, as opposed to manipulating artifacts of the game system. No game could possibly simulate everything realistically, but the best games pick some key challenges faced by the real-world commanders and make the players deal with the same problems. For example, the many games depicting the 1941 German invasion of the U.S.S.R. find the German player with near total military superiority in any given battle—but always wondering whether to outrun his supply lines, and conquer as much ground as possible, before the winter sets in. Other games make the players work on the delicate balance of combined arms—learning how to make infantry, tanks, and artillery work together in diverse terrain, and learning what to do when your tanks are all destroyed but the enemy still has fifteen left.

Some war-gamers prefer purely tactical games, such as plane-to-plane or ship-to-ship combat. These players come away with amazing amounts of knowledge about submarines, or fighter planes, or Greek triremes, or dreadnaughts. And since real war-gamers like lots of different games, many learn, in-depth, about many different military subjects.

Even the least successful games teach a good deal of geography and history. And they always demonstrate how the "right" answer to a military strategy question is usually clear only in hindsight.

The war-gaming magazines are all about military history, naturally, and most war-gamers end up reading military history and strategy books too. If you ask, "Who was Heinz Guderian?" most people will guess, "Some sort of ketchup genius?" War gamers will be ones who answer: "The German general who invented modern tank warfare, and who wrote a famous memoir, *Panzer Leader.*"

Most people who war-game don't become real warriors—although the games have always been especially popular at military academies. Anyone who spends a few hundred hours playing war-games (and many hobbyists put in thousands of hours) will soon know more about the nuts and bolts of warfare than most journalists who cover the subject or most politicians who vote on military matters.

So here's the funny thing. While the official American culture around, say, 1977 was revolted by anything military, a bunch of the nation's smartest young males—the "leaders of tomorrow"—were reading *Panzer Leader* and Sir Basil Henry Liddell Hart's *Strategy,*[7] and, of course, Sun Tzu's *Art of War,* long before it became a business-school cliché.

This was no accident. Many of those who founded the war-game publishing business feared that, with the antimilitarism caused by the Vietnam War and, later, with the adoption of the all-volunteer army, American society would become estranged from all things military, leaving ordinary citizens too ignorant to make meaningful democratic judgments about war. They hoped that realistic simulation games would teach important principles.

We're only now testing the societal effect of having such a large number of knowledgeable citizens. The Gulf War was too short, and too much of a set piece, for public military knowledge to play a major role. But there's reason to believe that it will be different this time—especially as the favored geek mode of communication, the Internet, is now pervasive. This means that geeks' knowledge, and their knowledgeable opinions, will have substantial influence. They will be able to put the military events of any given day into a much broader perspective, and they may be opinion leaders who help their friends and neighbors avoid the error of thinking that the last fifteen minutes of television footage tell the conclusive story of the war's progress. The role of warbloggers—and military bloggers—so far has certainly seemed to fit this bill.

The phenomenal educational effort of the war-game publishers has ensured that, despite the neglect of matters military by most educational institutions, important aspects of military knowledge were kept alive and taught to new generations of Americans, in a fashion so enjoyable that many didn't even realize they were being educated.

VIRTUAL DATING AND OTHER VITAL EDUCATIONAL TOOLS

Of course, the usefulness of computer games as an educational technique goes well beyond war, as I discovered recently firsthand when I heard my daughter and one of her friends having an earnest discussion: "You have to have a job to buy food and things, and if you don't go to work, you get fired. And if you spend all your money buying stuff, you have to make more."

All true enough, and worthy of Clark Howard or Dave Ramsey. And it's certainly something my daughter has heard from me over the years. But rather than quoting paternal wisdom, they were talking about *The Sims,* a computer game that simulates ordinary American life, which swept through my patch of Little-Girl Land at breakneck speed. Thanks to *The Sims,* the girls know how to make a budget and how to read an income statement—and to be worried when cash flow goes negative. They understand comparison shopping. They're also picking up some pointers on human interaction, though *The Sims* characters come up short in that department. (Then again, so do real people, now and then.)

Now *The Sims 2* has upped the stakes. Among other things, as its label makes clear, it allows players to "Mix Genes: Your Sims have DNA and inherit physical and personality traits. Take your Sims through an infinite number of generations as you evolve their family tree."

What more could a father want than a game that will teach his daughter that if you marry a loser, he'll likely stay a loser, and if you have kids with him, they'll have a good chance of being losers too? Thank God for technology.

All joking aside, I'm impressed with the things that these games teach. I've already mentioned the value of video games in teaching warlike skills, but of course those aren't the only skills games can impart, just the ones for which there was a large and early market. But as the technology improves, and people get more and more used to computers, I think we'll see a lot more games that teach as they entertain. SimWorld isn't the real world, of course. But it's a world in which actions have consequences, and not necessarily happy ones. (Your Sim characters can die, if you let them screw things up too much—and they can have extramarital affairs, which as in real life, usually turn out badly for all concerned.) It's a world in which narcissism, hedonism, and impulsiveness are punished, and in which traditional middle-class virtues, like thrift and planning, generally pay off. In short, it's a world that's a lot more like the real world than the fantasy worlds of movies, popular songs, and novels—the places where children and adolescents have traditionally gotten their non-parental information on how life works.

And kids find this stuff more interesting than movies, popular songs, and novels, at least judging from the degree of addiction *The Sims* has produced among my daughter's crowd. Which means that we have not only a powerful teaching tool, but a powerful teaching tool that people actually want to learn from. It's not quite *A Young Lady's Illustrated Primer,* the computerized tutorial from Neal Stephenson's novel *The Diamond Age,* but you can see things moving in that direction.

What's more, it's a powerful teaching tool that people buy. The government does not decree the use of such a game from on high; instead it's a creation of a free market that had entertainment, not instruction, as its primary goal. And it's teaching something that most kids don't get in school or at home. I don't think that *The Sims* will replace schools, but it's interesting to see a consumer product providing an education that is, in some ways, more rigorous than many schools provide.

THE KIDS ARE ALRIGHT

It may be making a difference. At the very least, the fears of the video-game critics seem to be stillborn. American teenagers are doing better than ever, and people are trying to figure out why. Games just might have something to do with it; at the very least, they don't seem to be hurting.

Teen pregnancy is down, along with teen crime, drug use, and many other social ills. There's also evidence that teenagers are more serious about life in general and are more determined to make something worthwhile of their lives. Where just a few years ago the "teenager problem" looked insoluble, it now seems well on the road to solving itself.[8] But why?

Reading about this change, it suddenly occurred to me that I had the answer: porn and video games. That's what's making American teens healthier!

It should have been obvious. After all, one of the great changes in teenagers' social environments over the past decade or so has been far greater exposure to explicit pornography, via the Internet; and violence, via video games. Where twenty or thirty years ago teenagers had to go to some effort to see pictures of people having sex, now those things are as close as a Google query. (In fact, on the Internet it takes some small effort to *avoid* such pictures.) Meanwhile, video games have gotten more violent, with efforts to limit their content failing on First Amendment grounds.

But, despite continued warnings from concerned mothers' groups, teenagers are less violent, and—according to some, if not all, studies—they're having less sex, notwithstanding the predictions of many concerned people that such exposure would have the opposite effect. More virtual sex and violence would seem to go along with less real sex and violence; certainly with less pregnancy and violence.[9]

The solution is clear—we need a massive government program to ensure that no American teenager goes without porn and video games. Let no child be left behind! Well, no. Not even I'm ready to argue for that kind of legislation, though I suppose candidates interested in the youth vote might want to give it a thought. But the real lesson is that complex social problems are, well, complex, and that the law of unintended consequences continues to apply.

When teen crime and pregnancy rates were going up, people looked at things that were going on—including increased availability of porn and violent imagery—and concluded that there might be something to that correlation. It turned out that there wasn't. Porn and *Duke Nukem* took over the land, and yet teenagers became more responsible and less violent.

Maybe the porn and the video games provided catharsis, serving as substitutes for the real thing. Maybe. And maybe there's no connection at all. (Or maybe it's a different one—the research indicates that teenagers, though safer and healthier, are also fatter—so perhaps the other improvements are the result of teens sitting around looking at porn and video games until they're too out-of-shape and unattractive for the real thing.) Most likely, the lesson is that—once again—correlation isn't causation, despite policy entrepreneurs' efforts to claim otherwise.

Regardless, the fears of the doomsayers have not come to pass. People can continue to claim that psychological research suggests that video games lead to violence and that porn leads to promiscuity, but in the real world the evidence suggests otherwise. So perhaps we should reconsider regulating video games. And we should definitely take claims of impending social doom with a grain of salt. (Hey, while we're at it, why not encourage surfing porn and playing shoot-'em-up games? After all, as the activists say, if it saves just one child, it's worth it!)

More seriously, such a lack of evidence is reason enough not to shut down the virtual worlds that kids are inhabiting. Instead, we may want to look at the lessons they learn. I don't think that *Duke Nukem* or *Grand Theft Auto* are particularly harmful, but it would be useful for people to think about ways of making those games teach productive real-world lessons, and I think that can be done without making them uninteresting. The real world is interesting, after all, and it's very, very good at teaching real-world lessons. The advantage of the virtual world is that those lessons can be learned without bloodshed, bankruptcy, or jail. Seems like a good thing to me.

9

EMPOWERING THE *REALLY* LITTLE GUYS

All sorts of new technologies promise to empower individuals, but the ultimate empowerer of ordinary people may well turn out to be nanotechnology, the much-hyped but still important technology of molecular manufacturing and computing. Indeed, for all the nano-hype, the reality of nanotechnology may turn out to exceed the claims. The result may be as big a change as the Industrial Revolution, but in a different direction.

Nanotechnology derives its name from the nanometer, or a billionth of a meter, and refers to the manipulation of matter at the atomic and molecular level. The ideas behind nanotechnology are simple ones: every substance on Earth is made up of molecules composed of one or more atoms (the smallest particles of elements). To describe the molecules that constitute a physical object and how they interrelate is to say nearly everything important about the object. It follows, then, that if you can manipulate individual atoms and molecules and put them together in certain configurations, you should be able to create just about anything you desire. And if technologies like computers and the Internet have empowered individuals by giving them drastically more control over the organization of information, the impact of nano-technology—which promises similar control over the material world—is likely to be much greater. This goes well beyond home-brewing beer, though, as with making beer, nanotechnology involves letting someone else do the hard work at the microscopic level.

Richard Feynman's first description of nanotechnology still serves:

The principles of physics, as far as I can see, do not speak against the possibility of maneuvering things atom by atom. . . . [I]t would be, in principle, possible for a physi-cist to synthesize any chemical substance that the chemist writes down. How? Put the atoms down where the chemist says, and so you make the substance. The problems of chemistry and biology can be greatly helped if our ability to see what we are doing, and to do things on an atomic level, is ultimately developed—a development which I think can-not be avoided.[1]

Modern nanotechnology researchers want to go beyond synthe-sizing "substances" (though that has great importance) to use nanotechnology's atom-by-atom construction techniques to pro-duce objects: tiny, bacterium-sized devices that can repair clogged arteries, kill cancer cells, fix cellular damage from aging, and (via what are called "assemblers") make other devices of greater size or complexity by plugging atoms, one at a time, into the desired arrangements, very quickly. Other researchers believe that nanotechnology will allow for a degree of miniaturization that might permit computers a millionfold more efficient than anything available now. Still others believe that nanotechnology's tiny devices will be able to unravel mysteries of the microscopic world (such as cell metabolism, the aging process, and cancer) in ways that other tools will not be able to.

So far, pioneers like Eric Drexler and Robert Freitas have worked out a lot of the details, and research has produced some small devices, but nothing as exotic as those described above. But nanotechnologists are refining both their instrumentation and their understanding of nanofabrication at an accelerating rate. Will they be able to fulfill the field's promise? Richard Feynman thought so. That raises a lot of interesting possibilities—and questions.

The digital revolution brought us a debate over the difference between virtual reality and physical reality, a distinction the courts are still trying to figure out. But we are also at the dawn of a new technological revolution—the nanotech revolution—that may challenge our definition of what physical reality is. Superman could create diamonds by squeezing lumps of coal, using heat and pressure to rearrange the carbon atoms. Nanotechnology could achieve the same transformation, with considerably less fuss, simply by plugging carbon atoms together, one at a time, in the correct manner—and without the embarrassing blue tights.

This sounds like the stuff of science fiction, and it is: In Michael Crichton's thriller, *Prey,* nanotech plays the bad guy. But in real life, nanotech is already being used by everyone from Lee Jeans, which uses nanofibers to make stain-proof pants, to the U.S. military, which uses nanotechnology to make better catalysts for rockets and missiles, to scientists who are using nano-technology to develop workable artificial kidneys.[2]

"JUST ADD SUNLIGHT AND DIRT"

Many scientists initially doubted that nanotechnology's precise positioning of molecules was possible, but that skepticism appears to have been misplaced. That's no surprise, really, since living organisms, including our own bodies, make things like bone and muscle by manipulating individual atoms and molecules. Yet as criticism has shifted from claims that nanotechnology won't work to fears that it might, there have been calls to stop progress in the field of nanotechnology before research really gets off the ground. The ETC Group, an anti-technology organization operating out of Canada, has proposed a moratorium on nanotechnology research and on research into self-replicating machines. (At the moment, the latter is like calling for a moratorium on antigravity or faster-than-light travel—nobody's doing it anyway.)

Proponents of this line of criticism face an uphill battle. What's attractive about devices that can be programmed to manipulate molecules is that they let you make virtually anything you want, and you can generally make it out of cheap and commonly available materials and energy—what nanotech enthusiasts call "sunlight and dirt." Selectively sticky probes on tiny bacterium-scale arms, attached either to tiny robots or to a silicon substrate and controlled by computer, can grab the atoms they need from solution, and then plug them together in the proper configuration. It's not quite molecular Legos, but it's close. General purpose devices that can do this are called "assemblers," and the process is known among nanotechnology proponents as "molecular manufacturing."

This process raises some problems of its own, though. Assemblers that can manufacture virtually anything from sunlight and dirt might, as the result of a program error, manufacture endless copies of themselves, which would then go on to make still more copies, and so on. The fear that nanobots might turn the world into mush is known in the trade as the "gray goo problem," the apocalyptic scenario raised in Crichton's novel.

Nanotech's backers, however, believe the real problem won't be accident, but abuse. With mature nanotechnology, it might be possible to disassemble enemy weapons. (Imagine bacterium-sized devices that convert high explosives into inert substances, a technique that would neutralize even nuclear weapons, whose detonators are made of chemical high explosive.) On a more threatening note, sophisticated nanodevices could serve as artificial "disease" agents of great power and subtlety. Highly sophisticated nanorobots could even hide out in people's brains, manipulating their neurochemistry to ensure that they genuinely loved Big Brother. Like nuclear weapons, these devices would be awesome in their destructiveness, and their misuse would be terrifying. Still, the race to harness this power is well underway: Defense spending on nanotechnology is climbing, and civilian spending is over $1 billion a year.[3]

In a world in which the promises of nanotechnology were realized, practically anyone could live a life that would be extraordinary by today's standards, in terms of health (thanks to nanomedicine) and material possessions. DNA damaged by radiation, toxins, or aging could be repaired; arterial plaque could be removed; and cancerous or senescent cells could be destroyed or fixed. Organs could be replaced or even enhanced. Researcher Robert Freitas surveys many of these issues in his book *Nanomedicine,* which explores such topics as "respirocytes"—tiny devices in the bloodstream that could deliver oxygen when the body wasn't able to, protecting against everything from drowning to heart attacks and strokes long enough to allow medical assistance. And this just scratches the surface in terms of potential enhancements, which might also involve stronger muscles, better nerves, and enhanced cognition—the last being the subject of an ongoing Department of Defense research project already.[4]

Most physical goods could be manufactured onsite at low cost from cheap raw materials. Imagine owning an appliance the size of a refrigerator, full of nanoassemblers, that ran on sunlight and dirt (well, solar electricity and cheap feedstocks, anyway) and made pretty much everything you need, from clothing to food. The widespread availability of such devices would make things very, very different. Material goods wouldn't be quite free, but they would be nearly so.

In such a world, personal property would become almost meaningless. Some actual physical items would retain sentimental value, but everything else could be produced as needed, then recycled as soon as the need passed. (As someone who writes on a laptop that was cutting edge last year and is now old news, with its value discounted accordingly, I sometimes think we're already there except for the recycling part. Don't even ask about my MP3 player.)

Real property would retain its value—as my grandfather used to say, "They're not making any more of it," especially oceanfront acreage—but what would "value" mean? Value usually describes an object's ability to be exchanged for another item. But with personal property creatable on demand from sunlight and dirt, it's not clear what the medium of exchange would be. Value comes from scarcity, and most goods wouldn't be scarce. Intellectual property—the software and designs used to program the nano-devices—would be valuable, though once computing power became immense and ubiquitous, developing such designs wouldn't be likely to pose much of a challenge.

One thing that would remain scarce is time. Personal services like teaching, lawyering, or prostitution wouldn't be cheapened in the same fashion. We might wind up with an economy based on the exchange of personal services more than on the purchase of goods. As I mentioned earlier, that's where we're headed already to a point. Even without nanotechnology, the prices of many goods are falling. Televisions, once expensive, are near-commodity goods, as are computers, stereos, and just about all other electronics. It's cheaper to build new ones than to fix old ones, and prices continue to fall as capabilities increase. Nanotechnology would simply accelerate this trend and extend it to everything else. Ironically, it may be the combination of capitalism and technology that brings about a utopia unblemished by the need for ownership, the sort that socialists (usually no fans of capitalism) and romantics (no fans of technology) have long dreamed of.

PIONEERS' PROGRESS

We're not there yet, but things are progressing faster than even I had realized. Recently, I attended an EPA Science Advisory Board meeting where nanotechnology was discussed. What struck me is that even for people like me who try to keep up, the pace of nanotechnology research is moving much too fast to catch everything.

One of the documents distributed at that meeting was a supplement to the president's budget request, entitled *National Nanotechnology Initiative: Research and Development Supporting the Next Industrial Revolution.*[5] I expected it to be the usual bureaucratic pap, but in fact, it turned out to contain a lot of actual useful information, including reports of several nanotechnology developments that I had missed.

The most interesting, to me, was the report of "peptide [ring] nanotubes that kill bacteria by punching holes in the bacteria's membrane." You might think of these as a sort of mechanical antibiotic. As the report notes, "By controlling the type of peptides used to build the rings, scientists are able to design nanotubes that selectively perforate bacterial membranes without harming the cells of the host."[6] It goes on to note, "In theory, these nano-bio agents should be far less prone than existing antibiotics to the development of bacterial resistance."[7] What's more, if such resistance appears, it is likely to be easier to counter. Given the way in which resistance to conventional antibiotics has exploded, this is awfully good news.

Another item involved the use of nanoscale particles of metallic iron to clean up contaminated groundwater. In one experiment, aimed at the contaminant trichloroethylene (TCE), the results were quite impressive: "The researchers carried out a field demonstration at an industrial site in which nanoparticles injected into a groundwater plume containing TCE reduced contaminant levels by up to 96 percent." The report goes on to observe, "A wide variety of contaminants (including chlorinated hydrocarbons, pesticides, explosives, polychlorinated biphenyls and perchlorate) have been successfully broken down in both laboratory and field tests."[8] Not too shabby.

And there's more: the development of nanosensors capable of identifying particular microbes or chemicals, of nanomotors, and dramatic advances in materials. These advances shouldn't be underestimated.

We tend to forget this, but it's possible for a technology to have revolutionary effects long before it reaches its maturity. The impact of high-strength materials, for example, is likely to be much greater than people generally realize. Materials science isn't sexy the way that, say, robots are sexy, but when you can cut the weight, or boost the strength, of aircraft, or spacecraft, or even automobiles by a factor of ten or fifty, the consequences are enormous. Ditto for killing germs, or even detecting them in short order. These sorts of things aren't as exciting as true molecular manufacturing, and they're not as revolutionary, but they're still awfully important, and awfully revolutionary, by comparison with everything else.

When I gave my talk at the Science Advisory Board, I divided nanotechnology into these categories:

- Fake: where it's basically a marketing term, as with nanopants

- Simple: high-strength materials, sensors, coatings, etc.,—things that are important, but not sexy

- Major: advanced devices short of true assemblers

- Spooky: assemblers and related technology (true molecular nanotechnology, capable of making most anything from sunlight and dirt, creating supercomputers smaller than a sugar cube, etc.)

I noted that only in the final category did serious ethical or regulatory issues appear, and also noted that the recent flood of "it's impossible" claims relating to "spooky" nanotechnology seem to have more to do with fear of ethical or regulatory scrutiny than anything else. People in the industry are hoping to keep the critics away with a smokescreen of doubt as to the capabilities of the technology. That probably won't work, especially as nanotechnology develops and is put to use in more and more ways.

Up to now, talk of nanotechnology has generally involved either the "fake" variety (stain-resistant pants) or the "spooky" variety (full-scale molecular nanotechnology with all it implies). But as what might be called midlevel nanotechnology—neither fake nor spooky—begins to be deployed, it's likely to have a substantial effect on the nature of the debate. It's one thing to worry about (fictitious) swarms of predatory nanobots, *a la* Michael Crichton's novel *Prey.* It's another to talk about nanotech bans or moratoria when nanotechnology is already at work curing diseases and cleaning up the environment.

LEARNING FROM EXPERIENCE

I think that these positive uses will probably shift the debate away from the nano-Luddites. But, on the other hand, as nanotechnology becomes commonplace, serious discussion of its implications may be short-circuited. I think that the nanotech business community is actually hoping for such an outcome, in fact, but I continue to believe that such hopes are shortsighted. Genetically modified foods, for example, came to the market with the same absence of discussion, but the result wasn't so great for the industry. Will nanotechnology be different? Stay tuned. Whatever happens, I think that trying to stand still might well prove the most dangerous course of action.

This may seem surprising, but experience suggests that it's true.

For an academic project I worked on awhile back, I reviewed the history of what used to be called "recombinant DNA research" and is now generally just called genetic engineering or biotechnology. Back in the late 1960s and early 1970s, this was very controversial stuff, with opponents raising a variety of frightening possibilities.

Not all the fears were irrational. We didn't know very much about how such things worked, and it was possible to imagine scary scenarios that at least seemed plausible. Indeed, such plausible fears led scientists in the field to get together, twice, holding conferences at Asilomar in California, to propose guidelines that would ensure the safety of recombinant DNA research until more was known.

Those voluntary guidelines became the basis for government regulations, regulations that work so well that researchers often voluntarily submit their work to government review even when the law doesn't require it—and standard DNA licensing agreements often even call for such submission. Self-policing was their key element, and it worked.

When the DNA research debate first started, scientific critics such as Erwin Chargaff met the notion of scientific self-regulation with skepticism. Chargaff predicted modern-day Frankensteins or "little biological monsters" and compared the notion of scientific self-regulation to that of "incendiaries forming their own fire brigade." Such critics warned that the harms that might result from permitting such research were literally incalculable, and thus it should not be allowed.

Others took a different view. Physicist Freeman Dyson, who admitted that (as a physicist, not a biologist) he had no personal stake in the debate, noted, "The real benefit to humanity from recombinant DNA will probably be the one no one has dreamed of. Our ignorance lies equally on both arms of the balance. The public costs of saying no to further development may in the end be far greater than the costs of saying yes." Harvard's Matthew Meselson agreed. The risk of not going forward, he argued, was the risk of being left open to "forthcoming catastrophes," in the form of starvation (which could be addressed by crop biotechnology) and the spread of new viruses. Critics like Chargaff pooh-poohed this view, saying that the promise of the new technology to alleviate such problems was unproven.[9]

Meselson and Dyson have been vindicated. Indeed, Meselson's comments about "forthcoming catastrophes" were made (though no one knew it at the time) just as AIDS was beginning to spread around the world. Without the tools developed through biotechnology and genetic engineering, the Human Immunodeficiency Virus could not even have been identified, and treatment efforts would have been limited. Had we listened to the critics, in other words, it's likely that many more people would have died. Meanwhile, the critics' Frankensteinian fears have not come true, and the research that was feared then has become commonplace, as this excerpt from John Hockenberry's *DNA Files* program on NPR illustrates:

Hockenberry: In those early days [Arthur] Caplan says people were concerned about what would happen if we tried to genetically engineer different bacteria.

Caplan: The mayor of Cambridge, Massachusetts, at one point said he was worried if there were scientific institutions in his town that were doing this, he didn't want to see sort of Frankenstein-type microbes coming out of the sewers.

Hockenberry: Today those early concerns seem almost quaint. Now even high school biology classes like this one in Maine do the same gene combining experiments that once struck fear into the hearts of public officials and private citizens.[10]

This experience suggests that we need to pay close attention to the downsides of limiting scientific research, and that we need to scrutinize the claims of fearmongering critics every bit as carefully as the claims of optimistic boosters. This is especially true at the moment, because, arguably, we're in a window of vulnerability where many technologies are concerned. For example, in 2002 researchers at SUNY-Stony Brook synthesized a virus using a commercial protein synthesizer and a genetic map downloaded from the Internet. This wasn't really news from a technical standpoint (I remember a scientist telling me in 1999 that anyone with a protein synthesizer and a computer could do such a thing), but many found it troubling.[11]

But at the moment, it's troubling because we know more about viruses than about their cures, meaning that it's easier to cause trouble by making viruses than it is to remedy viruses once made. In another decade or two, depending on the pace of research, developing a vaccine or cure will be just as easy. That being the case, doesn't it make sense to progress as rapidly as possible, to minimize the timespan in which we're at risk? It does to me.

Critics of biotechnology feel otherwise. But their track record hasn't been very impressive so far. What's more interesting is who's *not* criticizing nanotechnology. Typically Luddite Greenpeace, for instance, has been surprisingly moderate in its response. The environmental organization has sponsored a report entitled "Future Technologies, Today's Choices: Nanotechnology, Artificial Intelligence and Robotics; A Technical, Political and Institutional Map of Emerging Technologies"[12] that looks rather extensively at nanotechnology.

Surprisingly, the report rejects the idea of a moratorium on nanotechnology, despite calls to squelch nanotech from other environmental groups. Instead, it finds that a moratorium on nanotechnology research "seems both unpractical and probably damaging at present."[13] The report also echoes warnings from others that such a moratorium might simply drive nanotechnology research underground.

Though overlooked in the few news stories to cover the report, this finding is significant. With a moratorium taken off the table, the question then becomes one of how, not whether, to develop nanotechnology.

The report also takes a rather balanced view of the technology's prospects. It notes that there has been a tendency to blur the distinction between nanoscale technologies of limited long-term importance (e.g., stain-resistant "nanopants") and build-anything general assembler devices and other sophisticated nanotechnologies, so as to make incremental work look sexier than it is. This is important: the report's not-entirely-unreasonable worries about the dangers of nanomaterials are distinguishable from more science-fictional concerns of the Crichton variety. (Remember, Crichton rhymes with "frighten.") Thus, it will be harder for Greenpeace to conflate the two kinds of concerns itself, as has been done in the struggle against genetically modified foods where opponents have often mixed minor-but-proven threats with major-but-bogus ones in a rather promiscuous fashion.

Indeed, it seems to me that nano-blogger Howard Lovy is right in saying, "Take out the code words and phrases that are tailored to Greenpeace's audience, and you'll find some sound advice in there for the nanotech industry."[14] Greenpeace is calling for more research into safety. Now is a good time to do that—even for the industry, which currently doesn't have a lot of products at risk. Quite a few responsible nanotechnology researchers are calling for this kind of research as well. Such research is likely to do more good than harm at blocking Luddite efforts to turn nanotechnology into a political football—the next Genetically Modified Organism (GMO) derived food. Despite the vast promise of GMO foods (including vitamin-enhanced "golden rice" that can prevent widespread blindness among Third-World children), environmentalist hostility and fearmongering has kept most of them out of the market. As Rice University researcher Vicki Colvin noted in congressional testimony:

> The campaign against GMOs was successful despite the lack of sound scientific data demonstrating a threat to society. In fact, I argue that the lack of sufficient public scientific data on GMOs, whether positive or negative, was a controlling factor in the industry's fall from favor. The failure of the industry to produce and share information with public stakeholders left it ill-equipped to respond to GMO detractors. This industry went, in essence, from "wow" to "yuck" to "bankrupt." There is a powerful lesson here for nanotechnology.[15]

She's right, and the nanotechnology industry would do well to learn from the failings she outlines. As I noted above, some companies and researchers have tended to dismiss the prospects for advanced nanotechnology in the hopes of avoiding the attention of environmental activists. That obviously isn't working. The best defense against nano-critics is good, solid scientific information, not denial—especially given the strong promise of nanotechnology in terms of environmental improvement.

Nanotechnology legislation recently passed by Congress calls for some investigation into these issues of safety and ethics. I hope that there will be more emphasis on exploring both the scientific and the ethical issues involved in nanotechnology's growth. That sort of exploration—done by serious people, not the charlatans and fearmongers who are sure to target the area regardless—will be important in making nanotechnology succeed.

The critics won't shut up, of course, but some aspects of their criticism will have more weight than others, leaving the scaremongering less influential than the scaremongers hope. And if that's not enough, the argument for nanotechnology's role in maintaining military supremacy is likely to rear its head. Nanotechnology is likely to be as important in the twenty-first century as rocketry or nuclear physics were in the twentieth. The United States has a fairly competent nanotechnology research program, though many feel its efforts are misdirected. Europe has a substantial but comparatively muted one. Other countries seem very interested indeed.

In the United States, and especially in Europe, research into nanotechnology is facing growing resistance from the same forces that have opposed biotechnology—and, for that matter, nuclear energy and other new technologies. The claim is that concerns about the safety and morality of nanotechnology justify limitations on research and development. Even Prince Charles has weighed in against nanotechnology, although Ian Bell wonders if the real fuss is about something other than the science:

Charles is afraid that the science could, yes, run amok, with minuscule robots reproducing themselves and proceeding to turn the world into "grey goo."

Many might suspect that the only grey goo we have to worry about is between the ears of HRH, but scientists fear that the prince could do to them what he did to the reputation of contemporary architecture. Charles, clearly, can have no way of knowing what he is talking about, but the fear he

expresses is common: do any of us really know what we are
doing when we follow where science leads?[16]

The real problem isn't a distrust of science. It's a distrust of people.
Such fear is strongest when pessimism about humanity is at a
high. Europe, perhaps understandably pessimistic about humanity's prospects in light of recent history, leads the way in throwing
some people's only favored invention—the wet blanket—over
nanotechnology research.

In the more-optimistic United States, concerns exist, but they
haven't yet led to a strong interest in regulating nanotechnology.
Instead, the U.S. takes an ostrich-like approach to dealing with
the realities of the technology; scientific and corporate types try to
shift the focus to short-term technological developments while
scoffing at the prospects for genuine molecular manufacturing—
the "spooky" stuff, as I've labeled it. Some promising developments are taking place, both at the National Nanotechnology
Initiative and within the nanotechnology industry itself, but it's
still too early to tell whether this turnaround will really take hold.

MANDARINS AND MEMORIES

In the meantime, other cultures, unencumbered by the residual
belief in original sin plaguing even the most secular Westerners,
show far less reluctance. Perhaps they are less comfortable and
more ambitious than we are, as well. Chinese interest in military nanotechnology has begun to alarm some, especially as
China is already third in the world in nanotechnology patent
applications.[17]

India's president, Abdul Kalam, is also touting nanotechnology, and as a recent press account captured, he's quite straightforward in saying that one reason for treating nanotechnology as important is that it will lead to revolutionary weaponry:

> [Kalam] said carbon nano tubes and its composites would give rise to super strong, smart and intelligent structures in the field of material science and this in turn could lead to new production of nano robots with new types of explosives and sensors for air, land and space systems. "This would revolutionise the total concepts of future warfare," he said.[18]

Yes, it would. Westerners tend to forget it, but it was a few key technologies—primarily steam navigation and repeating firearms—that made the era of Western colonialism possible. (See Daniel Headrick's *The Tools of Empire*[19] for more on this.)

It is, no doubt, as hard for American and European Mandarins to imagine being conquered by Chinese troops equipped with superior weaponry as it was for Chinese Mandarins to imagine the reverse two hundred years ago. Will our mandarins be smart enough to learn from that experience? That's the question, isn't it?

But in the long run, the growth of nanotechnology means that we won't just be worrying about countries, but about individuals. With mature nanotechnology, individuals and small groups will possess powers once available only to nation-states. As with all powers possessed by individuals, these will sometimes be used for good, and sometimes for ill.

Of course, that's just an extension of existing phenomena. My own neighborhood has a few dozen families in it; between them, they probably have enough guns and motorized vehicles (conveniently, mostly SUVs) to wipe out a Roman legion, or a Mongol horde—forces that, in both cases, once represented the peak of military power on the planet. Nobody worries about the military power that my neighborhood represents, because it's (1) unlikely to be misused, and (2) negligible in a world where most anyone can afford guns and SUVs anyway.

What this suggests is that a world in which nanotechnology is ubiquitous is likely to be less threatening than one in which it's a closely held government monopoly. A world in which nanotechnology is ubiquitous is a rich world. That doesn't preclude bad behavior, but it helps. A world with such diffuse power makes abuse by smaller groups, or even governments, less threatening overall. The average Roman or Mongolian citizen didn't really need guns or SUVs. Back then, the hobbyist machine shop in my neighbor's basement would have been a tool of strategic, even world-changing, importance all by itself. Now, in a different world, it's just a toy, even though it could, in theory, produce dangerous weaponry. It's probably best if nano-technology works out the same way, with diffusion minimizing the risk that anyone will gain disproportionate power over the rest of us.

In his recent book, *The Singularity Is Near,* Ray Kurzweil notes that technology often suffices to deal with technological threats, even in the absence of governmental intervention:

When [the computer virus] first appeared, strong concerns were voiced that as they became more sophisticated, software pathogens had the potential to destroy the computer-network medium in which they live. Yet the "immune system" that has evolved in response to this challenge has been largely effective. Although destructive self-replicating software entities do cause damage from time to time, the injury is but a small fraction of the benefit we receive from the computers and communications links that harbor them.[20]

Software viruses, of course, aren't usually a lethal threat. But Kurzweil notes that this cuts both ways:

> The fact that computer viruses are not usually deadly to humans only means that more people are willing to create and release them. The vast majority of software-virus authors would not release viruses if they thought they would kill people. It also means that our response to the danger is that much less intense. Conversely, when it comes to self-replicating entities that are potentially lethal on a large scale, our response on all levels will be vastly more serious.[21]

I think that's right. In fact, prophetic works of science fiction—Neal Stephenson's *The Diamond Age*, for instance—generally feature such defensive technologies against rogue nanotechnology. Given the greater threat potential of nanotechnologies, we may have to rely on more than Symantec and McAfee for protection—but on the other hand, given the huge benefits promised by nanotechnology, we should be willing to go ahead anyway. And I expect we will.

10

LIVE LONG—
AND PROSPER!

One of the ways in which technology is empowering ordinary people involves helping us to live longer. Aristocrats always had much longer and healthier lives than the common folks, who were (more or less literally) plagued with disadvantages such as poor nutrition, unhealthy living conditions, and overwork. There's no longer such a huge discrepancy among classes. As historian Robert Fogel notes:

> [T]he life expectancy of the [British] lower classes increased from 41 years at birth in 1875 to about 74 years today, while the life expectancy of the elite increased from 58 years at birth to about 78 years. That is a remarkable improvement. Indeed, there was more than twice as much increase in life expectancies during the past century as there was during the previous 200,000 years. If anything sets the twentieth century apart from the past, it is this huge increase in the longevity of the lower classes.[1]

Now, however, technology seems likely to extend life expectancy even more—decades or centuries more, while featuring vastly better health and vigor in the bargain. That seems like terrific news to me, but not everyone is so sure.

There is now some reason to think that life spans may become considerably longer in the not-too-distant future. Experiments with rats, fruit flies, and worms have demonstrated that relatively simple modifications ranging from caloric restriction to changes in single genes can produce dramatic increases in life span. So far, these haven't been demonstrated in human beings (whose long life spans make us harder to work with than fruit flies, for whom a doubling only lengthens the experiment for a few days), but many researchers believe that such improvements are feasible.

At the moment, both dietary and genetic approaches to increasing longevity have proved successful. As Richard Miller writes, "In the past two decades, biogerontologists have established that the pace of aging can be decelerated routinely in mammals by dietary or genetic means. . . . There is now . . . incontrovertible evidence, from many fronts that aging in mammals can be decelerated, and that it is not too hard to do this."[2]

Caloric restriction is probably the better-established of the two approaches. Animals fed diets that contain all necessary nutrients, but that provide substantially fewer calories than normal diets (and I mean substantially, as in 40–60 percent fewer), seem to lead longer and healthier lives:

> Caloric restriction prolongs the life span by several different, but interrelated, mechanisms that attenuate oxidative stress. . . . The fundamental observation is that dietary

restriction reduces damage to cellular macromolecules such as proteins, lipids, and nucleic acids. . . . Caloric restriction leads to reduction in cellular oxidants such as hydrogen peroxide and increases the activity of endogenous antioxidant enzymes.[3]

In fact, animals on reduced-calorie diets are healthier, not simply longer-lived:

> Importantly, the CR diet does not merely postpone diseases and death; it seems to decelerate aging per se and in so doing retards age-related changes in (nearly) every system and cell type examined. . . . Calorie-restricted rodents remain healthy and active at ages at which control littermates have long since all died. . . . Autopsy studies of CR animals at the end of their life span typically show very low levels of arthritic, neoplastic, and degenerative change, and in functional tests of immunity, memory, muscle strength, and the like, they typically resemble much younger animals of the control group.[4]

No struldbrugs these.[5]

Some humans are experimenting with caloric restriction, but it does not seem likely to appeal to most people, as it may promise a long life—but a hungry one. Still, it's promising for two reasons. Most obviously it indicates that the aging process—often regarded with almost supernatural awe—is in fact susceptible to change through rather simple and crude interventions. Additionally, it seems likely that many of the processes impacted by caloric restriction can be artificially induced by other means.[6]

Genetics also seems to offer hope. Some species are notably longer-lived than others, and it turns out that those long-lived species tend to have many genetic characteristics in common. While one might, via a sufficiently long-term breeding program, produce long-lived humans without any external interventions, doing so would take many generations. And inserting new or modified genes in human beings, though likely possible in time, is difficult and poses significant political problems.

Scientists are, however, already researching drugs that activate or deactivate existing genes in order to retard aging:

> Once these two longevity extension mechanisms were identified, many scientists independently tried to develop pharmaceutical interventions by feeding various drugs suspected of regulating these two processes to their laboratory animals. Six of these experiments have shown various signs of success. Although these independent experimenters used different intervention strategies and administered different molecules to their laboratory animals, they each recorded significant increases in the animals' health span and/or a significant extension of the animals' functional abilities. . . . The pharmaceutical extension of longevity via a delayed onset of senescence has been proved in principle by these six experiments despite their individual limitations.[7]

Biogerontologists like Cambridge University's Aubrey de Grey are looking at far more dramatic interventions that would not merely slow the aging process, but stop or even reverse it, through eliminating DNA damage, replacing senescent cells with new ones, and so on.[8]

But won't we wind up with lots of sick old people to look after? No. In fact, we're actually likely to see fewer people in nursing homes even though we'll have many more old people around. That's because (as in the experiments above) people will be younger, in terms of both health and ability, for their ages. And, after all, who would buy a treatment that just promised to extend your drooling years?

Government programs and pharmaceutical company researchers will likely aim at producing treatments resulting in healthy and vigorous oldsters, not struldbrugs, and it seems even more likely that people will be willing to pay for, and undergo, treatments that promote youth and vigor, but not treatments that simply prolong old age. Today's approach of incremental, one-disease-at-a-time medical research does nothing to help old people in terrible condition, still around simply because they're not quite sick enough to die yet. Genuine aging research is likely to produce a different outcome, restoring youth and health. If it can produce treatments or medications that let people enjoy a longer health span—more youth, or at least more middle age, by several decades—then those treatments will sell. If not, then there won't likely be much of a market for treatments that merely extend the worst part of old age.

LADIES, MEET DON JUAN SR.

Thus, if we can expect anything, we can expect treatments that give us more of the good part of our lives—anywhere from a couple of extra decades to, at the most optimistic end, several extra centuries. And who could be against that?

Well, Leon Kass, the chair of the White House Bioethics Council during President Bush's first term and into the second, for one. "Is it really true that longer life for individuals is an unqualified good?" asks Kass, tossing around similar questions. "If the human life span were increased even by only twenty years, would the pleasures of life increase proportionately? Would professional tennis players really enjoy playing 25 percent more games of tennis? Would the Don Juans of our world feel better for having seduced 1250 women rather than 1000?"[9]

To me, it seems obvious that the answer to all these questions is yes. To Kass, it would seem, the answer is obviously no. But as it happens, we've conducted an experiment along these lines already, and the outcome is not in Kass's favor.

Life spans, after all, have been getting steadily longer since the turn of the twentieth century. According to the Centers for Disease Control, "Since 1900, the average life span of persons in the United States has lengthened by greater than thirty years."[10] That's an average, of course. Nonetheless, there are a lot more old people than there used to be, and they're working longer. Indeed, as *Discover* magazine has observed, "A century ago, most Americans lived to be about fifty. Today people over a hundred make up the fastest-growing segment of the population."[11] You can argue about the details, but it's clear that typical adults are living longer than at any time in human history.

So we've already tested out an extra twenty years of healthy life, more or less. And yet people—far from being bored, as Kass suggests they should be—seem quite anxious to live longer, play more tennis, have more sex, and so on. The market is proof of that: although it possesses little scientific basis at the moment, so-called "anti-aging medicine" is a rapidly growing field—rapidly growing enough, in fact, that biogerontologists fear it will give legitimate research in the field a bad name.[12] (That's proof that there's demand out there, anyway.) Nor does one hear of many otherwise healthy people who are anxious to die, even at advanced ages, out of sheer boredom. Instead, they seem eager to improve their lives, particularly their sex lives, as the booming sales of drugs like Viagra and Cialis indicate.

One might argue—and in fact bioethicist Daniel Callahan does argue—that these desires are selfish and will be satisfied at the expense of society as a whole.[13] All of those perpetually young old-sters, after all, will refuse to retire, and society will stagnate.[14]

That sounds plausible. But greater life expectancy is not the only recent achievement: the past hundred years have also been the most creative and dynamic period in human history. And our institutions certainly aren't controlled by a rigid gerontocracy. (In fact, one finds rigid gerontocracies mostly in communist coun-tries—the former Soviet Union, the current People's Republic of China—not in capitalist democracies. So those who fear geron-tocracy might do better by opposing communism than aging research.)

At any rate, I'm not too worried. The tendency in America seems to be toward more turnover, not less, in major institutions, even as life spans grow. CEOs don't last nearly as long as they did a few decades ago. University presidents (as my own institution can attest) also seem to have much shorter tenures. Second and third careers (often following voluntary or involuntary early retirements) are common now. As a professor, I see an increasing number of older students entering law school for a variety of reasons, and despite the alleged permanence of faculty jobs, more than half of my law faculty has turned over, in the absence of mandatory retirement, in the fifteen years that I have been teaching. And we've seen all of this in spite of longer lives, and in spite of the abolition of mandatory retirement ages by statute over a decade ago.[15] This is more dynamism, not less.

To his credit, Callahan says that he doesn't want to ban life-extension research or treatment: "I would not want to prohibit the research. I want to stigmatize it. I want to make it look like you are being an utterly irresponsible citizen if you would sort of dump this radical life extension on the rest of us, as if you expect your friends and neighbors to pay for your Social Security at age 125, your Medicare at 145."[16]

He's wise not to suggest a ban. It seems likely that such a ban on life-extension research or treatments would be unconstitutional, in light of the rights to privacy, medical treatment, and free speech established in a number of Supreme Court opinions. As a result of cases like *Lawrence v. Texas*[17] or *Griswold v. Connecticut*[18] that establish people's right to control their own bodies, and to pursue courses of medical care that they see as life-enhancing without moralistic interference from the state, such a ban would likely fail. (Would it make a difference that the Supremes tend to be rather long in the tooth? Maybe.)

It seems even more likely, however, that such a ban would be unpopular (and surely even the most hardened supporter of Social Security and Medicare would blanch at the claim that those programs create a moral obligation to die early on the part of their recipients). Nor does it seem likely that if life were extended to such lengths people would want to retire early and collect Medicare.

WHY RETIRE?

Today's notion of "retirement age" is a fairly recent one. Otto von Bismarck is often credited with craftily setting the retirement age at sixty-five because most people wouldn't live that long—though in fact, Bismarck set it at seventy and it wasn't lowered to sixty-five until later.[19] But the justification for retirement has always been that by retirement age people were nearly used up and deserved a bit of fun and then a comfortable and dignified decline until death. Get rid of the decline and death, and you've given up the justification for subsisting—as Social Security recipients, at least, do—off other people's efforts on what amounts to a form of welfare. Logically, retirement should be put off until people are physically or mentally infirm (and perhaps retirement should just be replaced entirely with disability insurance). Those who are able to work should do so, while those desirous of not working should save up as for a long vacation. Alan Greenspan—the very model of combined productivity and longevity—has argued repeatedly for extending retirement ages in tandem with increasing life expectancies, and it is possible that in some non-election year his advice may be followed.[20]

In this regard, increased longevity, with (at the very least) much higher retirement ages, could be the salvation of many nations' pension systems, which to varying degrees are facing an actuarial disaster already as the result of longer life spans and lower retirement ages, coupled with lowered birthrates.[21]

Indeed, although many people worry that longer life spans will lead to overpopulation, the world is now facing what Phillip Longman, writing in *Foreign Affairs,* calls a "global baby bust."[22] Longer lives and later retirements will help offset at least some of the consequences of falling birthrates—and people who expect to live longer might be more willing to take time out to bear and raise children, without feeling that it's such a career sacrifice to do so.

But what's surprising to me is that so many people see the idea of living longer as controversial, even morally suspect. Part of this, I suspect, has to do with the usual skepticism regarding the new. Ron Bailey notes:

> As history demonstrates, the public's immediate "yuck" reaction to new technologies is a very fallible and highly changeable guide to moral choices or biomedical policy. For example, in 1969 a Harris poll found that a majority of Americans believed that producing test-tube babies was "against God's will." However, less than a decade later, in 1978, more than half of Americans said that they would use in vitro fertilization if they were married and couldn't have a baby any other way.[23]

In fact, as Bailey also notes, many of those who oppose longer lives—including, for example, Leon Kass—previously opposed in vitro fertilization too.[24] They tend not to bring that subject up on their own now, though. And that's not all:

> New medical technologies have often been opposed on allegedly moral and religious grounds. For centuries autop-

sies were prohibited as sinful. People rioted against smallpox vaccinations and opposed the pasteurization of milk. Others wanted to ban anesthesia for childbirth because the Bible declared that after the Fall, God told Eve, "In sorrow thou shalt bring forth children" (Gen. 3:16).[25]

I suspect that people's inherent suspicion of longer life will fade too. In mythology, longer life is always offered by a supernatural force, with a hidden and horrible catch somewhere: you have to surrender your soul, or drink the blood of virgins, or live forever while growing more feeble. Or, in real life as opposed to mythology, such a prize was offered to the desperate and gullible by charlatans who couldn't deliver on their promises anyway.

Of course, cures for baldness and impotence used to be the domain of charlatans too (though they got less attention from evil deities). Now they're cured by products available in pharmacies, sometimes without a prescription. People may joke about Viagra or Rogaine, but they don't fear them. I suspect that's how treatments for extending our lives will come to be seen—unless those who oppose them manage to get them outlawed now, while they can still capitalize on people's inchoate fears. I doubt they'll succeed. But I'm sure they'll try.

AFTERWORD: AN INTERVIEW ON IMMORTALITY

Aubrey de Grey is a biogerontologist at Cambridge University in England, whose research on longevity—via an approach known as "Scientifically Engineered Negligible Senescence"—has gotten a great deal of attention. I think that this subject is on the technological (and political) cusp, and that we'll be hearing more about it, so I interviewed him (via email).

> *Reynolds:* What reasons are there to be optimistic about efforts to slow or stop aging?

> *de Grey:* The main reason to be optimistic is in two parts: First, we can be pretty sure we've identified all the things we need to fix in order to prevent—and even reverse—aging, and second, we have either actual therapies or else at least feasible proposals for therapies to repair each of those things (not completely, but thoroughly enough to keep us going until we can fix them better). The confidence that we know everything we need to fix comes most persuasively from the fact that we haven't identified anything new for over twenty years.

> *Reynolds:* What do you think is a reasonable expectation of progress in this department over the next twenty to thirty years?

> *de Grey:* I think we have a 50/50 chance of effectively completely curing aging by then. I should explain that I mean something precise by the suspiciously vague-sounding term "effectively completely." I define an effectively complete cure for aging as the attainment of "escape velocity" in the postponement of aging, which is the point when we're postponing aging for middle-aged people faster than time is passing.

> This is a slightly tricky concept, so I'll explain it in more detail. At the moment, a fifty-year-old

has roughly a 10 percent greater chance of dying within the next year than a forty-nine-year-old, and a fifty-one-year-old has a 10 percent greater chance than a fifty-year-old, and so on up to at least eighty-five to ninety (after which more complicated things happen). But medical progress means that those actual probabilities are coming down with time. So, since we're fifty only a year after being forty-nine, and so on, each of us has less than a 10 percent greater chance of dying at fifty than at forty-nine—it's 10 percent minus the amount that medical progress has achieved for fifty-year-olds in the year that we were forty-nine. Thus, if we get to the point where we're bringing down the risk of death at each age faster than 10 percent per year, people will be enjoying a progressively diminishing risk of death in the next year (or, equivalently, a progressively increasing remaining life expectancy) as time passes. That's what I call "escape velocity," and I think it's fair to call it the point where aging is effectively cured.

Reynolds: What sort of research do you think we should be doing that we're not doing now?

de Grey: Well, there are several approaches to curing aspects of aging that I think are very promising, but which most people seem to think are too hard to be worth trying. One is to obviate mitochondrial mutations, by putting suitably modified copies of the thirteen mitochondrial protein-coding genes into the nucleus. This is hard—some of those suitable modifications are hard to identify—but it's definitely feasible. A second one is to find enzymes in bacteria or fungi that can break down stuff that our cells accumulate because they can't break it down, like oxidized cholesterol. The idea here is to put such genes into our cells with gene therapy, thereby enabling them to break the stuff down. If we could do that, it would virtually eliminate strokes and heart attacks; and similar approaches could cure all neurodegenerative diseases and also macular degeneration, the main cause of age-related blindness. A third one is to look for chemicals or enzymes that can cut sugar-induced cross-links (advanced glycation end products). One such compound is known, but it only breaks one class of such links so we need more, and no one is really looking. And maybe the biggest of all is to cure cancer properly, by deleting our telomere-maintenance genes and thereby stopping cancer cells from dividing indefinitely even after they've accumulated lots and lots of mutations.

Reynolds: Some people regard aging research, and efforts to extend life span, with suspicion. Why do you think that is? What is your response to those concerns?

de Grey: I think it's because people don't think extending healthy life span a lot will be possible for centuries. Once they realize that we may be able to reach escape velocity within twenty to thirty years, all these silly reasons people currently present for why it's not a good idea will evaporate overnight. People don't want to think seriously about it yet, for fear of getting their hopes up and having them dashed, and that's all that's holding us back. Because of this, my universal response to all the arguments against curing is simple: don't tell me it'll cause us problems, tell me that it'll cause us problems so severe that it's preferable to sit back and send 100,000 people to their deaths every single day, forever. If you can't make a case that the problems outweigh 100,000 deaths a day, don't waste my time.

Reynolds: What are some arguments in favor of life extension?

de Grey: I only have one, really: It'll save 100,000 lives a day. People sometimes say no, this is not saving lives, it's extending lives, but when I ask what the difference is, exactly, no one has yet been able to tell me. Saying that extending old people's lives is not so important as extending young people's lives may be justified today, when older people have less potential life to live (in terms of both quantity and quality) than younger people, but when that difference is seen to be removable (by curing aging), one would have to argue that older people matter less because they have a longer past, even though their potential future is no different from that of younger people. That's ageism in its starkest form, and we've learned to put aside such foolish things as ageism in the rest of society; it's time to do it in the biomedical realm too.

Reynolds: Do you see signs of an organized political movement in opposition to life extension?

de Grey: No, interestingly. I see people making arguments against it, and certainly some of those people are highly influential (Leon Kass, for example), but really they're just using life extension as a vehicle for reinforcing their opposition to things that the public does realize we might be able to do quite soon if we try. They get the public on their side by exploiting the irrationality about life spans that I've described above, then it's easier to move to other topics.

Reynolds: For that matter, do you see signs of an organized movement in support of such efforts?

de Grey: Oh yes. There are really only isolated organizations so far, but they are increasingly cooperating and synergizing. The older ones, like the cryonics outfits and the Life Extension Foundation, are as strong as ever, and they're being joined by other technophile groups like the Foresight and Extropy Institutes and the World Transhumanist Association, plus more explicitly longevity-centric newcomers such as the Immortality Institute. Quite a few blogs are helping this process along nicely, especially Fight Aging! and Futurepundit, and I really appreciate that you're now among them. And of course there's the organization that I cofounded with David Gobel a couple of years ago, the Methuselah Foundation, which funds some of my work through donations but whose main activity is to administer the Methuselah Mouse Prize. [A prize of over $1 million for extending the life of laboratory mice beyond the present record.]

Reynolds: What might life be like for people with a life expectancy of 150 years?

de Grey: Well, we won't have a 150-year life expectancy for very long at all—we'll race past every so-called "life expectancy" number as fast as we approach it, as outlined above. So maybe I should give an answer to the analogous question regarding indefinite life spans. Life will be very much the same as now, in my view, except without the frail people. People will retire, but not permanently—only until they need a job again. Adult education will be enormously increased, because education is what makes life never get boring. There will be progressively fewer children around, but we'll get used to that just as easily as we got used to wearing these absurd rubber contraptions whenever we have sex just in order to avoid having too many kids once infant mortality wasn't culling them any more. Another important difference, I'm convinced, is that there will be much less violence, whether it be warfare or serious crime, because life will be much more valued when it's so much more under our control.

Reynolds: What is your response to concerns that life extension therapies might be too expensive for anyone
but the rich?

de Grey: This is a very legitimate concern, which society will
have to fix as soon as possible. Since 9/11 we all
know how bad an idea it is to make a lot of people
really angry for a long time—if the tip of that anger
iceberg is willing to sacrifice everything, lots of
other people lose everything too. Since rich people
will be paying for rejuvenation therapies as a way to
live longer, not as a way to get blown up by poor
people, everyone will work really hard to make
these treatments as cheap as possible as soon as possible. That'll be a lot easier with a bit of forward-
planning, though—e.g., an investment in training
a currently unnecessary-looking number of medical
professionals. But one way or another, these treatments will definitely become universally available
in the end, probably only a few years after they
become available at all, even though the cost of
doing this will be staggering. The only way to have
a sense of proportion about this period is to remember that it'll be the last chapter in what we can definitely call the War on Aging—people worldwide
will readily make the same sort of sacrifices that
they make in wartime, in order to end the slaugh-
ter as soon as possible.

Reynolds: Leon Kass has suggested various items of literature
as cautionary tales. What literary or science fiction

stories might you recommend for people interested in this subject?

de Grey: I used to give the obvious answer to this— [Robert A.] Heinlein. But now I have a new answer. Nick Bostrom, a philosopher at Oxford University here in the UK, has written a "fairy tale" about a dragon that eats 100,000 people a day and its eventual slaying. It's been published in the *Journal of Medical Ethics,* but it's also online in a great many places, including his website [http://www.nickbostrom.com]. It's absolutely brilliant.

11

SPACE: IT'S NOT JUST FOR GOVERNMENTS ANYMORE

Life on Earth was a total waste,
I don't care if I'm lost in space,
I'm on a rocket to nowhere!
—WEBB WILDER[1]

Webb Wilder wrote these words to describe the drawbacks of a swinging-single lifestyle, but they apply all too well to America's decidedly non-swinging space program. The old government-based approach hasn't done very well, but fortunately some smaller players, empowered by technology and competition, are stepping up to the plate. They may be just in time.

The aerospace industry as a whole is in trouble. Even in the aviation sector, there are too few companies for significant competition, and only one major company—Boeing—is really competitive in the civilian market. Today's airliners are modest improvements over the 707s that ruled the skies when I was born, but there's nothing on the drawing boards that will be much better.

Ditto for the space sector, only more so. Oh, it's not all bad: the civilian commercial space industry has been booming in terms of revenue. There's actually more commercial money spent on things like communications satellites and Earth observation than on government space programs, these days. But the technology of getting into space hasn't progressed much since the 1960s, industry concentration is even worse, and there's no prospect of any improvement.

Certainly the International Space Station isn't doing much to promote our future in space. Originally designed as a place that would support extensive experimentation, and the on-orbit construction of bigger-crewed structures and interplanetary spacecraft, it has now been pared down so thoroughly that it's little more than a jobs program—lots of people on the ground supporting three astronauts in orbit who spend most of their time simply doing maintenance. And the balky, expensive space shuttle may actually be a step backward.

NASA has gotten leaner, but not appreciably meaner. It's like the Space Station writ large: Most of what science and technology development goes on there is an afterthought, with the lion's share of the agency's revenue and energy going instead to supervise NASA bureaucrats who produce nothing.

This isn't entirely NASA's fault. At the White House there has been a policy vacuum regarding space programs for a over decade. NASA successfully used inflated cost estimates to kill President George H. W. Bush's 1991 Mars mission plan for fear it would compete with the Space Station. The Clinton administration—

which abolished the National Space Council that used to oversee space policy—never provided much new guidance beyond Al Gore's lame plan to launch a satellite that would broadcast pictures of Earth via the Internet.

Quite a depressing litany. I could spend another chapter or twenty dwelling on the sordid details. But instead let's address what to do about the dire situation that the interplay of space development and big government has created.

THE BIG ISSUES IN ORBIT

On the governmental front, the first thing we need is some direction at the top. It's virtually impossible to accomplish anything through bureaucracies without strong White House backing. So I suggest reconstituting the National Space Council (traditionally headed by the vice president), whose abolition was opposed by every major space group at the time. (Full disclosure: I was an advisor to the Space Council in 1991–1992.) Once reconstituted, the Space Council should set out to address several major problems:

1. Concentration. There aren't enough firms in the space industry to foster competition, and competition is what gives us expanded capabilities and lower costs. Whether this calls for the Justice Department to pursue a breakup of some of these companies, or whether the government should attempt to foster the growth of startups is unclear, but these options should be considered closely. Neither of these tactics constitutes unwarranted interference with the free market, since what we have now is in essence a cozy, government-supervised cartel anyway.

2. Caution. People in the established space enterprises are afraid to fail. In fact, they're afraid to even try things that might risk failure. A certain amount of caution, of course, is a good thing. But failure is one of the main ways we learn. For instance, the failure of the X-33 single-stage-to-orbit program yielded some important lessons and—because of the program's comparatively small scale—didn't produce a serious political backlash. Those lessons could prove useful, but only if a program is in place to take advantage of them. We need to institutionalize learning from failure, something NASA and the aerospace industry did very well in the 1950s, but not so much today. More thoughts on that later.

3. Civilians. The military has caught on to the importance of space to its mission; civilians in the federal government outside NASA (and a disturbing number within NASA) don't feel a comparable urgency. But space isn't a Cold War public-relations arena now. It's essential to economics, military strength, and cultural warfare. Agencies beyond NASA need to get more involved and more supportive: the FCC, for example. More thoughts on that later too.

4. Counting. It isn't sexy, but having a decent accounting system makes a huge difference. In conversations I've had, experts within the government have called NASA's financial management system "abominable." It's not that they don't know where the money goes, so much as that they don't know what they're getting back for it. (This may not be entirely an accident. Government programs seldom encourage that kind of transparency and accountability.) NASA administrator Sean O'Keefe was well positioned by experience to fix this problem

during his term, but didn't make enough progress, and the agency has yet to complete this essential first step toward fixing other problems.

5. Cost. Cost is the major barrier to doing things in space. The government is lousy at lowering costs. But it can help promote the technological and economic environments that will allow such things to become feasible on a self-sustaining basis. Sadly, while the federal government has the power to help, it has even greater power to screw things up in this department. NASA needs to rethink its core mission and focus on its original role of developing technologies that enable others to do things, rather than feeling that it must do things itself. NASA needs to see the space tourism industry, for example, as one of its offshoot accomplishments, not, as it sometimes does now, a competitor. It's the free market that lowers costs, and empowering a little friendly competition will do more to promote American supremacy in space than any single R&D program.

In addition, the government needs to do other things to smooth the path: streamlining regulation for commercial space (FAA); protecting radio spectrum needed by space enterprises (FCC); making some sense out of export controls (Commerce and State); and so on. Congress has actually made a start at this, but there's room for much more.

The good news, as Holman Jenkins notes in the *Wall Street Journal,* is that space advocates have used the Internet to end-run the usual interest groups affecting space policy. In 2004, space activists pressured Congress to pass a space tourism bill, and more recently they've been publicly criticizing NASA's new moon-Mars programs. As Jenkin notes, the old "iron triangle" of government contractors, NASA, and congressional delegations now faces "an effective peanut gallery, their voices magnified by the Web, which has sprouted numerous sites devoted to criticizing and kibitzing about NASA."[2] These grassroots supporters aren't just critiquing government policy, though. They're also working to get things going on their own.

REACHING FOR THE STARS VS. REACHING FOR THE PAPER

The year 2001 is now behind us, but we're a long way from the space stations, lunar bases, and missions to Jupiter that Kubrick and Clarke made so plausible way back when. It's time to get our act together, so that we won't find ourselves in the same straits in 2051. The good news is that some people are doing just that. In fact, private foundations, private companies, and even NASA itself are waking up to some new approaches.

The X-Prize Foundation, organized by space supporters who were frustrated by the slow progress of government programs, decided to resurrect an old surefire motivator: a prize. The X-Prize approach is based on the historic role played by privately funded prizes in developing aviation. (Charles Lindbergh crossed the Atlantic to win the $25,000 Orteig Prize.) Its founders and organizers hope that private initiative, and lean budgets coupled with clear goals, will produce more rapid progress than the government-funded programs organized by space bureaucrats over the past five decades or so. (More full disclosure: I was a *pro bono* legal advisor to the X-Prize Foundation in its early days.) In particular, the founders are interested in bringing down costs and speeding up launch cycles, so that space travel can benefit from aircraft-type cost efficiencies. And so far it looks as if they're having some success.

The X-Prize Foundation began by offering a $10 million private award for the first team that: "Privately finances, builds & launches a spaceship, able to carry three people to 100 kilometers (62.5 miles); Returns safely to Earth; Repeats the launch with the same ship within 2 weeks." The official prize winner was Burt Rutan's Scaled Composites, with its *SpaceShipOne* spacecraft. But the fact that *twenty-seven* competitors, from a number of different countries, competed for the prize indicates that the foundation itself is the real winner. The $10 million prize generated a lot more than $10 million worth of investment.

Which is, of course, the point. Ten million dollars in a government program won't get you much; by the time paper is pushed and overhead is allocated, it may not get you anything. A $10 million prize, however, can attract much more—with competitors driven as much by prestige as by the chance of making a profit.

Another great benefit is that prize-based programs allow for a lot of failure. By definition, if twenty-seven teams go for the prize, at least twenty-six will fail. And that's okay. Government programs, on the other hand, are afraid of failure. So they are either too conservative, playing it safe so as to avoid being blamed for failure, or too drawn out, dragging on so long that, by the time it's clear they're not going anywhere, everyone responsible has died or retired. (In government, or big corporations, it's okay not to succeed, so long as you aren't seen to fail.)

Since we usually learn more by taking chances and failing than by playing it safe and learning nothing, in the right circumstances a prize program is likely to produce more and faster progress. This isn't by accident. As X-Prize cofounder Peter Diamandis noted in recent congressional testimony:

> The results of this competition have been miraculous. For the promise of $10 million, over $50 million has been spent in research, development and testing. And where we might normally have expected one or two paper designs resulting from a typical government procurement, we're seeing dozens of real vehicles being built and tested. This is Darwinian evolution applied to spaceships. Rather than paper competition with selection boards, the winner will be determined by ignition of engines and the flight of humans into space. Best of all, we don't pay a single dollar till the result is achieved.[3]

Bureaucracies are good at some things, but doing new things quickly and cheaply isn't one of them. Foundations like X-Prize offer a different approach. I wonder what other government programs could benefit from this kind of thing?

Actually, NASA is starting some prizes of its own, devoting $400,000 over two years toward competitions aimed at developing some pretty cool technology: wireless power transmission (power-beaming) and high-strength space tethers or "elevators." More competitions are expected to follow.[4] It's not a lot of money, but—as the X-Prize demonstrated—you don't need a lot of money to accomplish a lot if you spend it well, something that NASA hasn't done historically. That's the real news here.

Both the tether technology and the power-beaming are important on their own, of course. Space "elevator" technology is rapidly moving out of the realm of science fiction, as progress in material science makes cables strong enough to reach from Earth's surface to a point beyond geosynchronous orbit feasible. At geosynchronous orbit, it takes a satellite twenty-four hours to circle Earth, meaning that a point in geosynchronous orbit remains above the same spot at Earth's equator. A cable (suitably counter-weighted) from the surface can thus go straight up to geosynchronous orbit, which conveniently enough is also the most useful orbit for satellites. With such a cable, it becomes possible to reach orbit via electric motors (which themselves can be solar powered by solar cells in space, above earthbound clouds, smog, and atmospheric haze) instead of rockets, making the prospect of cheap spaceflight look much more attainable. And if you can get to space cheaply, you can build big things there cheaply—instead of expensively and badly, as we do now—and if you can do that, among the things you can build are solar power satellites that convert the unfiltered twenty-four-hour sunlight of space into electricity to send back to Earth.[5]

So how do you get the power to Earth? Well, you could send it down a cable, if your satellite's at geosynchronous orbit, but you can also beam it, which lets you send power to a much wider variety of terrestrial locations, from a much wider variety of orbits. Hence the relevance of the power-beaming work.

Solar power satellites offer one answer to a question raised by the current wave of enthusiasm for hydrogen-fueled cars: Where will the hydrogen come from? You need electricity to produce hydrogen, and lots of it—hydrogen is really more like a power-storage system than a fuel—and if you get that electricity from burning coal or oil you pretty much vitiate the environmental benefits of hydrogen. That's just substituting smokestacks for tailpipes, which is no great improvement. Big nuclear plants are another option, of course, but some people have a problem with those.

What's really revolutionary today aren't these ideas—people have been talking and thinking about solar power satellites for pretty much my entire lifetime—but the means by which they are being achieved. Instead of going for a massive Apollo (or worse, space shuttle) sort of program, NASA is attacking these problems incrementally, and it's getting other minds involved. The way the prize program is structured (contestants get to keep their own intellectual property) encourages people to participate, and the goals get more ambitious over time.

What's more, NASA seems to have identified a suite of technologies to be developed by prize-winning competitions that, taken together, look pretty promising where more ambitious projects are concerned:

- aerocapture demonstrations

- micro reentry vehicles

- robotic lunar soft landers

- station-keeping solar sails

- robotic triathlon

- human-robotic analog research campaigns

- autonomous drills

- lunar all-terrain vehicles

- precision landers

- telerobotic construction

- power-storage breakthroughs

- radiation-shield breakthroughs

Put all this stuff together, and you've got the makings of an ambitious space program, with the R&D done on the cheap. Maybe there's hope for NASA yet. Or at least for our future in space.

MORE EGGS IN MORE BASKETS

There had better be, because our future may depend on getting a sizable chunk of humanity into outer space. I attended a conference on terrorism, war, and advanced technology a few years ago, and after hearing about everything from genetically engineered smallpox to military nanoplagues, one of the participants remarked, "This makes space colonization look a lot more urgent than I had thought."

He's not the only one to feel that way. Stephen Hawking says that humanity won't survive the next thousand years unless we colonize space. I think that Hawking is an optimist.

We've seen a certain amount of worry about smallpox, anthrax, and various other bioweapons since 9/11. At the moment, and over the next five or ten years, these worries, while not without basis, are probably exaggerated. At present there aren't any really satisfactory biological weapons. Anthrax is scary, but not capable of wiping out large (that is, crippling) numbers of people.

Smallpox, though a very dangerous threat, is hard to come by and easy to vaccinate against, and the populations whose members are the most likely to employ it as a weapon (say, impoverished Islamic countries) are also those most vulnerable to it if, as is almost inevitable, it gets out of hand once used.

That will change, though. Already there are troubling indications that far more dangerous biological weapons are on the horizon, and the technology needed to develop them is steadily becoming cheaper and more available.

That's not all bad—the spread of such technology will make defenses and antidotes easier to come up with too. But over the long term, by which I mean the next century, not the next millennium, disaster may hold the edge over prevention: a nasty biological agent only has to get out once to devastate humanity, no matter how many times other such agents were contained previously.

Nor is biological warfare the only thing we have to fear. Nuclear weapons are spreading, and there are a number of ways to modify nuclear weapons so as to produce lethal levels of fallout around the globe with surprisingly few of the devices. That's not yet a serious threat, but it will become so within a couple of decades.

More talked about, though probably less of a threat in coming decades, is nanotechnology. Biological weapons are likely to exceed nanotech as a threat for some time, but not forever. Again, within this century misuse of nanotech will be a danger.

Want farther-out scenarios? Private companies are already launching asteroid rendezvous missions. Perhaps in the not-too-distant future, a mission to divert a substantial asteroid from its orbit to strike Earth may be on the to-do list of small, disgruntled nations and death-obsessed terror groups (or perhaps Luddites who believe that smashing humanity back to the Neolithic would be a wonderful thing). Imagine the Unabomber with a space suit and better resources.

No matter. Readers of this book are no doubt sophisticated enough to come up with their own apocalyptic scenarios. The real question is, what are we going to do about it?

In the short term, prevention and defense strategies make sense. But such strategies take you only so far. As Robert Heinlein once said, Earth is too fragile a basket to hold all of our eggs. We need to diversify, to create more baskets. Colonies on the moon, on Mars, in orbit, perhaps on asteroids and beyond would disperse humanity beyond the risk of most catastrophes short of a solar explosion.

Interestingly, spreading human settlement to outer space is already official United States policy. Congress declared it such in the 1988 Space Settlements Act. Congress declared as a national goal "the extension of human life beyond Earth's atmosphere, leading ultimately to the establishment of space settlements," and required periodic reports from NASA on achieving those goals, though NASA has dropped the ball on them.[6] The policy was endorsed again by Presidents Reagan and Bush (the Clinton administration didn't exactly renounce this goal, but didn't emphasize it either). But talk is cheap; not much has been done.

What would a space policy aimed at settling humanity throughout the solar system look like? Not much like the one we've got, unfortunately.

The most important goal of such a policy has to be to lower

costs. Doing things in space is expensive—horribly so. In fact, in many ways it's more expensive than it was in the 1960s. This is no surprise: it's the tendency of government programs to drive up costs over time, and human spaceflight has up to now been an exclusively government-run program.

That's why promoting the commercialization of outer space is so important. Market forces lower costs; government bureaucracies drive them up. Among the cost-lowering programs likely to make the biggest difference is space tourism, which is beginning to look like a viable industry in the short term. (Just ask Dennis Tito, Greg Olsen, or Mark Shuttleworth, all of whom have already bought rides into space on Russian rockets, at a cost of many millions of dollars each). We should be promoting such commercialization any way we can, but especially through regulatory relief and liability protections.

Government programs should be aimed at research and development that will produce breakthroughs in lowering costs: cheaper, more reliable engines; new technologies like laser launch, solid-liquid hybrid rocket engines, space elevators. Once this technology is produced, it should be released to the private sector as quickly as possible.

Other research should aim at long-term problems: fully closed life support systems capable of supporting humans for extended periods (you might think that the International Space Station would provide a platform for this kind of research, but it doesn't); exploration of asteroids, the moon, and Mars with an eye toward discovering resources that are essential for colonization; and so on.

Putting these policies into place would require drastic change at NASA, which is now primarily a trucking-and-hotel company, putting most of its resources into the Space Station and the space shuttle, which now exists mostly to take people to and from the Space Station. But we've been stuck in that particular loop for nearly twenty years. President Bush has pushed a return to the moon and a mission to Mars as top goals, and Congress has recently endorsed them. But so far, actual movement seems small.

It's time for that to change. Like a chick that has grown too big for its egg, we must emerge or die. I prefer the former. Apparently, judging from the new proposals to return to the Moon and send humans to Mars, Congress and the Bush administration feel the same way. But there are some issues to be resolved before we go to Mars.

The first question is, how?

MARS OR BUST!

One well-known proposal that NASA has shown some interest in features Bob Zubrin's Mars Direct mission architecture, which uses mostly proven technology and which promises to be much, much cheaper than earlier plans. Mars Direct involves flying automated fuel factories to Mars in advance of astronauts; the astronauts land to find a fully fueled return vehicle waiting for them. The factories remain behind to make more fuel for future operations.

Zubrin thinks that we could do a Mars mission using this architecture for $30–40 billion—which, even if you double it, is still manageable. Back when I worked for Al Gore's presidential campaign in 1988, I did a paper on Mars missions that concluded that $80–90 billion (in 1988 dollars, about the cost of the Apollo program) was the maximum feasible expenditure on a Mars mission. This estimate would fall well below that figure. True, we have the war on terrorism to fight now, but in 1988 (and for that matter, during Apollo's development) we had the Cold War.

A more cogent criticism than cost is what we have to show for it when we're done. I'm a fan of Zubrin's approach. But I agree with other critics that the real key to successful space settlement over the long term is to take the work away from governments and turn it over to profit-making businesses—ordinary people working in market structures that maximize creativity and willingness to take risks. The government has an important early role to play in exploring new territories before they're settled—it wasn't private enterprise that financed Lewis and Clark, after all—but government programs aren't much good once the trail-breaking phase has passed. And the earlier commercial participation comes in, the better.

If you want settlement and development, you need to give people an incentive. One possibility, discussed by space enthusiasts for some time, is a property-rights regime modeled on the American West, with land grants for those who actually establish a presence on the moon or Mars. Some have, of course, derided the idea of a "Wild West" approach to space development, but other people like the idea of a "Moon Rush," which I suppose could be expanded in time to a "Mars Rush."

Could our "cowboy" president get behind a Wild West approach to space settlement? He'd be accused of unilateralism, disrespect for other nations, and, of course, of taking a "cowboy approach" to outer space that's sure to infuriate other nations who want to be players but who can't compete along those lines—like, say, the French. *Hmm.* When you look at it that way, there doesn't seem to be much doubt about what he'll do, does there?

One reason for optimism is that this time around, cost and technology are getting a lot more thought than when NASA was looking at Mars missions in the 1980s. Nuclear propulsion is at the forefront this time—back then, it was a political nonstarter. It's possible to go to Mars using chemical rockets alone, but just barely. Using nuclear space propulsion—where a reactor heats gases to form high-speed exhaust rather than using chemical explosions to do so—cuts travel times from six months to two, and, because of better specific impulse (efficiency), allows for higher payloads. (There are no plans, as far as I know, to use Orion-style nuclear-explosive propulsion. Should I turn out to be wrong about this, it will probably be a sign that somebody somewhere is very worried about something.)

The United States experimented with nuclear propulsion as part of the Kiwi and Nerva projects in the 1960s and early 1970s. The results were extraordinarily promising, but the projects died because, with the United States already abandoning the moon and giving up on Mars, there was no plausible application for the technology. Nuclear propulsion is mostly useful beyond low-earth orbit, and we were in the process of abandoning everything beyond low-earth orbit.

That appears to be changing, and it's a good thing. I think that the "settlement" part is as important as the "exploration" part. And while exploration is possible based on chemical rockets alone, settlement without using nuclear power will be much more difficult.

Nuclear space propulsion has had its critics and opponents for years, though weirdly their opposition stems largely from fears that it will lead to "nuclear-powered space battle stations." This isn't quite as weird as Rep. Dennis Kucinich's legislation to ban satellite-based "mind control devices,"[7] but it seems pretty far down the list of things we should be concerned about. With worries about earthbound nuclear weapons in the hands of Iran, North Korea, and perhaps assorted terrorist groups, it's hard to take seriously claims that possible American military activity in space, spun off from civilian Mars missions, might be our biggest problem. Indeed, the whole concern about "space battle stations" has a faintly musty air about it, redolent of circa-1984 "nuclear freeze" propaganda. Who would we fight in space today? Aliens? And if we needed to do that, wouldn't nuclear-powered space battle stations be a *good* thing?

Nor are environmental concerns significant. Space nuclear reactors would be launched in a "cold" (and thus safe) state and not powered up until they were safely in orbit. And again, compared with the environmental threat caused by rogue nuclear weapons, their dangers seem minuscule.

The administration's Mars proposal is at least a step in the right direction, and its adoption of nuclear space propulsion indicates more realism than the flags-and-footprints approach favored by the previous Bush administrations. What's more, the use of nuclear propulsion, which makes interplanetary travel both cheaper and faster, greatly increases the likelihood of going beyond flags and footprints to true space settlement. It's about time.

But there are still questions. Imagine that you've got a lot of money. No, more than that. A *lot* of money. Now imagine that you want to go to Mars. Oh, you already do? Me too. Then imagine that with your money you've built a spaceship—perhaps along the lines of Zubrin's Mars Direct mission architecture, though for our purposes the details don't matter. If you prefer, you may substitute antigravity or the Mannschenn Drive as your mechanism of choice.

Regardless of technology, you've got a craft that will take you to Mars and back, in one piece, along with sufficient supplies on the outbound leg and some samples when you come back. You're going to find out firsthand what Viking couldn't settle: whether there's life on Mars. You'll also do some research aimed at laying the groundwork for Martian colonization. Are you ready to go?

Not quite. You see, there might be life on Mars.

Well, *duh*. That's what you're going to find out, isn't it?

Yes. But if you find it's there, then what? You see, the 1967 Outer Space Treaty requires its signatories to conduct explorations of celestial bodies "so as to avoid their harmful contamination and also adverse changes in the environment of the Earth resulting from the introduction of extraterrestrial matter."[8] When you get to Mars you may create the first kind of contamination, and if there's life on Mars, you may create the second—assuming that you plan to return to Earth.

That human explorers will "contaminate" Mars is inevitable—humans contain oceans of bacteria, and a human presence on Mars is sure to leave some behind. Even if all wastes are bagged and returned to Earth (unlikely because of the expense involved), some germs are bound to escape via air leaks and transport on surfaces of Mars suits and other objects that exit the spacecraft.

NASA now takes extensive steps to sterilize unmanned

spacecraft so as to keep Earth germs from reaching other planets, something known in the trade as "forward contamination." Such precautions may be adequate for robotic missions, but it is simply impossible to ensure that missions involving people won't result in contamination. They will.

Given the impossibility of avoiding some sort of "contamination," the treaty obviously and sensibly does not forbid mere "contamination." It prohibits *harmful* contamination. What does that mean? Well, if Mars is lifeless, harmful contamination can only be contamination that interferes with human purposes. To scientists at the moment, any contamination seems harmful, since it may make it harder for them to determine if Mars has native life when it might have come from Earth. ("Hey, look, Mars has *E. Coli!*— er, or some space-probe-manufacturing guy on Earth has poor personal hygiene.") But once humans go to Mars, the framework is likely to change.

If Mars has life of its own (unlikely, but not impossible, especially in light of some intriguing new evidence), the situation gets harder. First, we may have to consider whether Martian bacteria or lichens or whatever may be harmed by any organisms humans bring. Then we have to decide whether we care about that. Is harm to bacteria the sort of harm the Outer Space Treaty was meant to prevent? Almost certainly not, but no doubt bacteria-rights advocates will do their best to get a debate fermenting here on Earth.

Martian bacteria raise another question: the question of "back contamination," as it's called—contamination of Earth by Martian organisms. That, too, will be difficult to rule out in the event of a manned mission. Oh, it's unlikely that bacteria that can survive in the Martian environment will flourish on Earth, and even less likely that they would prove harmful to Earth life. But unlikely isn't the same as impossible, and people are likely to worry. In fact, they already have worried about it in the context of robotic sample-return missions.

Mars colonization fans—of whom I am certainly one—need to ensure that the same questions have been addressed long before any humans set out for Mars. As we've learned in many other contexts, sometimes the environmental impact statement takes longer than the underlying project.

Of course, this may all be much ado about nothing—as the National Research Council has noted, nontrivial quantities of Martian material have been deposited on Earth as meteorites, blasted loose from Mars by asteroidal impacts, and it is entirely possible that bacteria could have survived the journey.[9] Smaller quantities (because of Earth's greater gravity) of Earth material have presumably gone to Mars in the same fashion. And in the early days of the solar system, when life was new, the greater degree of celestial bombardment on both planets would have made such exchanges far more frequent. So if we find life on Mars, it may simply be Earth life that has beaten us there. Or perhaps it will be our ancestral Mars life welcoming us home. In neither case will we have to worry much about harmful contamination.

But what about *beneficial* contamination?

Mars, as far as we can tell, is a dead world. Even if it turns out to host some forms of life, they are almost certain to be limited to bacteria, akin to the extremophiles that populate places like volcanoes, undersea thermal vents, and deep subsurface rock formations; and their distribution is likely to be similarly circumscribed. Algae would be big, big news.

But Mars needn't remain dead (or near-dead). For several decades people have been looking at "terraforming" Mars by giving it an earthlike—or at least more earthlike—climate. (For the technically inclined, a superb engineering textbook on the subject is Martyn Fogg's *Terraforming: Engineering Planetary Environments,* a thoroughly practical book published by the thoroughly practical SAE.[10]) In essence, the process would involve setting up factories that would produce artificial greenhouse gases (Bob Zubrin and Chris McKay suggest perfluoromethane, CF4). In his recent book *Entering Space,* Zubrin notes:

> If CF4 were produced and released on Mars at the same rate as chlorofluorocarbon (CFC) gases are currently being produced on Earth (about 1000 tonnes per hour), the average global temperature of the Red Planet would be increased by 10 degrees C within a few decades. This temperature rise would cause vast amounts of carbon dioxide to outgas from the regolith, which would warm the planet further, since CO2 is a greenhouse gas. . . . The net result of such a program could be the creation of a Mars with acceptable atmospheric pressure and temperature, and liquid water on its surface within fifty years of the start of the program.[11]

The resultant atmosphere wouldn't be breathable by humans yet, but it would support crops and allow people to walk around outside with no more than an oxygen mask in the years before a fully breathable atmosphere could be established. How much is a whole new planet worth?

Mars currently has a dry-land area approximating that of Earth. A terraformed Mars would have a smaller dry-land area, of course, because it would have oceans, or at least seas. Nonetheless, we are talking about a huge new area for human settlement. A colonized Mars would also be a way of spreading humanity and other Earth life to new places, making the species, and human civilization, less vulnerable to natural or artificial calamity. Perhaps even more importantly, we would also derive the protection from social, cultural, and political stagnation that a frontier provides.

IT'S MY PLANET AND I'LL GRIPE IF I WANT TO

Naturally, this will make some people unhappy. Though terraforming would not, in my opinion, violate the Outer Space Treaty—which prohibits only "harmful," not beneficial, contamination—there are sure to be vigorous objections raised from certain quarters. Indeed, such objections have already appeared in a few scattered locations.

Objections to terraforming can be roughly categorized as follows:

- the Peter Sellers objection ("Now is not the time," as Inspector Clouseau kept telling his valet, Cato.)

- the scientific objection

- the theological objection

- the human-cancer objection

The *Peter Sellers objection* is that terraforming efforts should not begin until we have extensive knowledge of the Martian geology and climate. Efforts that are begun too soon may not work as anticipated and might conceivably interfere with more knowledgeable (and thus more prepared) efforts later.

Little to argue with here. Though of course experts may disagree as to when we know enough, and undoubtedly people opposed to terraforming on other grounds may for political reasons raise this objection rather than reveal their true motives, the basic principle is sound. Martian terraforming efforts should not go off half-cocked. The good news is that the need for a solid database on Martian climate and geology makes today's unmanned missions—which space settlement enthusiasts view as unexciting—quite valuable. We're simply not in a position to begin terraforming efforts on Mars now, but by advancing our knowledge of important factors we nonetheless hasten the day when it will take place. Think of the robotic probes visiting Mars as the latter-day equivalents of Lewis and Clark or Zebulon Pike.

The *scientific objection* may be viewed as a near-cousin of the Sellers objection. Once terraforming efforts begin in earnest, information about the primeval Mars will be lost. Scientists can thus be expected to protest that terraforming should not begin until all interesting data about Mars in its current state have been extracted. Unfortunately, that is a task that will never be entirely completed, meaning that we will have to weigh the value of additional scientific data (which is likely to be significant) against the value of an entire new world for settlement, which is likely to be colossal.

The *theological objection* involves no such trade-offs, but rather an assertion that human beings simply are not meant to settle other planets—a variation on the old "If man were meant to fly he'd have wings" argument from the nineteenth century. Variants of this argument, in keeping with certain ideas of quasi-religious Deep Ecology adherents, might say that the "pristine" character of an "unspoiled" Mars is of such enormous, even "sacred," value that no development—or perhaps even human exploration—should be permitted.

As the use of words like "unspoiled" and "pristine" suggests, this is fundamentally an aesthetic view masquerading as a religious one. (And, indeed, the world's major religions offer precious little support to such a view.) One might plausibly prefer an empty, dead Mars over a living, vibrant one, just as one might plausibly prefer the Backstreet Boys to the Beatles. But, since such views are founded in taste, such views do not lend themselves well to rational debate, nor are they likely to prove persuasive to those who are not already predisposed to them.

The *human-cancer objection* is essentially a stronger version of the theological objection: humanity is so awful, such a blight on the face of the earth, that the last thing we should want is for people to spread everywhere else, carrying their nastiness with them and polluting everything they contact.

It is always a surprise to me that people who view humanity as a cancer somehow continue to live, and even to raise children, rather than committing the honorable suicide that self-diagnosis as a cancer cell would seem to call for. But the human mind is entirely capable of holding contradictory views as it operates. And this view does characterize certain members of the environmental movement, more concerned with saving nature from evil humans than preserving it for our enjoyment.

I predict that these peculiarly gnostic environmentalists will be most vocal in opposing terraforming efforts. And by speaking out against the terraforming of a dead Mars, or even a Mars inhabited by bacteria and lichens, such people will be showing their true colors. After all, one may be motivated to protect a sequoia forest either from hatred of loggers or for love of trees. But those opposing development of rocks and sand are pretty obviously not acting out of concern for any kind of life.

So pay attention to who denounces proposals for Martian terraforming as they begin to appear more frequently in mainstream discourse. It will not only be of interest in itself, but will tell you something about how you ought to view the denouncers' other positions.

I'm not the only one to look at this question. Robert Pinson recently wrote an article for the *Environmental Law Reporter* on the environmental ethics of terraforming Mars. After surveying the arguments pro and con, Pinson concludes:

The most applicable environmental ethic to terraforming Mars is anthropocentrism. It puts our interests at the forefront while still ensuring the existence of all life. It seems obvious that we should give ourselves the highest level of intrinsic worth since we are the ones placing the value. Life, of course, has the ultimate intrinsic worth, but we are a part of that life. It is in our best interest to preserve and expand life. What better way than by changing a planet that is currently unable to sustain life into one that can. Not only will we enrich our lives but also the life around us. We cannot, of course, begin terraforming today, but we can research and plan for the future.[12]

Of course, it's possible that the people who will be making such decisions won't be inhabitants of Earth, but rather settlers on Mars.

A MARTIAN CONSTITUTION

In response to a column of mine on Mars awhile back, reader Philip Shropshire posted a comment asking: "I'm curious as to what you think. Would you prefer to live under the American Constitution on Mars, or a new constitution that you designed yourself . . . in case you're looking for next week's column material."

Well, I'm always happy for suggestions (and, in fact, I did get a column out of this one), but this isn't actually a new idea. In fact, the Smithsonian Institution, in cooperation with Boston University's Center for Democracy, produced a set of principles for creating a new constitution to govern human societies on Mars and elsewhere in outer space. Fellow lawyer John Ragosta and I drafted an alternative proposal that was published in the American Bar Association's journal of law, science, and technology, *Jurimetrics*.[13]

Shropshire makes it easy, of course: I'd rather live under a new constitution that I designed myself. It's the constitutions designed by *other* people that worry me. On second thought, the United States Constitution isn't perfect, but it's lasted a long time, through all sorts of stresses, without producing the sort of tyranny or genocide that has been all-too-common elsewhere, even in countries we generally regard as civilized. So perhaps it's been demonstrated to be "fault tolerant."

But the interesting (and worrying) thing about proposals for new constitutions for outer space is that they mostly take it for granted that the United States Constitution offers too much freedom. Writing in *Ad Astra* magazine some years ago, William Wu observed that "[s]pace colonists may face life on a political leash," and compared space colony life to that in an oppressive company town.

> In a company town, freedom of expression may be in danger. Democracy permits citizens to make public statements about political figures that they would never say openly about their immediate bosses or top-level officers of the companies for which they work. The security and efficiency of a well-organized and well-run company town in space might be politically stifling. . . . The colonization of space may point toward a weakening of individual rights and a strengthening of government power.[14]

The participants in the Smithsonian conference on space governance seemed to feel the same way, stressing the need to balance individual freedoms against the needs of the community and emphasizing a wide array of social controls: "The imperatives of the community safety," they wrote, "and individual survival within the unique environment of outer space shall be guaranteed in harmony with the exercise of such fundamental individual rights as freedom of speech, religion, assembly, contract, travel to, in and from outer space, media and communications."[15]

There's no similar provision in the United States Constitution, and this probably reflects the participants' belief that in space we won't be able to afford as much freedom as we can on Earth. Space as less free than Earth? This view is probably wrong, but nonetheless it concerns me a great deal. It is probably wrong because all of the available evidence is that things don't work this way. Although there are some simulated Mars bases on Earth now, the closest current analogs to a space colony are Antarctic bases. But these are not harsh, dictatorial environments. By contrast, the kinds of conditions that Antarctic crews face tend to force the abandonment of traditional hierarchical systems in favor of more flexible ones. It's more freedom for the little guy, not less. As Andrew Lawler writes:

> A winter base in Antarctica is a unique world, where the cook often has greater prestige than the officer-in-charge and the radio operator can have more influence than an accomplished scientist. The traditional hierarchical structure of the military, and of government as a whole, breaks down among a small group of people isolated from others for months at a time. This was a controversial and embarrassing realization for the Navy. Flexible authority and sharing of tasks among everyone are vital for the well-being of a small, isolated group. This can run against the grain of highly specialized scientists and career military officers.[16]

Experience, thus, tends to suggest that overly rigid and controlled environments are harmful to survival under such conditions, not essential to it. George Robinson and Harold White agree, stressing in their book *Envoys of Mankind* that "the real answer to [space] community success probably lies in motivated, self-actualized, strong, adventurous, unconventional, yet disciplined and well-trained human beings."[17] In other words, empowering ordinary people is the key to success.

A proscriptive attitude toward liberties in space societies (or even the suggestion of such an attitude) worries me because I believe that, consciously or unconsciously, the way we envision space societies mirrors the way we see our own society in many ways. Many characteristics of space societies, such as strong dependence on advanced technology; problems with maintaining environmental quality; the need for people to work together under stress; and individuals' strong dependence upon their society for basic necessities such as food and water are simply amplified images of characteristics already present, and growing, in our own society.

This is a good reason for being interested in space societies, since by studying their problems we gain a window into our future on Earth. It is also a reason to be worried. For if there is a general belief that a high level of interdependence and environmental fragility means that space settlers will not be able to afford individual rights, then what of those of us who remain on Earth under similar conditions? I don't think that the march of technology has made individual rights obsolete, but I worry that others may think so. And I believe that it is wrong. Just as space societies will need access to the creativity and individual initiative of their inhabitants to flourish, so will societies on Earth. Surely the failure of totalitarian societies worldwide to achieve any kind of social—or even material—greatness illustrates that.

The role of technology has generally been to make us freer, not less free.

In fact, I think that although early Mars societies will not offer certain kinds of freedoms that we enjoy on Earth—such as the freedom to be nonproductive sponges living off the labors of others—they will offer more freedom for individuals to make something of themselves. Mars visionary Bob Zubrin agrees and compares the settlement of Mars to the settlement of the American West:

> The frontier drove the development of democracy in America by creating a self-reliant population that insisted on the right to self-government. It is doubtful that democracy can persist without such people. . . .
>
> Democracy in America and elsewhere in western civilization needs a shot in the arm. That boost can only come from the example of a frontier people whose civilization incorporates the ethos that breathed the spirit into democracy in America in the first place. As Americans showed Europe in the last century, so in the next the Martians can show us the way away from oligarchy.[18]

I think he's probably right, and it is this notion of space as an empowering frontier that animates many space advocates. I also suspect that, being populated by people willing to undertake a tremendous life-altering journey in order to make something of themselves, Mars will be home to those who are unwilling to be subjected to the sort of pointless regulation that is all too often the rule on Earth. In the face of such regulation, they'll start writing their own constitutions, and what we earthlings have to say about it will matter very little.

This is as it should be. But it's not clear whether those people will be descended from Americans or other nations—most notably China—that have considerable interest in space themselves.

RED STAR RISING?

China's agenda is ambitious. Crews of two astronauts. Space walks. Docking. There are two responses to this. One is dismissive: "Ho, hum. We did this with Gemini forty years ago. The Chinese are way behind the curve." The other is paranoid: "Oh, no! The Chinese are going to take over outer space!"

Both are unjustified, though the first probably more than the second. Yes, China is playing catch-up, doing things we used to do that to them are new. It's easy to dismiss this sort of thing, I suppose, just as it was easy to make fun of the first wave of Japanese automobiles to hit American shores. They really weren't very good, compared to the American cars of the day. Yet, as Detroit learned, such amusement was temporary and expensive: the American cars stayed about the same, while the Japanese cars got steadily better. The same thing may be happening in space; at least, we shouldn't ignore the possibility.

Although the Chinese are playing catch-up right now, they're likely to experience the second-mover's advantage. It's easier to catch up than to forge new ground. And although China is vastly poorer and weaker than the United States is today, in terms of absolute capabilities, the gap between the China of today and the

United States of, say, 1965 is much closer, with China actually ahead in quite a few capabilities. Plus, they know what's possible; we were trying to figure that out.

Then, too, the absence of any real forward progress since the 1970s on the part of the United States means that China doesn't have all that much catching up to do.

The bottom line: Our position is not so advanced that we can afford to look down on the Chinese. A determined China could leapfrog us in a variety of ways in a surprisingly short time. But that, of course, is no reason to be paranoid either. While China could surpass us, competition between the United States and China might just be a good thing.

First, as I've noted here before, there's good reason to believe that humanity won't survive over the long term (or even the not-so-terribly-long term) if we don't settle outer space. From that perspective, anything that jumpstarts the process again should be welcome. It's no coincidence that the United States' forward progress in space started to fade as soon as the contest with the Soviets ended. A new competition might encourage more effort—and more focus—on our part.

Second, the United States and China are, almost inevitably, going to begin competing more across a variety of fronts. Better that we should be competing in space than in some more dangerous arenas here on Earth. Many people believe, in fact, that the space race helped to defuse the tensions of the Cold War, and some think that this was part of President Kennedy's purpose in setting out a lunar landing as a public goal. (Jerome Wiesner, who served as an adviser to JFK, once told me that this was very much Kennedy's intent.)

GOLIATHS IN SPACE

As much as I am a fan of small-scale approaches like the X-Prize, smaller is only sometimes better, and Goliaths have their own virtues. In the case of space travel there's one big approach that was abandoned long ago, but that may well come back, with help from the Chinese.

In the old science fiction movies, spaceships looked like, well, ships. They had massive steel girders, thick bulkheads, and rivets everywhere. And big crews, with bunks, staterooms, and mess halls. Now we know better of course: spaceships aren't big, massive constructions made of steel. They're cramped gossamer contraptions of composites and exotic alloys designed to keep the weight down.

It might have turned out differently. In his recent book *Project Orion: The True Story of the Atomic Spaceship,*[19] George Dyson tells the story of an engineering effort that, but for a treaty or two and a lot of bureaucratic infighting, might have given us spaceships with rivets.

Orion was a nuclear-propelled spaceship. And by "propelled," I mean *propelled.* The idea was to propel a spaceship by means of nuclear explosions. The explosions would come from specially constructed bombs. The bombs would be ejected and explode a few dozen meters behind a large pusher plate. The plate would absorb much of the blast, convert it to momentum, and transfer that momentum to the rest of the ship via a system of shock absorbers.

It's not terribly surprising, of course, that if you set off a nuclear explosion next to a large object, the object in question will *move.* The surprising discovery was that you could do that without out destroying said object. But experiments demonstrated that properly treated substances could survive intact within a few meters of an atomic explosion, protected from vaporization by a thin layer of stagnating plasma.[20] The original idea had been Stanislaw Ulam's in 1948, but beginning in 1958 physicists Ted Taylor and Freeman Dyson (author George Dyson's father) worked with numerous other scientists and engineers to design a 4,000-ton spacecraft that would take advantage of this fact to extract motive force from atomic explosions. And, yes, I really did write *4,000 tons.* Orion was big, clunky, and mechanical—featuring springs, hydraulic shock absorbers, and other nineteenth-century-style accoutrements. To handle the shock, it needed to be big. It probably would have had rivets.

In fact, one of the greatest appeals of Orion was that the bigger you made it, the better it worked. While chemical rockets scale badly—with big ones much harder to build than small ones— Orion was just the opposite. That meant that large spacecraft, capable of long missions, were not merely possible, but actually easier to build, for a variety of reasons, than small ones. Bigger spaceships meant more mass for absorbing radiation and shock, more room to store fuel, and so on. As Freeman Dyson wrote in an early design study from 1959, "The general conclusion of the analysis is that ships able to take off from the ground and escape from the Earth's gravitational field are feasible with total masses ranging from a few hundred to a few million tons. The payloads also range from zero to a few million tons."[21]

The appeal of the project was such that its unofficial motto became "Saturn by 1970,"[22] and those working on it believed that they would be able to build a ship capable of exploring the outer planets—indeed, capable of crossing the solar system in mere months—in time to make that trip. And why not? America was already very good at building atomic bombs and had plenty of them. The other design problems (chiefly involving resonances in the pusher plate against which the nuclear shock wave struck, and in the shock-absorption system coupling the plate to the rest of the ship) were genuine, but they were mechanical engineering problems more akin to those involved in locomotive design than rocket science. In many ways, Orion was the ultimate "Big Dumb Booster." And though it was big, the program that designed it was small.

The scientists and engineers who worked on Orion were confident. "It was dead serious," as one says. "If we wanted to do it, if there were any good reason for wanting to have high specific impulse and high thrust at the same time, we could go out and build Orion right now. And I think it would make a lot of sense."[23]

But it didn't happen, of course.

There were several problems. One was the 1963 Limited Test Ban Treaty,[24] which forbids nuclear explosions in the atmosphere and in outer space. As Dyson makes clear, the United States might well have negotiated an exception to the treaty for projects like Orion, but chose not to because it was already committed to a chemical-rocket path to the moon, and NASA was uninterested in another big project. Meanwhile, the Air Force, another potential sponsor, couldn't come up with any plausible military reasons for 4,000-ton interplanetary spacecraft. There were some half-hearted efforts by space enthusiasts within the USAF to come up with such missions, which led to President Kennedy being deeply unimpressed by a more-than-man-sized model of an Orion-powered "space battleship," but no one was fooled. This bureaucratic warfare was another problem; Orion lacked a sufficient constituency, and it threatened too many people's rice bowls.

So what about now? Could Orion ever come back? The answer is yes. The Test Ban Treaty is a real obstacle to any future deployment of Orion; however, it binds only a few nations, and many nations (like India and China) that are both nuclear-capable and interested in outer space have never signed it. For an up-and-coming country looking to seize the high ground in space in a hurry, Orion could have considerable appeal. And, of course, even the United States could withdraw from the treaty, on three months' notice, under its own terms.

Orion's scientists weren't worried about fallout. Orion would have produced some, but the amount would have been tiny compared to what was being released already from above-ground tests, and there was hope that additional work would have produced even cleaner bombs designed specifically for propulsion. Today, people are much more nervous about radiation, and under current political conditions a ground-launched Orion is a nonstarter, at least in Western countries. But not everyone cares as much about radiation, and indeed the countries that worry about it the least are those most likely to find Orion appealing as a way to attain space supremacy in a hurry. What's "Orion" in Chinese?

Some have suggested that the 1967 Outer Space Treaty, which forbids placing "nuclear weapons or any other kinds of weapons of mass destruction" in outer space, would also be a barrier to Orion, but I don't think so.

A nuclear "bomb" used for space travel, arguably, isn't a "weapon." It's a tool—just as the Atlas rockets that launched the Mercury astronauts were, because of their use, different from the otherwise identical Atlas missiles aimed at the Soviet Union. (When asked about the difference, Kennedy responded: "attitude."[25])

The technical data from Orion are still around. (In fact, much of the design software is still in use, applied to other military and nuclear projects.) Dyson's book contains a large technical appendix, listing much declassified information. Much other information is still classified, even after nearly forty years. Will Orion come to pass in the twenty-first century? I wouldn't bet against it. Hmm. Saturn by 2020? It could happen—but not necessarily because of anything Americans do.

At any rate, a China (or, for that matter, perhaps even an India) looking to make a splash and anxious to get around the United States' supremacy in military (and civilian) space activity might well consider Orion to be appealing. China is not a signatory to the Limited Test Ban Treaty,[26] so that legal barrier would be out of the way. China has acceded to the 1967 Outer Space Treaty, but that treaty bans only the stationing of nuclear "weapons" in outer space, and there is, as I've noted, a plausible argument that nuclear explosives designed to propel a spacecraft are not "weapons."

With international law thus neutralized, the only remedy would be for people to either (1) start a war; or, short of that, (2) to threaten to shoot down the spacecraft, which probably would amount to starting a war anyway. (Jimmy Carter, the least bellicose of American presidents, said that an attack on a U.S.

satellite or spacecraft would be treated as an act of war, and it seems unlikely that the Chinese would take a more pacific approach than Carter.[27]) And even if shooting down the spacecraft were thought unlikely to lead to war, it would be unlikely to succeed—the Orion spacecraft would be huge, fast, and designed to survive in the neighborhood of a nuclear explosion: a very difficult target indeed.

The chief restraint on China would thus be world opinion, something to which the Chinese have not shown themselves particularly susceptible.

Much of the physics and engineering behind Orion is already well-known, and—given that American designers working with puny 1960-vintage computer technology saw the problems as tractable—it's very likely that the Chinese could manage to design and build an Orion craft within a few years of deciding to.

Hiding Orion-related work probably wouldn't be very hard either. China already has extensive space and nuclear-weapons programs, which would tend to conceal the existence of Orion-type research. And much of the necessary research and design work on Orion, involving, as it does, things like the resonance of huge steel plates and massive hydraulic shock absorbers, wouldn't look like space-related research, even to an American intelligence agency that discovered it. At least, not unless the intelligence analysts were familiar with Orion and had the possibility in mind. And how likely is that, unless they've read this book, or George Dyson's?

SPACE IN TIME

Will we wake up one day to find that a 4,000-ton Chinese spacecraft has climbed to orbit from inner Mongolia on a pillar of nuclear fireballs and is now heading to establish a base on the moon? It wouldn't be the first time America has had such a surprise, now would it?

I hope, however, that things will take a different path. While the "big dumb booster" approach embodied by Orion has its virtues, I'd rather see lots of small, smart boosters, of the sort pioneered by Burt Rutan and the other X-Prize contestants. The twentieth-century dystopian view of space as a barren battlefield dominated by big government could still come true, but it's more likely that we'll see something like the nineteenth-century American West: space settled by companies and groups of individuals, using the best available technology, with help from the government but not as a government enterprise. With luck, the result will be the kind of society of empowered individuals envisioned by Bob Zubrin.

J. Storrs Hall believes we'll see something like that and thinks that the vastly greater capabilities and lowered costs made possible by nanotechnology will be the key. Hall writes that the technology that has already revolutionized information will soon revolutionize matter. When your word processor launches, the brief pause before the screen opens involves the equivalent of about two thousand years of pen-and-paper calculation, made almost instantaneous by the superior information-processing ability of computers. The superior matter-processing power of nanotechnology will make launching spacecraft more efficient, too: "As nanotechnology matures, the same ability to throw what would have been enormous efforts at the most trivial problems will come to the physical world as we have in the software world now. Living in space is dangerous and prohibitively expensive with current technology; it will be cheap, easy, and safe with advanced nano-technology."[28]

Space development and advanced technology will produce a virtuous circle. Advances in science and engineering will let us settle outer space by empowering people technologically. Space societies, by empowering people politically and socially as frontiers tend to do, will produce new technologies that will expand human potential even further.

Let us make it so.

12

THE APPROACHING
SINGULARITY

I ndividuals are getting more and more powerful. With the current rate of progress we're seeing in biotechnology, nanotechnology, artificial intelligence, and other technologies, it seems likely that individuals will one day—and one day relatively soon—possess powers once thought available only to nation-states, superheroes, or gods. This sounds dramatic, but we're already partway there.

Futurists use the term "Singularity" to describe the point at which technological change has become so great that it's hard for people to predict what would come next. It was coined by computer scientist and science fiction writer Vernor Vinge, who wrote that the acceleration of technological progress over the past century has itself taken place at an accelerating rate, leading him to predict greater-than-human intelligence in the next thirty years, and developments over the next century that many would have expected to take millennia or longer. He concluded: "I think it's fair to call this event a singularity. . . . It is a point where our old models must be discarded and a new reality rules. As we move closer to this point, it will loom vaster and vaster over human affairs till the notion becomes commonplace. Yet when it finally happens it may still be a great surprise and a greater unknown. In the 1950s there were very few who saw it."[1]

A lot more people see it coming now—in fact, a lot more people see it coming, and are writing about it now, than in 1993 when Vinge wrote these words.

WE'RE ALL SUPERMEN NOW

One question is just how much, using technologies like nanotechnology and genetic engineering, we should improve on the human condition. My own feeling is "a lot"—it seems to me that there's plenty of room for improvement—but others may feel differently. If we choose to improve, will we become superheroes or something like them?

Should we?

My six-year-old nephew, Christopher, wants to be a superhero. It was Superman for a while, then Spiderman. (Short-lived enthusiasm for the Incredible Hulk didn't survive the lameness of the film, apparently.)

And really, who *wouldn't* want to be a superhero of some sort? It's not so much the cape or the crime fighting that lies behind this sentiment. It's the way that superheroes don't have to deal with the limitations that face the rest of us. It's easy to see why kids, whose everyday limitations place them in a position that is obviously inferior to that of adults, would be so excited about super powers. But even as adults we face limitations of speed and strength and—especially—vulnerability to all kinds of pain, to death. The idea of being able to do better seems pretty attractive sometimes, even if we don't fantasize about being members of the Justice League any more.

Will ordinary people have better-than-human powers one day? It's starting to look possible and some people are talking about the consequences. Joel Garreau makes the superhero angle explicit in his book *Radical Evolution*:

> Throughout the cohort of yesterday's superheroes—Wonder Woman, Spiderman, even The Shadow, who knows what evil lurks in the hearts of men—one sees the outlines of technologies that today either exist, or are now in engineering . . . . Today, we are entering a world in which such abilities are either yesterday's news or tomorrow's headlines. What's more, the ability to create this magic is accelerating.[2]

Yes, it is. The likely consequences are substantial. Running as fast as light, *a la* The Flash, might be out of the question, and web slinging is unlikely to catch on regardless of technology. But other abilities, like super strength, x-ray vision, underwater breathing, and the like are not so remote. (The dating potential promised by The Elongated Man's abilities, meanwhile, may produce a market even for those second-tier superpowers.) Regardless, transcending human limitations is part of what science and medicine are about. We're already doing so, in crude fashion, with steroids, human growth hormone, and artificial knees. More sophisticated stuff, like cochlear implants, is already available, and far better is on the way.

Would I like to be smarter? Yes, and I'd be willing to do it via a chip in my brain, or a direct computer interface. (Actually, that's already prefigured a bit in ordinary life too, as things like Google and Wi-Fi give us access to a degree of knowledge that would have seemed almost spooky not long ago, but that everyone takes for granted now.) I'd certainly like to be immune to cancer, or viruses, or aging. But these ideas threaten some people who feel that our physical and intellectual limitations are what make us human.

But *which* limitations, exactly? Would humanity no longer be human if AIDS ceased to exist? What about Irritable Bowel Syndrome? Was Einstein less human? If not, then why would humanity be less human if everyone were that smart? It may be true, as Dirty Harry said, that "a man's got to know his limitations." But does that mean that a man *is* his limitations? Some people think so, but I'm not so sure. Others think that overcoming limitations is what's central to being human. I have to say that I find that approach more persuasive.

These topics (well, probably not the Irritable Bowel Syndrome) were the subject of a conference at Yale on transhumanism and ethics. The conference was covered in a rather good article in *The Village Voice,* which reports that many in the pro-transhumanist community expect to encounter considerable opposition from Luddites and, judging by the works of antitechnologists like Francis Fukuyama and Bill McKibben, that's probably true.[3]

I suspect, however, that although opposition to human enhancement will produce some cushy foundation grants and book contracts, it's unlikely to carry a lot of weight in the real world. Being human is hard, and people have wanted to be better for, well, as long as there have been people. For millennia, various peddlers of the supernatural offered answers to that longing—from spells and potions in this world, to promises of reward in the next. Soon they're going to face stiff competition from science. The success of these students of human nature suggests that the demand for human improvement is high—probably high enough to overcome any barriers. (As Isaac Asimov once wrote, "It is a chief characteristic of the religion of science, that it works."[4])

At any rate, nothing short of a global dictatorship—whether benevolent, as featured in some of Larry Niven's future histories, or simply tyrannical, as seems more likely—or a global catastrophe is likely to stop the rush of technological progress. In fact, as I look around, it seems that we're living in science fiction territory already.

Take, for example, this report from the *Times of London*: "Scientists have created a 'miracle mouse' that can regenerate amputated limbs or badly damaged organs, making it able to recover from injuries that would kill or permanently disable normal animals." From nose to tail, the mouse is totally unique in the animal kingdom for its ability to regrow its nose and tail—and heart, joints, toes, and more. But the revolution isn't complete with Mickey's new limbs. The more fascinating prospect is that this trait can be replicated in other mice by transplanting cells from the "miracle mouse." "The discoveries raise the prospect that humans could one day be given the ability to regenerate lost or damaged organs, opening up a new era in medicine."[5]

Limb regeneration and custom-grown organs! Bring it on! Then there are the ads I'm seeing for offshore labs offering stem cell therapy to Americans. I don't know whether this particular therapy lives up to its claims, but if it doesn't, the odds are that other places soon will be offering therapy that does (see the mouse story above).

Meanwhile, Cambridge University just held the second conference on Scientifically Engineered Negligible Senescence. At the conference, people discussed ways of slowing, halting, or even reversing the aging process.[6] There was also a conference on medical nanotechnology,[7] while elsewhere nanotechnologists reported that they had produced aggregated carbon nanorods[8] that are harder than diamond.

On a more personal note, my wife recently went to the doctor, where they downloaded the data from the implanted computer that watches her heart, ready to step in to pace her out of dangerous rhythms or shock her back into normal rhythms if things went too badly. I remember seeing something similar in a science fiction film when I was a kid, but now it's a reality. And, of course, I now get most of my news, and carry on most of my correspondence, via media that weren't in existence fifteen years ago.

THE FUTURE ISN'T THE FUTURE

I mention this because as we look at the pace of change, we tend to take change that has already happened for granted. But these stories now (except for my wife's device, which isn't even newsworthy today) are just random minor news items that I noticed over a period of a week or two, even though they would have been science-fictional not long ago. Much as we get "velocitized" in a speeding car, so we've become accustomed to a rapid pace of technological change. This change isn't just fast, but continually accelerating. The science-fictional future isn't science-fictional. Sometimes, it's not even the future any more.

Nonetheless, we'll probably see much more dramatic change in the next few decades than we've seen in the last. So argues Ray Kurzweil in his new book, *The Singularity Is Near: When Humans Transcend Biology.*

Kurzweil notes the exponential progress in technological improvement across a wide number of fields and predicts that we'll see artificial intelligences of fully human capability by 2029, along with equally dramatic improvements in biotechnology and nanotechnology. (In fact, these developments tend to be self-reinforcing—better nanotechnology means better computers and better understanding of biology; better computers mean that we can do more with the data we've got, and progress more rapidly toward artificial intelligence, and so on.)

The upshot of this is that capabilities now available only to nation-states will soon be available to individuals. That's not surprising, of course. I've probably got more computing power in my home (where we usually have nine or ten computers at any one time) than most nation-states could muster a few decades ago, and it does, in fact, allow me to do all sorts of things that individuals couldn't possibly have done on their own until such power became available. But the changes go beyond computers, which merely represent the first wave of exponential technological progress. People will have not only intellectual but physical powers previously unavailable to individuals. Changes will come faster and thicker than we have seen from the computer revolution so far.

Kurzweil discusses the Singularity, and what it's likely to

mean, in excerpts from the following interview originally done for my blog, InstaPundit.[9] I encourage you to read his book, though, because the Singularity is, in a sense, the logical endpoint of the many near-term trends and events described in this book. The world is changing in a big way, and my reports might be likened to those from a frontline correspondent, while Kurzweil's writings are more in the nature of a strategic overview.

Reynolds: Your book is called *The Singularity Is Near* and—as an amusing photo makes clear—you're spoofing those "The End is Near" characters from the New Yorker cartoons.

For the benefit of those who aren't familiar with the topic, or who may have heard other definitions, what is your definition of "The Singularity"? And is it the end? Or a beginning?

Kurzweil: In chapter 1 of the book, I define the Singularity this way: "a future period during which the pace of technological change will be so rapid, its impact so deep, that human life will be irreversibly transformed. Although neither utopian nor dystopian, this epoch will transform the concepts that we rely on to give meaning to our lives, from our business models to the cycle of human life, including death itself. Understanding the Singularity will alter our perspective on the significance of our past and the ramifications for our future. To truly understand it inherently changes one's view of life in general and one's own particular life. I regard someone who understands the Singularity and who has reflected on its implications for his or her own life as a 'singularitarian.'"

The Singularity is a transition, but to appreciate its importance, one needs to understand the nature of exponential growth. On the one hand, exponential growth is smooth with no discontinuities, and values remain finite. On the other hand, it is explosive once we reach the "knee of the curve." The difference between what I refer to as the "intuitive linear" view and the historically correct exponential view is crucial, and I discuss my "law of accelerating returns" in detail in the first two chapters. It is remarkable to me how many otherwise thoughtful observers fail to understand that progress is exponential, not linear. This failure underlies the common "criticism from incredulity" that I discuss at the beginning of the "Response to Critics" chapter.

To describe these changes further, within a quarter century, nonbiological intelligence will match the range and subtlety of human intelligence. It will then soar past it because of the continuing acceleration of information-based technologies, as well as the ability of machines to instantly share their knowledge. Intelligent nanorobots will be deeply integrated in our bodies, our brains, and our environment, overcoming pollution and poverty, providing vastly extended

longevity, full-immersion virtual reality incorpo-
rating all of the senses, "experience beaming," and
vastly enhanced human intelligence. The result will
be an intimate merger between the technology-
creating species and the technological evolution-
ary process it spawned. But all of this is just the
precursor to the Singularity. Nonbiological intelligence will have access to its own design and will
be able to improve itself in an increasingly rapid
redesign cycle. We'll get to a point where technical progress will be so fast that unenhanced
human intelligence will be unable to follow it.
That will mark the Singularity.

Reynolds: Over what time frame do you see these things happening? And what signposts might we look for that
would indicate we're approaching the Singularity?

Kurzweil: I've consistently set 2029 as the date that we will
create Turing test-capable machines. We can break
this projection down into hardware and software
requirements. In the book, I show how we need
about 10 quadrillion (10^{16}) calculations per second
(cps) to provide a functional equivalent to all the
regions of the brain. Some estimates are lower than
this by a factor of 100. Supercomputers are already
at 100 trillion (10^{14}) cps, and will hit 10^{16} cps
around the end of this decade. Two Japanese
efforts targeting 10 quadrillion cps around the end
of the decade are already on the drawing board. By
2020, 10 quadrillion cps will be available for

around $1,000. Achieving the hardware require-
ment was controversial when my last book on this
topic, *The Age of Spiritual Machines*, came out in
1999, but is now pretty much of a mainstream
view among informed observers. Now the controversy is focused on the algorithms. . . .

In terms of signposts, credible reports of computers passing the full Turing test will be a very
important one, and that signpost will be preceded
by non-credible reports of successful Turing tests.

A key insight here is that the nonbiological
portion of our intelligence will expand exponentially, whereas our biological thinking is effectively
fixed. When we get to the mid-2040s, according to
my models, the nonbiological portion of our civilization's thinking ability will be billions of times
greater than the biological portion. Now that represents a profound change.

The term "Singularity" in my book and by the
Singularity-aware community is comparable to the
use of this term by the physics community. Just as
we find it hard to see beyond the event horizon of
a black hole, we also find it difficult to see beyond
the event horizon of the historical Singularity. How
can we, with our limited biological brains, imagine
what our future civilization, with its intelligence
multiplied billions and ultimately trillions of trillions fold, will be capable of thinking and doing?
Nevertheless, just as we can draw conclusions about

the nature of black holes through our conceptual thinking, despite never having actually been inside one, our thinking today is powerful enough to have meaningful insights into the implications of the Singularity. That's what I've tried to do in this book.

Reynolds: You look at three main areas of technology, what's usually called GNR for Genetics, Nanotechnology, and Robotics. But it's my impression that you regard artificial intelligence—strong AI—as the most important aspect. I've often wondered about that. I'm reminded of James Branch Cabell's Jurgen, who worked his way up the theological food chain past God to Koschei The Deathless, the real ruler of the Universe, only to discover that Koschei wasn't very bright, really. Jurgen, who prided himself on being a "monstrous clever fellow," learned that "Cleverness was not on top, and never had been."[10] Cleverness isn't power in the world we live in now—it helps to be clever, but many clever people aren't powerful, and you don't have to look far to see that many powerful people aren't clever. Why should artificial intelligence change that? In the calculus of tools-to-power, is it clear that a ten-times-smarter-than-human AI is worth more than a ten megaton warhead?

Kurzweil: This is a clever—and important—question, which has different aspects to it. One aspect is what is the relationship between intelligence and power? Does power result from intelligence? It would seem that there are many counterexamples.

But to piece this apart, we first need to distinguish between cleverness and true intelligence. Some people are clever or skillful in certain ways but have judgment lapses that undermine their own effectiveness. So their overall intelligence is muted.

We also need to clarify the concept of power as there are different ways to be powerful. The poet laureate may not have much impact on interest rates (although conceivably a suitably pointed poem might affect public opinion), but s/he does have influence in the world of poetry. The kids who hung out on Bronx street corners some decades back also had limited impact on geopolitical issues, but they did play an influential role in the creation of the hip hop cultural movement with their invention of break dancing. Can you name the German patent clerk who wrote down his daydreams (mental experiments) on the nature of time and space? How powerful did he turn out to be in the world of ideas, as well as on the world of geopolitics? On the other hand, can you name the wealthiest person at that time? Or the U.S. secretary of state in 1905? Or even the president of the U.S.? . . .

Reynolds: It seems to me that one of the characteristics of the Singularity is the development of what might be seen as weakly godlike powers on the part of individuals. Will society be able to handle that sort of thing? The Greek gods had superhuman powers (pretty piddling ones, in many ways, compared to what we're talking about) but an at-least-human degree of egocentrism, greed, jealousy, etc. Will post-Singularity humanity do better?

Kurzweil: Arguably, we already have powers comparable to the Greek gods, albeit, as you point out, piddling ones compared to what is to come. For example, you are able to write ideas in your blog and instantly communicate them to just those people who are interested. We have many ways of communicating our thoughts to precisely those persons around the world with whom we wish to share ideas. If you want to acquire an antique plate with a certain inscription, you have a good chance of quickly finding the person who has it. We have increasingly rapid access to our exponentially growing human knowledge base.

Human egocentrism, greed, jealousy, and other emotions that emerged from our evolution in much smaller clans have nonetheless not prevented the smooth, exponential growth of knowledge and technology through the centuries. So I don't see these emotional limitations halting the ongoing progression of technology.

Adaptation to new technologies does not occur by old technologies suddenly disappearing.

The old paradigms persist while new ones take root quickly. A great deal of economic commerce, for example, now transcends national boundaries, but the boundaries are still there, even if now less significant.

But there is reason for believing we will be in a position to do better than in times past. One important upcoming development will be the reverse-engineering of the human brain. In addition to giving us the principles of operation of human intelligence that will expand our AI tool kit, it will also give us unprecedented insight into ourselves. As we merge with our technology, and as the nonbiological portion of our intelligence begins to predominate in the 2030s, we will have the opportunity to apply our intelligence to improving on—redesigning—these primitive aspects of it. . . .

Reynolds: If an ordinary person were trying to prepare for the Singularity now, what should he or she do? Is there any way to prepare? And, for that matter, how should societies prepare, and can they?

Kurzweil: In essence, the Singularity will be an explosion of human knowledge made possible by the amplification of our intelligence through its merger with its exponentially growing variant. Creating knowledge requires passion, so one piece of advice would be to follow your passion.

That having been said, we need to keep in

mind that the cutting edge of the GNR revolutions is science and technology. So individuals need to be science and computer literate. And societies need to emphasize science and engineering education and training. Along these lines, there is reason for concern in the U.S. I've attached seven charts I've put together (that you're welcome to use) that show some disturbing trends. Bachelor degrees in engineering in the U.S. were 70,000 per year in 1985, but have dwindled to around 53,000 in 2000. In China, the numbers were comparable in 1985 but have soared to 220,000 in 2000, and have continued to rise since then. We see the same trend comparison in all other technological fields, including computer science and the natural sciences. We see the same trends in other Asian countries such as Japan, Korea, and India (India is not shown in these graphs). We also see the same trends on the doctoral level as well.

One counterpoint one could make is that the U.S. leads in the application of technology. Our musicians and artists, for example, are very sophisticated in the use of computers. If you go to the NAMM (National Association of Music Merchants) convention, it looks and reads like a computer conference. I spoke recently to the American Library Association, and the presentations were all about databases and search tools.

Essentially every conference I speak at, although diverse in topic, look and read like computer conferences.

But there is an urgent need in our country to attract more young people to science and engineering. We need to make these topics cool and compelling.

THE FUTURE

W e've seen all sorts of ways in which people are being empowered, from blogs and multimedia, to home-based manufacturing and other cottage industries, to the longer-term promise of molecular manufacturing and related technologies. So what's the big picture in a world where the small matters more?

Making predictions is always difficult. And considering the changes that strong technologies like nanotech, artificial intelligence, and genetic engineering are likely to make, predicting beyond the next few decades is especially difficult. But here are some thoughts on what it's all likely to mean, and what we should probably do to help ensure that the changes are mostly beneficial.

eBAY NATION

We're not all going to wind up working for eBay or Amazon, but as large organizations lose the economies of scope and scale that once made them preferred employers, more people are going to wind up working for themselves or for small businesses. That's probably a good thing. There doesn't seem to be a huge wellspring of love for the *Dilbert* lifestyle though, as I've mentioned before, most people wouldn't mind Dilbert's big-company benefits package. So eBay, with its health coverage for sellers, may be a prototype for future solutions to this dilemma.

If people are going to be doing more outside the big-organization box, and if most of our current infrastructure of health and retirement benefits and the like is built around the implicit or explicit expectation that most people will work for big businesses, it's probably time for a change.

On the smaller scale, this would suggest that it's time to make things like health insurance and retirement benefits more portable, and to make the tax code more friendly to small businesses and the self-employed. There's always a lot of lip service in that direction, but not so much actual movement. Some people might even go so far as to claim that this is an argument for single-payer national health insurance, which in theory would facilitate entrepreneurship. Given its poor record elsewhere—and the fact that places like Canada, Britain, and Germany aren't exactly hotbeds of independent entrepreneurial activity—I don't think I'd endorse that approach. But a mechanism that would let people operate on their own, without the very real problems that a lack of big-employer health insurance creates, would do a lot to facilitate independence. I know quite a few people who stay in their jobs because they need the health benefits; they'd be gone in a shot if they could get these benefits another way.

On a larger scale, though, it's worth looking at the role of government in general. I mentioned earlier that the big organizations in the twenty-first century will be more likely to flourish if they're organized so as to help individuals do what they want—to take the place of older, bigger organizations in a more disintermediated way. That's what eBay, Amazon, and others do. Could a similar approach work for the government? We're a long way from that right now.

In theory, of course, our government is all about maximizing individual potential and choices. In practice, well, not so much, as Joel Miller notes in his book *Size Matters: How Big Government Puts the Squeeze on America's Families, Finances, and Freedom.*[1] Miller mostly describes the problem rather than solutions. Thoughts on how to reorganize government to further those goals could easily occupy another book, but it strikes me that now is a good time to start trying to figure these things out.[2]

THE SWARM

In the chapter "Horizontal Knowledge," I discuss the rapid appearance of the World Wide Web, without any centralized planning effort, as evidence of how important horizontal knowledge and spontaneous organization have become. I've made this point before, as long ago as 2003,[3] and Kevin Kelly echoes it in a history of the Web published in *Wired:*

> In fewer than 4,000 days, we have encoded half a trillion versions of our collective story and put them in front of 1 billion people, or one-sixth of the world's population. That remarkable achievement was not in anyone's 10-year plan. . . . Ten years ago, anyone silly enough to trumpet the above . . . as a vision of the near future would have been confronted by the evidence: There wasn't enough

money in all the investment firms in the entire world to fund such a cornucopia. The success of the Web at this scale was impossible.[4]

But it happened. As Kelly notes, everyone who pondered the Web, including many very smart people who had been thinking about communications and computers for decades and who had substantial sums of money at stake, nonetheless missed the true story: the power of millions of amateurs doing things because they wanted to do them, not because they were told to. It was an Army of Davids, doing what the Goliaths never could have managed.

Because information is easier to manipulate than matter, the Army of Davids has appeared first in areas where computers and communications are involved. But new technologies will extend the ability of people to cooperate beyond cyberspace, as well as increasing what people can do in the real world. What's more, this process will feed back upon itself. New technologies will help people cooperate, which will lead to further improvements in technology, which will lead to more efficient cooperation (and individual effort), which will lead to further improvements, and so on. This means that "swarms" of activity will start to happen on all sorts of fronts. I can imagine good swarms (say, lots of people working on developing vaccines or space technology) and bad ones (lots of people working on viruses or missiles). I expect we'll see more of the good than the bad—just as we've seen far more coordinated good activity on the Web than bad—but the changes are likely to surprise the experts just as they have in the past.

HORIZONTAL POLITICS

Political power used to be a pyramid. In the old days, there was a king at the top, with layers of scribes, priests, and aristocrats below. In modern times things were more diffuse, sort of. Ordinary people who wanted to have an impact needed to find an interlocutor—typically an industrial-age institution like a labor union, a newspaper, or a political machine. And getting their ear was hard.

Not any more, as this email from a blog-reader illustrates:

> I wrote you a few weeks ago about the Illinois High School Association (IHSA) adding rules to stop Catholic schools from winning too many championships. My 15-year-old son came up with his own solution. He put together his own website (www.GoHomeIHSA.com), added a blog section, did a press release, got a bunch of publicity in the newspaper, and now he has been asked to make a brief presentation of his ideas at the IHSA Board meeting tomorrow. He spent under $10 for the domain name and set up the blog for free. Three years ago this never could have happened. Is it any wonder that many of our traditional institutions hate the Internet?

No wonder at all, as you've figured out already if you've read this far. The Internet makes the middleman much less important.

This poses a real challenge to traditional political institutions. Political parties are obviously in trouble. As a commenter on a blog I read awhile back noted, mass democracy is a thing of the past—the only problem is that it's nearly the only kind of democracy we've ever been able to make work.

Athens, of course, had a more fluid democracy, but the framers of our Constitution didn't regard its experience as a success; they were trying to prevent its problems, not emulate its excesses. There are lots of reasons to believe that unmediated democracy is a poor decision-making method, which is one reason why, in our constitutional system, democracy has always been mediated. Voters choose decision makers, rather than making decisions themselves.[5]

But if a fear of unmediated democracy led Americans to choose a system that was mediated, we must now deal with pressures toward disintermediation. The additional transparency added by the Internet is a good thing, limiting insider back scratching and deals done at the expense of constituents. On the other hand, the pressure toward direct democracy, or something very close to it, is likely to build. Is that a good idea? Probably not, unless you think that America would do better if it were run like your condo association.

The challenge in coming decades will be to take advantage of the ability for self-organization and horizontal knowledge that the Internet and other communications technologies provide without letting our entire political system turn into something that looks like an email flamewar on Usenet. I think we'll be able to do that—most people's tolerance for flaming is comparatively low, and in a democracy, what most people tolerate matters—but things are likely to get ugly if I'm wrong.

EXPRESS YOURSELF

But it's not just politics. People are hardwired to express themselves. Imagine two tribes of cavemen approaching a cave. Which tribe is more likely to survive—the one where someone says, "You know, I think there's a bear in there," or the one where nobody talks? I'm pretty sure we're descended from the talkative ones.

Until pretty recently, self-expression on any sizable scale was the limited province of the rich and powerful, or their clients. Only a few people could publish books, or write screenplays that might be filmed, or see their artwork or photographs widely circulated, or hear their music performed before a crowd. Now, pretty much anyone can do that. You can post an essay (or even an entire book) on the Web, make a film, or circulate your art and photos from anywhere and have them available to the entire world.

Now that more people can do that, more people *are* doing it, and it seems to make them happy. Naturally, some critics complain that much of what results isn't very good. That's true, but if you look at books, films, or art from the pre-Internet era, you'll find that much of that stuff wasn't very good either. (*Heaven's Gate* and *Gigli* were not Internet productions.) As science fiction writer Ted Sturgeon once said in response to a critic's claim that 90 percent of science fiction was crap: "Ninety percent of *everything* is crap."[6]

And if you doubt this, spend a few minutes channel-surfing or perusing bookstore stacks at random. You may conclude that Sturgeon was being generous, not just to science fiction, but to, well, everything.

On the other hand, "crap" is always a matter of opinion. Many people write books that are very valuable to them as self-expression, regardless of whether they get good reviews or sell millions of copies. (I myself have written two novels and enjoyed the writing process very much, even though neither has ever been published.) And regardless of whether they sell millions or please critics, such books probably please some people and can now sell in smaller quantities thanks to niche publishing markets and improved printing technologies.

Novelist Bill Quick, who has published many books through traditional publishers, tried the Internet publication route with a novel of his own and was pretty happy with the results. A few weeks after placing his novel *Inner Circles* on the Internet, he reported that despite not having paid for advertising or an agent, selling only via an automated website linked from his weblog, he had made over $4,500. Chicken feed? No. Quick said that his book, if it had been salable at all, would have brought an advance of about $10,000, payable in two installments, which after deducting the agent's commission would have produced a first check of about $4,250. He concluded, "I have taken in more than that as of now, because I am getting all of the 'cover price,' not eight percent of it (the usual author cut on a paperback)."[7]

Quick isn't just anyone, of course. He's a widely read blogger who's published many novels in the past. He warns his readers of this, but observes, "This outcome is a godsend for those of us professionals who think of ourselves as midlist, and who used to grind out two or three books a year in order to make thirty or forty grand before taxes." This is an important point. Once you realize how little money books on paper usually pay, Internet publication looks a lot better. More significantly, money or not, I think we'll see more authors able to earn an income, or at least a second income, as the Web grows.

Before the Industrial Revolution, you couldn't really make a living as a writer unless you had someone rich funding you. Books just didn't make enough money. In the nineteenth and twentieth centuries it was possible to do well as a writer, but books and then films were necessarily mass-marketed. You had to be able to sell a lot of them to recoup the substantial cost of producing them. The products had to be somewhat appealing to a large audience because of that—and because it was hard to find a smaller audience and hard for a smaller audience to find its author.

That's different now. It's become something of a truism to note that the Web is like a rainforest, full of niches that the well-adapted can flourish in, but like a lot of things, the expression is a truism because it's, well, true. And it's getting truer all the time as the number of people on the Web grows, thus expanding the number of potential customers; and as the tools that let people find what they really want, and not some mass market first-approximation thereof, get steadily better. Some people, of course, will always want to read the book, or see the film, or listen to the songs that lots of other people are, so there will always be a kind of mass market. But even that will be a niche of sorts, in place to address people's preferences rather than because of technological necessity.

Usually, too, when people talk about what "everyone" is reading or watching, they really mean not everyone, but everyone they know. As mass markets fragment, that may mean that people will really define things by their niches, rather than by true mass media. In fact, we're already seeing a lot of that. Another Internet truism is the replacement of Andy Warhol's line that in the future, everyone will be famous for fifteen minutes, with the statement that in the future, everyone will be famous to fifteen people. (As a so-called "celebrity blogger," I was once recognized by a gushing waitress in a restaurant while the rest of the staff stood by, uncomprehending. I wasn't in their niche, and they weren't in mine.)

At any rate, I think we're certain to see a future in which many more people think of themselves as writers, filmmakers, musicians, or journalists than in the past. This may feed back into the political equation noted above, but it could go either way. On the one hand, creative people tend to lean leftward, which suggests that if more people see themselves as creators, the country might move left. On the other hand, people have been complaining that the left has disproportionate influence in creative industries, meaning that if more people can get involved, those fields might shift back the other way, and the overrepresentation of leftist viewpoints might be countered. I suspect we'll see the latter rather than the former.

THE SINGULARITY IS NEAR

As I mentioned in the previous chapter, futurists write about something they call "The Singularity," meaning a point in the future where technological change has advanced to the point that present-day predictions are likely to be wide of the mark. By definition, it's hard to talk about what things will be like then, but the trend of empowered individuals is likely to continue. As the various items we've surveyed demonstrate, technology seems to be shifting power downward, from large organizations to individuals and small groups. Newer technologies like nanotechnology, artificial intelligence, and biotechnology will move us much further along the road, but advances in electronics and communications have gotten us started. You can write—heck, I have written—about the wonders to come in the future, but, in fact, we've moved a considerable distance in that direction already.

While a world of hugely and vastly empowered souls may lurk in the future, we're already living in a world in which individuals have far more power than they used to in all sorts of fields. Yesterday's science fiction is today's reality in many ways that we don't even notice.

That's not always good. With technology bestowing powers on individuals that were once reserved to nation-states, the already-shrinking planet starts to look very small indeed. That's one argument for settling outer space, of course, and many will also see it as an argument for reducing the freedom of individuals on Earth. If those latter arguments carry the day, it could lead to global repression. In its most benign form, we might see something like the A.R.M. of Larry Niven's science fiction future history, a global semisecret police force run by the United Nations that quietly suppresses dangerous scientific knowledge. In less benign forms, we might see harsh global tyranny, justified by the danger of man-made viruses and similar threats. (As I write this, scientists in a lab in Atlanta have resurrected the long-dead 1918 Spanish Flu and published its genome, meaning that people with resources far below those of nation-states will now be able to recreate one of the deadliest disease agents in history.[8])

I doubt that even a science-fictional tyranny could stamp out pervasive and inexpensive technology. Worse, it would leave most of the work in underground labs or rogue states and give people an incentive to put it to destructive use. That doesn't mean that some people won't be tempted to give tyranny a chance, especially if they can put themselves in the tyrant's seat.

On the other hand, there are lots of hopeful signs in the present—trends that will probably continue. Today's revolutionary communications technologies led to a massive mobilization of private efforts in response to disasters like the Indian Ocean tsunami and Hurricane Katrina, and it was text-messaging, websites, and email that broke the Chinese government's SARS cover-up. The phenomenon of "horizontal knowledge" is likely to result in people organizing, both spontaneously and with forethought, to deal with future crises; and there's considerable reason to think that those responses will be more effective than top-down governmental efforts. Indeed, we may see distributed efforts—modeled on things like SETI@home or NASA's SpaceGuard asteroid-warning project—that will incorporate empowered individuals to look for and perhaps even respond to new technological threats.

MAKING CONNECTIONS

When I want to know something about big events in India, I tend to look first to blogs like India Uncut, by Indian journalist Amit Varma. When I want to know about military affairs, I look at blogs like The Belmont Club, The Fourth Rail, The Mudville Gazette, or military analyst Austin Bay's site. When I want to know what's going on in Iraq, I look at Iraqi blogs and blogs by American soldiers there. When one Iraqi blogger reported war crimes by American troops, I called attention to his post, got an American military blogger in Iraq to point it out to authorities, and the soldiers involved wound up being court-martialed and convicted.

Yeah, so, I read a lot of blogs. I'm a blogger, after all. But so are a lot of people, and the person-to-person contact that blogs and other Internet media promote tends to encourage person-to-person relationships across professional, political, and geographic boundaries. This is just another form of the horizontal knowledge that I wrote about before, but it may play an important role in breaking down barriers and defusing animosities across those same boundaries.

People have been saying for a century, of course, that increased international understanding would prevent war, and yet we've seen rather a lot of war over the past century. Still, it may simply be that we haven't reached the tipping point yet. Certainly there's a qualitative, as well as a quantitative difference, as more and more people make person-to-person contact on their own. It's a very different thing from watching other countries' television programs and movies, or having a few people go on tourist expeditions and attend feel-good conferences of the Pugwash variety. While this isn't likely to eliminate hostility, it will certainly transform current understanding and cultural definitions. Overall, I think that the effect is more likely to be positive than negative.

THE WORLD AS WE KNOW IT (I FEEL FINE)

And that's probably the bottom line regarding all the changes described in this book. Technology is empowering individuals and small groups in all sorts of ways, producing fairly dramatic changes as compared to the previous couple of centuries. Not all of those changes are positive—there's bitter along with the sweet. But the era of Big Entities wasn't so great. From the Napoleonic

Wars to the Soviet Gulags, the empowerment of huge organizations and bureaucracies wasn't exactly a blessing to the human spirit. A return to some sort of balance, in which the world looks a bit more like the eighteenth century than the twentieth, is likely to be a good thing.

In some sense, of course, how you view these changes depends a lot on how you view humanity. If you think that people are, more often than not, good rather than bad, then empowering individuals probably seems like a good thing. If, on the other hand, you view the mass of humanity as dark, ignorant, and in need of close supervision by its betters, then the kinds of things I describe probably come across as pretty disturbing.

I fall into the optimistic camp, though I acknowledge that there's evidence pointing both ways. Those who think I'm taking too rosy a view, however, had better hope that I turn out to be right after all. That's because the changes I describe aren't so much inevitable as they are already here, and are just in the process of becoming, as William Gibson would have it, more evenly distributed.

The Army of Davids is coming. Let the Goliaths beware.

NOTES

INTRODUCTION—Do It Yourself
1. Damien Cave, "Rage for the Machine," Salon.com, 12 April 2000, http://www.salon.com/tech/log/2000/04/12/joy_song/. See also Dave Hallsworth, "Mobius Dick vs. the Luddites," Spiked-Online.com, 4 July 2001, http://www.spikedonline.com/Articles/00000002D16F.htm.

CHAPTER 1— The Change
1. Adam Smith, *An Inquiry into the Nature and Causes of the Wealth of Nations*, 4-5 (Modern Library, 1937). Smith got some details wrong in his description but nothing that affects his point.
2. David L. Collinson, "Managing Humor," *Journal of Management Studies* (May 2002), quoted in Daniel H. Pink, *A Whole New Mind* (Riverhead Books, 2005), 179.
3. Robert William Fogel, *The Escape from Hunger and Premature Death: 1700–2100* (Cambridge University Press, 2004).
4. Fogel, 2.
5. John Kenneth Galbraith, *The New Industrial State* (Houghton Mifflin, 1966).
6. Neil Gershenfeld, *Fab: The Coming Revolution on Your Desktop—From Personal Computers to Personal Fabrication* (Basic Books, 2005).
7. See Glenn Reynolds, "Backyard Auteurs," *Popular Mechanics*, October 2005, 56.

CHAPTER 2—Small Is the New Big
1. Jeff Jarvis, Buzzmachine blog. Available online at http://www.buzzmachine.com/index.php/2005/07/25/smallisthenewbighrdepartment/.
2. Louis Uchitelle, "Defying Forecast, Job Losses Mount for a 22nd Month," *New York Times*, 6 September 2003. Available online at http://www.nytimes.com/2003/09/06/business/06JOBS.html?ex=1378180800&en=81557ae4e610f624&ei=5007&partner=USERLAND.
3. Mickey Kaus, "Weaving the Gloom," *Slate*. Available online at http://slate.msn.com/id/2087872/.

4. John Scalzi, Scalzi.com. Available online at http://www.scalzi.com/whatever/archives/000483.html.

5. Daniel Pink, *Free Agent Nation: The Future of Working for Yourself* (Warner Business, 2002).

6. Virginia Postrel, *The Substance of Style: How the Rise of Aesthetic Value Is Remaking Commerce, Culture, and Consciousness* (HarperCollins, 2003), 164-67.

7. Ralph Kinney Bennett, "Car Country," TechCentralStation, 5 September 2003. Available online at http://www.techcentralstation.com/090503A.html.

8. The FAQ on eBay's program is available online here: http://pages.ebay.com/services/buyandsell/powerseller/healthcareprog.html. eBay doesn't pay for the insurance, but does use its buying power to make a group plan available. Once qualified, power sellers get to keep the coverage even if their sales fall below the required minimum.

9. According to Wal-Mart's website: "We insure more than 568,000 associates and more than 948,000 people in total, who pay as little as $17.50 for individual coverage and $70.50 for family coverage bi-weekly. Unlike many plans, after the first year, Wal-Mart's Associates' Medical Plan has no lifetime maximum for most expenses, protecting our associates against catastrophic loss and financial ruin." They also match 401(k) contributions and subsidize child care. Available online at http://www.walmartfacts.com/associates/default.aspx#a42.

10. Virginia Postrel, "In New Age Economics, It's More about the Experience Than about Just Owning Stuff," *New York Times*, 9 September 2004, C2.

11. Virginia Postrel, "A Prettier Jobs Picture?" *New York Times Magazine*, 22 February 2004, 16.

CHAPTER 3—The Comfy Chair Revolution

1. Ray Oldenburg, *The Great Good Place: Cafes, Coffee Shops, Bookstores, Bars, Hair Salons, and Other Hangouts at the Heart of a Community* (Marlowe & Co., 1999).

2. Carol Anne Douglas, "Support Feminist Bookstores!" *Off Our Backs*, 31 December 2000, 1.

3. Nick Hornby, *High Fidelity* (Riverhead, 1996).

4. Linda Baker, "Urban Renewal: The Wireless Way," *Salon*, 29 November 2004. Available online at http://www.salon.com/tech/feature/2004/11/29/digital_metropolis/index_np.html.

5. "The Internet in a Cup," *The Economist*, 18 December 2003. Available online at http://www.economist.com/World/europe/displayStory.cfm?story_id=2281736.

6. Virginia Postrel, *The Substance of Style: How the Rise of Aesthetic Value Is Remaking Commerce, Culture, and Consciousness* (HarperCollins, 2003).

7. Beth Mattson, "Where Town Square Meets the Mall," *Minneapolis-St. Paul Business Journal*, 27 August 1999. Available online at http://www.bizjournals.com/twincities/stories/1999/08/30/focus3.html?page=1.

8. Scott Morris, "A Third Place for Camano," *Daily Herald (Everett, WA)*, 5 September 2003. Available online at http://www.heraldnet.com/Stories/03/9/5/17437484.cfm.

9. For much more on the subject of malls, private property, and free speech, see Jennifer Niles Coffin, "The United Mall of America: Free Speech, State Constitutions, and the Growing Fortress of Private Property," Volume 33, University of Michigan J.L., Reform 615 (2000).

10. *Branzburg v. Hayes*, 408 U.S. 665, 794 (1972).

11. *Reno v. American Civil Liberties Union*, 521 U.S. 844, 870 (1997).

12. Charles L. Black Jr., "He Cannot Choose but Hear: The Plight of the Captive Auditor," Volume 53, *Columbia Law Review* (1953), 960.

CHAPTER 4—Making Beautiful Music, Together

1. "Mandela Steals the Show from Live 8 Rockers," *Cape Argus (Cape Town)*, 4 July 2005. Available at http://www.iol.co.za/index.php?set_id=1&click_id=126&art_id=vn20050704112543593C157427.

2. Telephone interview with Ali Partovi, 6 July 2005.

3. Walter Mossberg, "Podcasting Is Still Not Quite Ready for the Masses," *Wall Street Journal*, 6 July 2005, D5.

4. Lawrence Lessig, "The Same Old Song," *Wired*, July 2005, 100.

5. Jesse Walker, "Free Your Radio: Three Liberties We've Lost to the FCC," *Reason*, December 2001. Available online at http://www.reason.com/0112/cr.jw.radio.shtml.

6. Available online at http://www.diymedia.net/archive/0703.htm#071103.

7. James Plummer, "Real Media Reform," TechCentralStation, 20 June 2003. Available online at http://www.techcentralstation.com/062003F.html.

8. For more on this, see J.D. Lasica, *Darknet: Hollywood's War Against the Digital Generation* (Wiley, 2005).

CHAPTER 5—A Pack, Not a Herd

1. Galt's original website is at http://www.geocities.com/johnathanrgalt/; the newer version of his movement, Internet Haganah, is at http://haganah.us/haganah/index.html.

2. John Hawkins, "An Interview with Jon David." Available online at http://www.rightwingnews.com/interviews/jondavid.php.

3. Hawkins.

4. Brad Todd, "109 Minutes," originally published on FrankCagle.com. Available online at http://web.archive.org/web/20041010182414/http://216.111.31.12/details.asp?PRID=32.

5. Richard Aichele, "A Shining Light in Our Darkest Hour," *Professional Mariner*, December/January 2002. Available online at http://www.fireboat.org/press/prof_mariner_jan02_1.asp.

6. Mark Steyn reports one example of missing some pretty obvious warning signs:

With hindsight, the defining encounter of the age was not between Mohammed Atta's jet and the World Trade Center on September 11, 2001, but that between Mohammed Atta and Johnelle Bryant a year earlier. Bryant is an official with the US Department of Agriculture in Florida, and the late Atta had gone to see her about getting a $US650,000 government loan to convert a plane into the world's largest cropduster. A novel idea.

The meeting got off to a rocky start when Atta refused to deal with Bryant because she was but a woman. But, after this unpleasantness had been smoothed out, things went swimmingly. When it was explained to him that, alas, he wouldn't get the 650 grand in cash that day, Atta threatened to cut Bryant's throat. He then pointed to a picture behind her desk showing an aerial view of downtown Washington—the White House, the Pentagon, et al—and asked: "How would America like it if another country destroyed that city and some of the monuments in it?"

Fortunately, Bryant's been on the training course and knows an opportunity for multicultural outreach when she sees one. "I felt that he was trying to make the cultural leap from the country that he came from," she recalled. "I was attempting, in every manner I could, to help him make his relocation into our country as easy for him as I could."

Mark Steyn, "Mugged by Reality?" *The Australian*, 25 July 2005. Available online at http://www.theaustralian.news.com.au/common/story_page/0,5744,16034303%5E7583,00.html. Even government employees are likely to be more sensitive to the warning signs nowadays.

7. Jim Henley, "Unqualified Offerings," http://www.highclearing.com/uoarchives/week_2002_10_20.html#003796. Henley is quoting an anonymous bystander.

8. Colby Cosh, ColbyCosh.com, available online at http://www.colbycosh.com/old/october02.html#sscd.

9. Kathleen Tierney, "Strength of a City: A Disaster Research Perspective on the World Trade Center Attack," Social Science Research Council. Available online at http://www.ssrc.org/sept11/essays/tierney.htm. See also Monica Schoch-Spana, "Educating, Informing, and Mobilizing the Public," in Barry S. Levy and Victor Sidel, *Terrorism and Public Health: A Balanced Approach to Strengthening Systems and Protecting People* (Oxford University Press, 2003), 118. (Describes spontaneous organization in response to 9/11 attacks and recommends strategies to encourage such responses in the future).

10. Tierney; Schoch-Spana.

11. David Brin, "The Value—and Empowerment—of Common Citizens in an Age of Danger." Available online at http://www.futurist.com/portal/future_trends/david_brin_empowerment.htm.

12. J. B. Schramm, "The Best Anti-Terror Force: Us," *Washington Post*, 23 June 2004, A21. Available online at http://www.washingtonpost.com/wpdyn/articles/A624542004Jun22.html.

13. Jeff Cooper, *Principles of Personal Defense* (Paladin, 1989).

14. Sara Miller, "In War on Terror, an Expanding Citizens' Brigade," *Christian Science Monitor*, 13 August 2004. Available online at http://www.csmonitor.com/2004/0813/p01s02ussc.html.

15. The homepage is at http://www.americaswaterwaywatch.org/index.htm.

16. The homepage is at http://public.afosi.amc.af.mil/eagle/index.asp.

17. The homepage is at http://www.highwaywatch.com/.

18. Lisa Zagaroli, "Nation's 3 Million Truckers Enlist in War on Terrorism," *Detroit News*, 5 June 2002. Available online at http://www.detnews.com/2002/nation/0206/05/a05506969.htm.

19. Neil Samson Katz, "Amateur Astronomers Help NASA Find Killer Asteroids," Columbia News Service, 5 April 2004. Available online at http://www.jrn.columbia.edu/studentwork/cns/20040405/664.asp.

20. Katz.

21. S. M. Stirling, *Dies the Fire* (Roc, 2004).

22. The homepage is at http://www.legionxxiv.org/Default.htm.

23. The homepage is at http://albionswords.com/armor/roman/lorica.htm.

24. Allan Breed, "French Quarter Holdouts Create 'Tribes,'" Associated Press, 4 September 2005. Available online at http://www.wwltv.com/sharedcontent/nationworld/katrina/stories/090405cckatrinajrfrenchquarter.26851646.html.

25. This didn't get much press attention, but Houston blogger John Little posted a report with photos. It's available online at http://www.blogsofwar.com/looters_strike_in_advance_of_rita.

CHAPTER 6—From Media to We-dia

1. Eric Hoffer, *The Ordeal of Change* (Harper & Row, 1963), 109.

2. Zeyad's original blog post can be found at http://healingiraq.blogspot.com/archives/2003_12_01_healingiraq_archive.html#107107940577248802. A blog report from another Iraqi blogger can be found at http://iraqthemodel.blogspot.com/2003_12_01_iraqthemodel_archive.html#107107057634357719.

3. Pro-democracy rallies in Iraq and more. *Weekly Standard*, 22 December 2003. Available online at http://weeklystandard.com/Content/Public/Articles/000/000/003/494vhvue.asp.

4. Wagner James Au, "Silence of the Blogs: Why Did the New York Times Ignore Baghdad Blogger Announcements and Accounts of a Big Pro-Democracy Demonstration?" Salon.com, 23 January 2004. Available online at http://www.salon.com/tech/feature/2004/01/23/baghdad_gamer_two/index_np.html.

5. Kennedy School of Government, Case Study No. C-14-04-1731.0, "'Big Media' Meets 'The Bloggers': Coverage of Trent Lott's Remarks at Strom Thurmond's Birthday Party," http://www.ksg.harvard.edu/presspol/Research_Publications/Case_Studies/1731_0.pdf. See also Howard Kurtz, "Why So Late on Lott?" *Washington Post*, 10 December 2002, http://www.

washingtonpost.com/ac2/wp-dyn?pagename=article&contentId=A34186-2002Dec10&notFound=true; Noah Schachtman, "Blogs Make Headlines," *Wired News*, 23 December 2002. ("It's safe to assume that, before he flushed his reputation down the toilet, Trent Lott had absolutely no idea what a blog was.")

6. The original of this now-famous saying is available online at http://web.archive.org/web/20011214072915/http://kenlayne.com/2000/2001_12_09_logarc.html.

7. James C. Bennett, "The New Reformation?" Available online at http://www.upi.com/view.cfm?StoryID=281220010507337164r.

8. See generally James Fallows, *Breaking the News: How the Media Undermine American Democracy* (Pantheon Books, 1996); Andrew Kreig, *Spiked: How Chain Management Corrupted America's Oldest Newspaper* (Peregrine Press, 1987); Ben Bagdikian, *The New Media Monopoly* (Beacon Press, 2004).

9. Kennedy School of Government; pro-democracy rallies in Iraq and more, supra.

10. Available online at http://jimtreacher.com/archives/001281.html.

11. Alex Beam, "Standing Alone against Apple," *Boston Globe*, 24 May 2005. Available online at http://www.boston.com/news/globe/living/articles/2005/05/24/standing_alone_against_apple/.

12. See Robert Pierre and Ann Gerhart, "News of Pandemonium May Have Slowed Aid: Unsubstantiated Reports of Violence Were Confirmed by Some Officials, Spread by News Media," *Washington Post*, 5 October 2005, A08. Available online at http://www.washingtonpost.com/wpdyn/content/article/2005/10/04/AR2005100401525.html; Matt Welch, "Echo Chamber in the SuperDome," Reason.com, 4 October 2005, http://www.reason.com/links/links100405.shtml.

13. Garrett Hardin, "The Tragedy of the Commons," 162, *Science*, 1243 (1968).

14. Nick Denton, "Comments and Communities," Nickdenton.com, http://www.nickdenton.org/archives/004219.html.

15. Jeff Jarvis, "Exploding Porn," Buzzmachine.com, http://www.buzzmachine.com/archives/2004_10_22.html#008254.

16. Jonathan Peterson, "Breaking Down Peter Chernin's Comdex Keynote," Way.nu,http://www.way.nu/archives/000493.html.

17. Daniel Lyons, "Attack of the Blogs," Forbes.com, 14 November 2005. Available online at http://www.forbes.com/forbes/2005/1114/128.html.

18. Dan Gillmor, *We the Media* (O'Reilly, 2004).

19. Joe Trippi, *The Revolution Will Not Be Televised: Democracy, The Internet, and the Overthrow of Everything* (ReganBooks, 2004).

20. Hugh Hewitt, *Blog: Understanding the Information Revolution That's Changing Your World* (Nelson Books, 2005).

INTERLUDE—Good Blogging

1. Available online at http://web.archive.org/web/20021113004102/http://www.lileks.com/bleats/archive/02/1002/100202.html.

CHAPTER 7—Horizontal Knowledge

1. The Hephthalite, or "White" Huns, ruled Central Asia in the fifth and sixth centuries, until they were exterminated by the Persians. For more information, visit http://www.silkroad.com/artl/heph.shtml.

2. The rocket equation tells how high a rocket can fly and how great a velocity it can achieve, given its exhaust velocity, fuel, etc. For more information, visit http://web.media.mit.edu/~sibyl/projects/cognition/science/rocket.html.

3. As I write this, Biden has received $75,150 from the TV/movies/music industries for the 2006 election cycle. More information is available at http://opensecrets.org/politicians/indus.asp?CID=N00001669&cycle=2006.

4. That's actually true. I looked up all these things in under five minutes total while writing this. At least so long as "draw me a beer" means "draw me a beer and bring it to my table."

5. Nick Denton, "Organizational Terrorism," Nickdenton.org, http://www.nickdenton.org/archives/006004.html#006004.

6. William J. Broad, "At Los Alamos, Blogging Their Discontent," *New York Times*, 1 May 2005.

7. JoAnn S. Lublin, "The Open Inbox," *Wall Street Journal*, 10 October 2005, B1. Available online at http://online.wsj.com/public/article/SB1128 90006139064049PNxxU56QuvTOicPmJSXQnDrVmn8_20061010.html?mod=blogs. Excerpt: "Technology has really made this staff dialogue possible," observes Henry A. McKinnell Jr., CEO of New York-based Pfizer Inc., the world's largest drug maker. While being driven to meetings, the 62-year-old executive reports, "I don't look out the window. I use my BlackBerry and answer my email." He calls the roughly seventy-five internal emails he gets every day "an avenue of communication I don't otherwise have." He adds, "I really consider this an early-warning system." I think he's right to look at it that way.

8. Julia Scheeres, "Pics Worth a Thousand Protests," *Wired News*, 17 October 2003, http://wired-vig.wired.com/news/culture/0,1284,60828-2,00.html?tw=wn_story_page_next1.

9. Jesse Walker, "Is That a Computer in Your Pants? Cyberculture Chronicler Howard Rheingold on Smart Mobs, Smart Environments, and Smart Choices in an Age of Connectivity," Reason.com, April 2003. Available at http://www.reason.com/0304/fe.jw.is.shtml.

10. Clive Thompson, "On the Media," WNYC, 20 December 2002. Transcript available at http://www.onthemedia.org/transcripts/transcripts_122002_mobs.html.

CHAPTER 8—How the Game Is Played

1. "Violent Video Games under Attack," *Wired News*, 4 July 2004, http://wired.com/news/games/0,2101,64101,00.html?tw=wn_tophead_3.

2. See her website at www.violentkids.com for more information.

3. James Dunnigan, "Troops Game Their Way out of Ambushes," StrategyPage.com, 5 July 2004, http://www.strategypage.com/dls/articles/200475.asp.

4. Frank Vizard, "Couch to Combat: A Popular Computer Game Called 'America's Army' Has Evolved into a High-Tech Tool for Training Today's Soldiers," *Popular Mechanics*, June 2005, 80.

5. Dave Kopel and Glenn Reynolds, "Computer Geeks and War," NationalReview.com, 1 October 2001, http://www.nationalreview.com/kopel/ kopel100101.shtml.

6. Andrew Leonard, "Gun Mad," Salon.com, 18 April 1998, http://archive. salon.com/21st/feature/1998/04/cov_20feature2.html.

7. B. H. Liddell Hart, *Strategy* (Praeger, 1967).

8. See James Glassman, "Good News! The Kids Are Alright," TechCentralStation. com, http://techcentralstation.com/071604E.html. (Summarizes results of National Youth Survey and related studies.)

9. It's dangerous to make too much of any one study, of course, and studies of sexual behavior—and in particular teen sexual behavior—are probably less trustworthy than most. Another study suggests that teens are having more oral sex—which may account for the lowered pregnancy rates. See National Center for Health Statistics, "Sexual Behavior and Selected Health Measures: Men and Women 15-44 Years of Age," 2002. Available online at http://www.cdc.gov/nchs/products/pubs/pubd/ad/361-370/ad362.htm. See also Laura Sessions Stepp, "Study: Half of Teens Have Had Oral Sex," *Washington Post*, 16 September 2005, A07. Available online at http:// www.washingtonpost.com/wp-dyn/content/article/2005/09/15/ AR2005091500915.html.

   On the other hand, perhaps online porn—which often emphasizes oral sex—is behind this change as well. While some may feel that oral sex without pregnancy is no improvement over traditional sex with the risk of pregnancy, I suppose I regard this substitution, to the extent it's genuine, as some degree of progress. At any rate, there seems to be no disagreement about the decline in the pregnancy rate, regardless of cause.

CHAPTER 9—Empowering the *Really* Little Guys

1. Richard P. Feynman, *There's Plenty of Room at the Bottom*, ed. Horace D. Gilbert (1961), 295-96.

2. On the artificial kidneys, see "Nanotechnology Used to Help Develop Artificial Kidney," ABC News Online, http://www.abc.net.au/news/newsitems/ 200509/ s1461541.htm.

3. Information on the National Nanotechnology Initiative can be found at its website, http://www.nano.gov—but information on classified Defense Department work is, of course, classified.

4. Robert J. Freitas, *Nanomedicine, Volume I: Basic Capabilities* (Landes Bioscience, 1999). See also Robert J. Freitas, *Nanomedicine, Volume IIA: Biocompatibility* (Landes Bioscience, 2003). On enhanced cognition, see Kelly Hearn, "Future Soldiers Could Get Enhanced Minds," UPI, 19 March

2001, LexisNexis Library, UPI File (describing planned use of nanotechnology to enhance soldiers' cognition and decision-making under stress).

5. National Science and Technology Council (2004), available online at http://nano.gov/nni04_budget_supplement.pdf.

6. National Science and Technology Council, 27.

7. National Science and Technology Council.

8. National Science and Technology Council, 33.

9. For a summary of this debate, see Judith P. Swazey, et al., "Risks and Benefits, Rights and Responsibilities: A History of the Recombinant DNA Research Controversy," Volume 51, *Southern California Law Review* (1978), 1019.

10. Available online at http://www.dnafiles.org/PDFs/therapy.pdf.

11. See David Whitehouse, "First Synthetic Virus Created," BBC News, 11 July 2002. Available online at http://news.bbc.co.uk/2/hi/science/nature/2122619.stm.

12. Available online at http://www.greenpeace.org.uk/MultimediaFiles/Live/FullReport/ 5886.pdf.

13. Available online at http://www.greenpeace.org.uk/MultimediaFiles/Live/FullReport/5886.pdf.

14. Howard Lovy, Nanobot blog, http://nanobot.blogspot.com/2003_07_20_nanobot_archive.html#105905157013774164.

15. Testimony of Dr. Vicki L. Colvin, director, Center for Biological and Environmental Nanotechnology (CBEN), and associate professor of chemistry, Rice University, Houston, Texas, before the U.S. House of Representatives Committee on Science, in regard to "Nanotechnology Research and Development Act of 2003," 9 April 2003. Available online at http://www.house.gov/science/hearings/full03/apr09/colvin.htm.

16. Ian Bell, "Upgrading the Human Condition," *Sunday Herald (Glasgow)*, 1 August 2004. Available online at http://www.sundayherald.com/43701.

17. "China's Nanotechnology Patent Applications Rank Third in World," InvestorIdeas.com, 3 October 2003, http://www.investorideas.com/Companies/Nanotechnology/Articles/China'sNanotechnology1003,03.as. See also Dennis Normile, "China's R&D Power, Truth about Trade & Technology," 2 September 2005, http://www.truthabouttrade.org/article.asp?id=4364. ("Ernest Preeg, senior fellow in trade and productivity for the Manufacturers Alliance/MAPI, warns in his just released book, *The Emerging Chinese Advanced Technology Superstate* (jointly published by the Manufacturers Alliance/MAPI and the US Hudson Institute in June 2005) that 'China is right up there with the US in nanotechnology and coming on strong in biotech and in genetically modified agriculture.'")

18. "Indian Scientists Should Make Breakthrough in Nano Technology: Kalam," IndiaExpress.com, 1 July 2004, http://www.indiaexpress.com/news/technology/20040701-0.html.

19. Daniel Headrick, *The Tools of Empire: Technology and European Imperialism in the Nineteenth Century* (Oxford University Press, 1981).

20. Ray Kurzweil, *The Singularity Is Near: When Humans Transcend Biology* (Viking, 2005), 415.

21. Kurzweil.

CHAPTER 10—Live Long—and Prosper!

1. Robert Fogel, *The Escape from Hunger and Premature Death, 1700-2100: Europe, America, and the Third World* (Cambridge University Press, 2004), 40.

2. Richard A. Miller, "Extending Life: Scientific Prospects and Political Obstacles," in Stephen G. Post and David Binstock, eds., *The Fountain of Youth: Cultural, Scientific, and Ethical Perspectives on a Biomedical Goal* (Cambridge University Press, 2004), 228-29.

3. Gemma Casadesus, et al., "Eat Less, Eat Better, and Live Longer: Does It Work and Is It Worth It? The Role of Diet in Aging and Disease," in *The Fountain of Youth*, 201, 203-4.

4. Casadesus, 235.

5. Jonathan Swift's "struldbrugs" lived a very long time, but aged all the while, with deeply unfortunate results. See Jonathan Swift, *Gulliver's Travels*, ed., Paul Turner (Oxford University Press, 1998), 199-206.

6. Robert Arking, "Extending Human Longevity: A Biological Probability," in *The Fountain of Youth*, 177, 191-92.

7. Arking, 192-93.

8. Aubrey D.N.J. de Grey, "An Engineer's Approach to Developing Real Anti-Aging Medicine," in *The Fountain of Youth*, 249.

9. Leon Kass, "L'Chaim and Its Limits: Why Not Immortality?," in *The Fountain of Youth*, supra note 2, at p. 304, 309, 312.

10. Centers for Disease Control, "Ten Great Public Health Achievements: United States, 1900-1999," Volume 48, *Morbidity and Mortality Weekly Report* (1999), 241. Available at http://www.cdc.gov/epo/mmwr/preview/mmwrhtml/00056796.htm.

11. Karen Wright, "Staying Alive," *Discover*, November 2003, 11.

12. S. Jay Olshansky, Leonard Hayflick, and Thomas Perls, "Anti-Aging Medicine: The Hype and the Reality—Part I," Volume 59, *J. Gerontology: Biological Sciences* (2004), 513.

13. Gregory Stock and Daniel Callahan, "Point-Counterpoint: Would Doubling the Human Life Span Be a Net Positive or Negative for Us Either as Individual or as a Society?" Volume 59, *J. Gerontology: Biological Sciences* (2004), B554, B558. ("[T]o run a society, you have to both say no to people and to require people to do what they don't want to do. There are some higher goods than what we personally want.")

14. Stock and Callahan, 557: "[W]e could get a pretty good sense of likely possibilities based on our present experience. For instance, I've become interested

in universities: What happens now in universities that don't have mandatory retirement? First of all, some people stay beyond seventy, between 5 percent and 10 percent in the universities I've looked at. . . . Most importantly, they block the entry of young people onto the faculty."

15. On the abolition of mandatory environment, both within and without the academic world, see Pamela Perun, "Phased Retirement Programs for the Twenty-First Century Workplace," Volume 35, *John Marshall Law Review* (2002), 633.

16. Perun, 559.

17. 539 U.S. 558 (2003).

18. 381 U.S. 479 (1965).

19. Douglas Clement, "Why 65?" *FedGazette*, March 2004, http://minneapolisfed.org/pubs/fedgaz/04-03/65.cfm.

20. See, for example, Alan Greenspan, "U.S. Must Pare Retirement Benefit Promises," *Washington Post*, 29 February 2004, A3. ("Greenspan again recommended gradually raising the eligibility age for both Medicare and Social Security, to keep pace with the population's rising longevity.")

21. Sebastian Moffett, "For Ailing Japan, Longevity Begins to Take its Toll," *Wall Street Journal*, 11 February 2003, A1. See also Phillip Longman, "The Coming Baby Bust," *Foreign Affairs*, May/June 2004, 64.

22. Longman, 64.

23. Ronald Bailey, *Liberation Biology: The Scientific and Moral Case for the Biotech Revolution* (Prometheus Books, 2005), 242.

24. Bailey, 18.

25. Bailey, 132.

CHAPTER 11—Space: It's Not Just for Governments Anymore

1. Webb Wilder, "Rocket to Nowhere," *Acres of Suede* (Watermelon Records, 1996).

2. Holman W. Jenkins, "NASA's Coming Crackup," *Wall Street Journal*, 5 October 2005, A21. Available online at http://online.wsj.com/article_print/SB112847638707060287.html.

3. *NASA Contests and Prizes: How Can They Help Advance Space Exploration*, Hearings before the Subcommittee on Space and Aeronautics, Committee on Science, U.S. House of Representatives, 15 July 2004 (testimony of Peter Diamandis). Available online at http://commdocs.house.gov/committees/science/hsy94832.000/hsy94832_0.htm.

4. Alan Boyle, "NASA Announces Prizes for Space Breakthroughs," MSNBC.com, 24 March 2005, http://msnbc.msn.com/id/7280483/.

5. For more on space elevator technology, see Bradley Carl Edwards, "A Hoist to the Heavens," IEEE Spectrum, 21 August 2005, http://www.spectrum.ieee.org/aug05/1690.

6. Pub. L. 100-685, Title II § 217, 102 Stat 4094 (1988), codified at 42 USC §2451 (2000).

7. Kucinich's bill is discussed in Glenn Harlan Reynolds, "Moonstruck," TechCentralStation.com, 25 September 2002, http://www.techcentralstation.com/092502A.html.

8. *Treaty on Principles Governing the Activities of States in the Exploration and Use of Outer Space, Including the Moon and Other Celestial Bodies* (1967), 18 UST 2410 (1969).

9. National Research Council, "Task Group on Issues in Sample Return, Mars Sample Return: Issues and Recommendations: The Significance of Martian Meteorites," available at http://www.nap.edu/books/0309057337/html/17.html.

10. Martyn Fogg, *Terraforming: Engineering Planetary Environments* (SAE International, 1995).

11. Robert Zubrin, *Entering Space: Creating a Spacefaring Civilization* (Tarcher, 1999), 227.

12. Robert Pinson, "Ethical Considerations for Terraforming Mars," 32, *Environmental Law Reporter*, 11333, 11341 (2002).

13. John A. Ragosta Jr. and Glenn H. Reynolds, "In Search of Governing Principles," Volume 28, *Jurimetrics: Journal of Law, Science, and Technology* (1988), 473.

14. William Wu, "Taking Liberties in Space," *Ad Astra*, November 1991, 36. This point is reinforced by recent movies, such as *Outland* and *Total Recall*, that depict life in space colonies as harshly controlled.

15. "Governance in Space Project, Declaration of First Principles for the Governance of Space Societies," reprinted in Glenn H. Reynolds and Robert P. Merges, *Outer Space: Problems of Law and Policy* (Westview Press, 1997), 401–2.

16. Andrew Lawler, *Lessons from the Past: Toward a Long-Term Space Policy*, in *Lunar Bases and Space Activities of the Twenty-First Century* (Lunar & Planetary Institute, W.W. Mendell ed., 1985), 757, 762-63.

17. George Robinson and Harold White, *Envoys of Mankind: A Declaration of First Principles for the Governance of Space Societies* (Smithsonian Institute, 1986).

18. Bob Zubrin, "The Significance of the Martian Frontier." Available online at http://www.newmars.com/archives/000026.shtml.

19. George Dyson, *Project Orion: The True Story of the Atomic Spaceship* (Henry Holt & Co., 2002).

20. In addition, the 1957 Pascal-B underground nuclear test accidentally launched a manhole cover at speeds that may have exceeded escape velocity, though it isn't clear whether Orion researchers knew about this. The story of this test, often misnamed "Operation Thunderwell," which was actually the name of another nuclear-spacecraft project, has sparked many Internet legends.

21. Dyson, *Project Orion*.

22. For Freeman Dyson's firsthand account, see "Saturn by 1970" in Freeman Dyson, *Disturbing the Universe* (Harper & Row, 1979), 107.

23. Dyson, *Project Orion,* 119.
24. *Multilateral Treaty Banning Nuclear Weapon Tests in the Atmosphere, in Outer Space, and Under Water* (1963), 14 UST 1313 (1963). For more on this, see Glenn H. Reynolds and Robert P. Merges, *Outer Space: Problems of Law and Policy,* 2nd edition (Westview Press, 1997).
25. Quoted in Jack H. McCall, "The Inexorable Advance of Technology: American and International Efforts to Curb Missile Proliferation," Volume 32, *Jurimetrics: Journal of Law, Science, and Technology* (1992), 387, 426.
26. McCall.
27. 14 Weekly Comp. Pres. Doc. 1135, 1136 (20 June 1978). ("Purposeful interference with space systems shall be viewed as an infringement upon sovereign rights.")
28. J. Storrs Hall, *Nanofuture: What's Next for Nanotechnology* (Prometheus Books, 2005), 284.

CHAPTER 12—The Approaching Singularity
1. Vernor Vinge, "What Is the Singularity?" Available online at http://www.ugcs.caltech.edu/~phoenix/vinge/vinge-sing.html.
2. Joel Garreau, *Radical Evolution: The Promise and Peril of Enhancing Our Minds, Our Bodies, and What It Means to be Human* (Doubleday, 2005), 21. For more on this topic, see Ramez Naam, *More than Human: Embracing the Promise of Biological Enhancement* (Broadway Books, 2005); Ron Bailey, *Liberation Biology: The Scientific and Moral Case for the Biotech Revolution* (Prometheus Books, 2005); Gregory Stock, *Redesigning Humans: Choosing Our Genes, Changing Our Future* (Mariner Books, 2003).
3. Erik Baard, "Cyborg Liberation Front: Inside the Movement for Posthuman Rights," *Village Voice,* 30 July/5 August 2003. Available online at http://www.villagevoice.com/news/0331,baard,45866,1.html.
4. Isaac Asimov, *Foundation* (Doubleday, 1966), 112.
5. Jonathan Leake, "'Miracle Mouse' Can Grow Back Lost Limbs," *Times (London),* 28 August 2005. Available online at http://www.timesonline.co.uk/article/0,,2087-1754008,00.html.
6. See Mark Honigsbaum, "Maverick Who Believes We Can Live Forever," *Guardian,* 10 September 2005. Available online at http://www.guardian.co.uk/print/0,3858,5282378-103690,00.html.
7. "Nanotechnology and Health," *Nature,* 10 September 2005. Available online at http://www.nature.com/news/2005/050905/full/050905-2.html.
8. "Diamonds Are Not Forever," PhysicsWeb.org, http://physicsweb.org/articles/news/9/8/16/1?rss=2.0.
9. Ray Kurzweil, "The InstaPundit Interview," InstaPundit.com, 2 September 2005, http://instapundit.com/archives/025289.php.
10. James Branch Cabell, *Jurgen: A Comedy of Justice* (IndyPublish.com, 2004), 292.

CONCLUSION—The Future

1. Joel Miller, *Size Matters: How Big Government Puts the Squeeze on America's Families, Finances, and Freedom* (Nelson Current, 2006).

2. This topic actually gets some attention from Gene Sperling in his book, *The Pro-Growth Progressive: An Economic Strategy for Shared Prosperity* (Simon & Schuster, 2005), which calls for empowering individuals as a substitute for restricting markets.

3. Glenn Harlan Reynolds, "Horizontal Knowledge," TechCentralStation.com, 4 June 2003, http://www.techcentralstation.com/060403A.html.

4. Kevin Kelly, "We Are the Web," *Wired*, August 2005. Available online at http://wired.com/wired/archive/13.08/tech.html.

5. For some extended thoughts on the pluses and minuses of democracy, and its role in American constitutional thought, see Glenn Harlan Reynolds, "Is Democracy Like Sex?" Volume 48, *Vanderbilt Law Review* (1995), 1635.

6. This is known in some circles as Sturgeon's Law. According to the Wikipedia entry, there are multiple anecdotes regarding the origins of this observation. See "Sturgeon's Law," Wikipedia. Available online at http://en. wikipedia.org/wiki/Sturgeon's_law.

7. Bill Quick, "Book Sales," DailyPundit.com, http://www.dailypundit.com/newarchives/005081.php#005081.

8. Charles Krauthammer doesn't like that one bit. See Charles Krauthammer, "A Flu Hope, or Horror?" *Washington Post*, 14 October 2005, A19. Available online at http://www.washingtonpost.com/wp-dyn/content/article/2005/10/13/AR2005101301783.html.

INDEX